Forschung zur Digitalisierung der Wirtschaft | Advanced Studies in Business Digitization

Digitalisierung verändert Unternehmen und Behörden, unser Privatleben und unsere Gesellschaft. Organisationen, die wettbewerbsfähig bleiben wollen, müssen die dadurch notwendigen Veränderungen aktiv mitgestalten. Die Rolle der IT muss sich in diesem Zusammenhang vom Kostenfaktor zum Werttreiber wandeln. Weiterentwicklungen der IT-Kernkompetenzen sind nötig. In dieser Reihe werden wissenschaftlich fundierte und praktisch relevante Erkenntnisse zur Digitalisierung veröffentlicht. Praktiker finden darin vielfältige Anregungen für die Gestaltung und Verbesserung von Strukturen, Prozessen und IT-Systemen. Wissenschaftler erhalten Impulse für die Beschreibung, Erklärung, Prognose und Gestaltung der Digitalisierung.

Digitalization is changing businesses and governments, our private lives and our societies. Organizations that want to remain competitive must actively shape the changes that are necessary as a result. In this context, the role of IT must change from a cost factor to a value driver. Further developments of the IT core competencies are necessary. This series publishes scientifically sound and practically relevant findings on digitization. Practitioners will find many suggestions for the design and improvement of structures, processes and IT systems. Scientists receive impulses for the description, explanation, prediction and design of digitisation.

Maximilian Horn

Technology Acceptance, Path Dependence, and the Demand for Robo-Advisory Services

Springer Gabler

Maximilian Horn
Bonn, Germany

This dissertation was written at the University of Bremen and defended in the examination colloquium before the reviewers Prof. Dr. Martin Missong and Prof. Dr. Kristina Klein on July 11, 2023.
Diese Dissertation wurde an der Universität Bremen erstellt und im Prüfungskolloquium vor den Gutachtern Prof. Dr. Martin Missong und Prof. Dr. Kristina Klein am 11. Juli 2023 verteidigt.

ISSN 2662-4788 ISSN 2662-4796 (electronic)
Forschung zur Digitalisierung der Wirtschaft | Advanced Studies in Business Digitization
ISBN 978-3-658-44678-9 ISBN 978-3-658-44679-6 (eBook)
https://doi.org/10.1007/978-3-658-44679-6

This Springer Gabler imprint is published by the registered company Springer Fachmedien Wiesbaden GmbH, part of Springer Nature.
The registered company address is: Abraham-Lincoln-Str. 46, 65189 Wiesbaden, Germany

Paper in this product is recyclable.

Acknowledgements

I extend my deepest gratitude to my doctoral supervisor, Prof. Dr. Martin Missong, who made my doctoral studies an instructive journey with his imaginative suggestions, strong commitment, and high quality standards. His great openness to new ideas enabled me to shape this journey in a self-determined way. I would like to emphasize his strong sense of humor, which has always made working with him a great pleasure.

Special thanks are also due to Prof. Dr. Stefan Mittnik, who contributed his theoretical expertise and practical experience as co-founder of Scalable Capital on the topic of robo-advisors at the CEQURA 2021 conference and as an external reviewer in the colloquium. I am equally grateful to Prof. Dr. Martin Möhrle, whose input improved the quality of the dissertation in the final stage.

I would like to thank all the partners of Berg Lund & Company, especially Markus Berg and Dr. Torsten Lund, who initiated the contact to Prof. Dr. Martin Missong and made it financially possible through a flexible part-time model. In addition, they gave me the opportunity to present the most important findings of my dissertation at a major conference in the field of retail banking.

My thanks extend to Philipp Wierzchowski for his diligent support with data collection and to Lea Hashagen for her invaluable graphical contributions and recommendations. Mary Trost contributed to the linguistic development of the thesis, who, as a Brit, managed to recognize British spelling in a text based on American English.

The emotional support that I received was particularly important during my doctoral journey: My parents, Eva-Maria Horn and Rolf-Ulrich Horn, have been my pillars throughout the doctoral phase, especially when I needed a sympathetic ear. They also actively supported me in making the best possible use of my time through (partly joint) workations. I would like to thank my partner,

Noor-A-Kasida Maria Islam, who has been a constant source of support and understanding, which enabled me to concentrate fully on my dissertation. Her dedication, reflected in numerous readings and invaluable feedback during the culmination of my doctorate, was crucial to my dissertation's completion.

As the true contribution of my parents and my partner cannot be put into words, I would like to dedicate this thesis to them.

Abstract

This thesis aims at modeling and investigating the demand for robo-advisory services empirically. Thus, it seeks to contribute to the accessibility of financial markets for private investors. This objective is pursued by applying two approaches: the integration of individual path dependence into established models of technology acceptance (TAM and UTAUT) and the analysis of the impact of product features (services, cost structures etc.) on the demand for robo-advisory services. Relevant insights for the information systems (IS) community, suppliers of robo-advisory services, and governmental institutions are derived based on the theoretical and empirical results.

I expanded the unified theory of acceptance and use of technology (UTAUT) with the idea of path dependence deriving a path dependence augmented UTAUT model (PDA-UTAUT model). The path dependence in this model is operationalized as the acceptance of a basic product or technology, e.g., the investment on the stock market, which enables the usage of a new or advanced technology, e.g., robo-advisor technology, and influences the attitudes towards the new or advanced technology, e.g., the performance expectancy attributed to robo-advisor technology. The PDA-UTAUT model was adapted to robo-advice by including additional relevant constructs. I tested this robo-advisor-specific model using online survey data from Germany (n = 1102) and the USA (n = 1093) employing partial least square (PLS) regressions. The results demonstrate that path dependence is an important factor for the acceptance of and attitudes towards the advanced technology of robo-advisory. Furthermore, the PDA-UTAUT model can account for factors with diverging effects on the basic and new technology conclusively. Other technologies warranting an explicit modeling of path dependence are pointed out and recommendations on the application of the PDA-UTAUT model are provided.

The decisive role of product attributes for technology acceptance is mirrored by their inclusion in the first technology acceptance model (TAM) by Davis 1985. Nevertheless, the focus of academic research has shifted away from them. A structured process to identify product attributes which impact technology acceptance is presented and applied to robo-advisors: A longlist of attributes was derived from the academic, industry, and consumer literature. The empirical data for these attributes were collected for 40 German and 34 American robo-advisors allowing a statistical comparison of both markets. The relative importance of selected attributes for customers' decision making was evaluated with a choice-based conjoint analysis (CBC) relying on online survey data from Germany (n = 330) and the USA (n = 288). The most relevant attributes were subsequently included in an adapted PDA-UTAUT model accounting for supply effects and tested using online survey data from the USA (n = 750) employing PLS regressions finding support for the effect of selected attributes on the intention to adopt robo-advisor technology and the influence of path dependence on the attitudes towards robo-advisors.

Contents

Abbreviation

AGE	Age
AI	Artificial intelligence
API	Application programming interface
AuM	Assets under management
AVE	Average variance extracted
CA	Conjoint analysis
CBC	Choice-based conjoint analysis
DOI	Diffusion of innovations
EDU	Education
EE	Effort expectancy
EI	External influence
ESSM	Ethical stance (towards the stock market)
ET	Emotional trust
ETF	Exchange-traded fund
FAM	Familiarity (with the use of robots)
FinTech	Financial technology
FL	Financial literacy
FL_A	Advanced financial literacy
FL_B	Basic financial literacy
FR	Financial risk attitude
GEN	Gender
HB	Hierarchical-Bayes-analysis
HTMT	Heterotrait-monotrait ratio
I	Income
IDT	Innovation diffusion theory
II	Interpersonal influence

IINV	(Behavioral) intention to invest (on the stock market)
IIRA	(Behavioral) intention to invest with a robo-advisor
INRA	Investors not invested using robo-advisors
INV	Investment on the stock market
IS	Information systems
IURA	(Behavioral) intention to use robo-advisor technology
IWRA	Investment with a robo-advisor
MM	Motivational model
MNL	Multinomial logistic regression
MPCU	Model of PC utilization
NFC	Near-field communication
NI	Non-investors
OLS	Ordinary least squares
PE	Performance expectancy
PEOU	Perceived ease of use
PI	Personal innovativeness
PLS	Partial least squares
PPR	Perceived privacy risk
PU	Perceived usefulness
RA	Robo-advisor(s)
REIT	Real estate investment trust
RLH	Root likelihood
RPA	Robotic process automation
RUM	Random utility model
SCT	Social cognitive theory
SD	Standard deviation
TAM	Technology acceptance model
TC	Trust in competence
TI	Trust in integrity
TPB	Theory of planned behavior
TRA	Theory of reasoned action
UTAUT	Unified theory of acceptance and use of technology
VIF	Variance inflation factor
Vs.	Versus
WEA	Wealth
WTP	Willingness to pay

Introduction 1

Financial markets bring together actors seeking financing (e.g., private companies or the government) with actors seeking to invest their money profitably (e.g., private investors). Thus, the efficiency and accessibility of financial markets are in the interest of the overall economy as well as of the individuals within an economy.

Digitization and process automation enable business models that were not possible or profitable before. In banking and finance, these new businesses are known as financial technology (FinTech) companies. FinTech companies utilize emerging technologies as algorithms, artificial intelligence (AI), big data, blockchain, open application programming interfaces (API), or robotic process automation (RPA). FinTech companies cover areas as diverse as peer-to-peer-lending, open banking, social trading, and robo-advisors. Using these new technologies, FinTech companies can increase the efficiency and accessibility of financial markets.

This thesis concentrates on the financial technology of robo-advisory services, which have flourished in the last decade. Notably, robo-advisors allow private investors to access financial markets at relatively low costs and often with a lower minimum investment as compared to traditional advisors. Thus, robo-advisors might provide an opportunity for those who are not invested on the stock market yet. Non-investors currently constitute 82.9% of the German population in 2021 (Balonier et al. 2022 from *Deutsches Aktieninstitut*) and 42% of the US-American population in 2022 (Saad and Jones 2022 from *Gallup*).

Robo-advisors are automated and algorithm-based services to invest on the stock and bond markets without requiring human interaction or judgment. These services are offered by banks, financial advisory firms, or start-ups relying on standardized questionnaires on investors' risk attitudes, investment goals and

M. Horn, *Technology Acceptance, Path Dependence, and the Demand for Robo-Advisory Services*, Forschung zur Digitalisierung der Wirtschaft | Advanced Studies in Business Digitization, https://doi.org/10.1007/978-3-658-44679-6_1

planning intervals. They provide a recommendation on how to split assets between different classes and offer the asset management to execute the recommendation. Some robo-advisors offer additional services like tax loss harvesting. Robo-advisors typically derive revenues from their services by charging fees in proportion to the assets under management (AuMs) invested in them.[1,2]

Whether robo-advisory will replace, augment or simply co-exist with established advisory approaches is yet to be seen. Hybrid models of human advisors augmented with robo-advisor technology are already on the market (e.g., TD Ameritrade and Fidelity). They offer the advantages of robo-advisory (e.g., 24/7 availability and cost efficiency) combined with the traditional focus on human relationships and trust of established financial advisory and wealth management firms (Chowney and Fragnière 2014).

This thesis aims at providing a model and empirical investigation of the private demand for robo-advice. This investigation shall allow a better understanding of the demand behavior of private investors. These findings can substantiate the strategies of suppliers of robo-advisory services to achieve profitable growth as well as public institutions to increase the share of stock investors in the population.

Governmental institutions of major economies promote financial market participation, especially for the purpose of retirement planning. This objective is often motivated by the vulnerabilities that pay-as-you-go, as opposed to funded pension schemes, exhibit due to an aging population. In January 2023, the German Federal Minister of Finance, Christian Lindner, proposed a program called "Aktienrente". The aim of the program is to introduce stock market investment as an additional pillar of the German public retirement insurance ("gesetzliche Rentenversicherung") to counteract the effects of demographic change and allow a participation in the returns achieved on global financial markets. In a similar vein, the government of the USA has been granting tax breaks to

---

[1] An example of a wider definition of robo-advisory can be found in D'acunto and Rossi 2019, who study a portfolio optimizer offered by an Indian brokerage firm. The tool uses Markowitz 1959 based mean-variance optimization to construct and visualize portfolio weights using Indian stocks. Trading operations had to be approved by consumers.

[2] D´Acunto and Rossi 2021 discuss the expansion of the term robo-advisory to all personal finance choices households face. Examples for this broader view of robo-advice are the online real estate marketplace Zillow, the discount real estate brokerage Redfin and the social financial management app Status Money. Although this broader definition might become mainstream in the future, this dissertation confines itself to tackling adoption of portfolio allocation technologies. To the author's knowledge none of the said companies market their services as robo-advisory up until now.

the employer-sponsored, defined-contribution, personal pension 401(k) accounts since 1978.

Traditional models of technology acceptance serve as a starting point to analyze the demand for robo-advisory services.[3] The most prominent models of technology acceptance are the unified theory of adoption and use of technology (UTAUT) developed by Venkatesh et al. 2003 and its predecessor the technology adoption model (TAM) developed by Davis 1985. UTAUT and TAM have been widely adopted to investigate the adoption intention and behavior of different information technologies. The UTAUT model assumes that the behavioral intention (to use a technology) alongside facilitating conditions influence usage behavior (of a technology). The behavioral intention is influenced by performance expectancy, effort expectancy, and social influence. The relationship between independent and dependent constructs can be moderated by different mostly demographic factors. Various factors have been considered in addition to the main constructs of the UTAUT and TAM to model the adoption of diverse technologies without changing the core models. The details of the models will be explained in Chapter 2.

Although the UTAUT model serves as a baseline, it is not sufficient to model the usage of robo-advisors, as their acceptance is influenced by the stock market participation of their potential clients. Stock market participation directly affects the acceptance of robo-advisor technology, as it constitutes a necessary condition. I refer to stock market investments as a basic product/technology for the new technology of robo-advisory.

The process by which investment behavior influences the demand for robo-advisors can be conceptualized as a case of individual path dependence (Nelson and Winter 1982; Arthur 1989; Arthur 1996). A general framework will be provided on how to model individual path dependence in UTAUT models. This general framework will be adjusted to robo-advice.

Building on this theoretical basis, an empirical analysis using PLS regressions on survey data from Germany and the USA shall provide answers to **research question 1:**

> *How does the individual investment behavior influence the demand for robo-advisory services?*

---

[3] Thus, this thesis can be seen as part of the information systems (IS) literature.

Evidence for the importance of product features[4] on product adoption can be found throughout the history of technology. Features have played a decisive role in the breakthrough or prevention of various technologies. The following examples illustrate the importance of features for technology adoption:

- **Electric cars:** At the dawn of the car industry in the late 19th century, electrically powered cars were competitors to gasoline-powered cars.[5] However, electric cars lost out to gasoline-powered cars, due to a lack of range, long charging times, and expensive production.
- **iPhones:** Apple's iPhone was not the first attempt to make smartphones mass marketable, however, the first one successfully establishing a new mass market (Gartner 2022). According to home users' preferences elicited by surveys, the iPhone was easy to use and equipped with the following features: 3G compatibility, third-party software integration, GPS, e-mail, and voice recognition.
- **Flash memories**[6]: Initially, flash memories were unsuccessful in the traditional hard disk markets (e.g., PCs) because of their low capacity and reliability. However, due to their small size, low power consumption and high speed, they were used in USB sticks, digital cameras, and MP3 players. Based on these increased sales, flash memories continued their success in laptops and other mobile devices.

Thus, it can be assumed that product features also play a role for the demand for robo-advisory services. Hence, I investigate how to integrate objective product features of robo-advisors, i.e., features that can be quantified and do not constitute attitudes and perceptions, into the PDA-UTAUT model. Suitable features of robo-advisors are identified using a systematic market overview of current features of robo-advisors in Germany and the USA. A choice-based conjoint analysis (CBC) using survey data from Germany and the USA allows a selection of features by their relative impact on customer decision making. These features are included and tested within an adapted PDA-UTAUT model using data from a second survey from the USA providing evidence on **research question 2:**

---

[4] The terms "feature" and "attribute" are used synonymously in this thesis. The terms are defined and discussed in depth in Chapter 5.

[5] The first speed record over 100 km/h was achieved by an electric car (Bourgarit and Plateau 2005).

[6] This example was adapted from Christensen 1997.

How do features influence the demand for robo-advisory services?

The ideas behind both research approaches of this thesis are established for a long time: While the concept of path dependence is known at least since the 1980s (Nelson and Winter 1982; Arthur 1989; Arthur 1996), product features were an integral part of the first model of technology acceptance, TAM, proposed by Davis 1985. The implication of individual path dependence for technology acceptance has not been conclusively discussed in the IS literature.[7] I argue that individual path dependence is not limited to the technology of robo-advice, but it can be expected to play a role for the acceptance of other technologies or products as well. An example for a basic product might be a mobile phone with near-field communication (NFC) for the new technology of mobile payment. Arthur 1996 took the software Java as an example which serves as a basic technology to other computer programs, i.e., advanced technologies.

Although some researchers in the field of IS recommend product features to influence the constructs of models of technology acceptance (Belanche et al. 2019; Wu and Gao 2021), empirical investigations of product features remain scarce. Thus, this thesis follows the recommendation of members of the IS community to analyze the role of product features empirically, e.g., Benbasat and Barki 2007 in the *Journal of the Association for Information Systems.*

This thesis provides a theoretical basis and empirical methods to investigate the following questions structured by their imputed target audience:

IS researchers might find answers to the following questions relevant:

- How can the impact of basic technologies on the adoption of a new technology be represented in a UTAUT model and for which technologies is this useful?
- What is a systematic process for evaluating and testing the impact of product features on customer demand?

Providers of robo-advisory services and governmental institutions might be interested in answers to the following questions:

- What is the impact of stock market investment on the adoption of robo-advisory services?

[7] Some recent studies on the acceptance of robo-advice have dealt with path dependence only indirectly by excluding participants who do not invest without referring to path dependence explicitly (Fan and Chatterjee 2020; Todd and Seay 2020).

- Can robo-advisors increase the share of stock market investors in Germany and the USA?
- Do German and American robo-advisors match customer preferences with the product features that they currently offer?
- Which product features are relevant for the acceptance of robo-advisors?

As the empirical methods are applied on convenience samples, although trying to approximate representative samples as closely as possible, and are based on new theoretical approaches, the empirical findings of this thesis can be considered as exploratory.

The following chapters structure this thesis:

- Chapter 2 combines the established UTAUT model and the theory of path dependence to derive a path dependence augmented UTAUT model (PDA-UTAUT model) including recommendations on its applicability to other technologies.
- Chapter 3 adapts the PDA-UTAUT model to the specificities of the robo-advisor technology.
- Chapter 4 tests the robo-advisor specific PDA-UTAUT model with partial least squares (PLS) regressions using online survey data from Germany and the USA.
- Chapter 5 conducts a market survey of product features of German and American robo-advisors based on a list of features derived from the academic and industry literature.
- Chapter 6 includes notable product features derived from Chapter 5 in a choice-based conjoint study (CBC) based on online survey data from Germany and the USA deriving the relative importance of these features for private customers.
- Chapter 7 derives a PDA-UTAUT model accounting for supply effects which is adapted to robo-advisor technology. This model is tested with PLS regressions employing online survey data from the USA.
- Chapter 8 summarizes the findings of the thesis deriving theoretical and empirical implications, especially for providers of robo-advisory services as well as governmental institutions. Furthermore, it points out limitations and opportunities for future research.

Figure 1.1 summarizes the structure of the thesis.

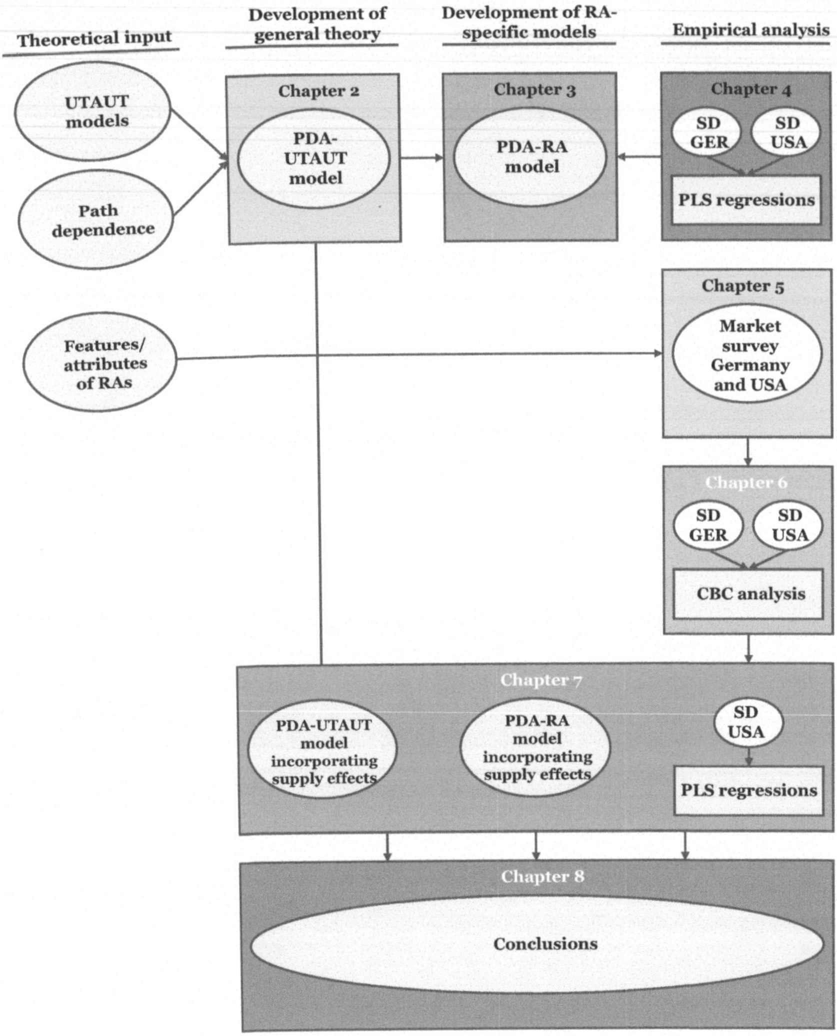

RA:	Robo-advisors	SD:	Survey data
UTAUT:	Unified theory of acceptance and use of technology	PLS:	Partial least squares
PDA:	Path dependence augmented	CBC:	Choice-based conjoint

Figure 1.1 Structure of the dissertation

2 Uniting Individual Path Dependence and UTAUT: The PDA-UTAUT Model

Accounting for path dependence in the modeling of the acceptance of robo-advisor technology will be organized in the following way. In Chapter 2, a path dependence augmented UTAUT (PDA-UTAUT) model will be deducted based on general and robo-advisor-specific technology acceptance as well as path dependence research. In Chapter 3, the PDA-UTAUT model will be adapted to the specific traits of robo-advisor technology. In Chapter 4, the robo-advisor-specific PDA-UTAUT model will be tested deriving practical implications from the empirical findings.

2.1 Introduction to UTAUT

The technology acceptance model (TAM) (Davis 1985; Davis 1989) and the unified theory of acceptance and use of technology (UTAUT) (Venkatesh et al. 2003) are widely used models to investigate the acceptance of information technologies. Additional constructs are added to these models to adapt them to specific contexts and technologies (Srite and Karahanna 2006; Venkatesh et al. 2012; Nistor et al. 2014; Belanche et al. 2019). It is important to consider that both TAM and UTAUT were originally developed in the context of business organizations and were later adapted to the consumer context. Adoption behavior and behavioral intention to adopt the information technology are chosen as dependent constructs contingent on the context.

The predictive role of behavioral intention for usage is decisive, but well established in the information systems (IS) literature, as described by Ajzen 1991 for the literature on the theory of planned behavior (TPB) and by Sheppard et al.

M. Horn, *Technology Acceptance, Path Dependence, and the Demand for Robo-Advisory Services*, Forschung zur Digitalisierung der Wirtschaft | Advanced Studies in Business Digitization, https://doi.org/10.1007/978-3-658-44679-6_2

1988 in their meta-study summarizing the empirical research on the theory of reasoned action (TRA). They focused on the distinction between behavior which can be performed at will, e.g., eating at a fast food restaurant (Brinberg and Durand 1983), and goals which involve a degree of uncertainty, e.g., having a child in the next two years (Davidson and Jaccard 1979). They found that intentions better predict behavior than goals. This finding supports the importance of facilitating conditions (Venkatesh et al. 2003). Taylor and Todd 1995b demonstrated the predictive significance of intention on behavior for making use of the resources of a computer resource center at a university with over 750 participants within the technology acceptance model (TAM) and two versions of the theory of planned behavior (TPB).

Based on the theory of reasoned action (TRA) (Fishbein and Ajzen 1975), Davis 1985 proposes the following constructs to explain the acceptance of specific information technologies:

- Perceived usefulness is defined as "the degree to which a person believes that using a particular system would enhance his or her job performance".
- Perceived ease of use is defined as "the degree to which a person believes that using a particular system would be free of physical and mental efforts".

Later, the construct of subjective norm ("the person's perception that most people who are important to him think that he should or should not perform the behavior in question" Fishbein and Ajzen 1975) was added to TAM (Venkatesh and Davis 2000). TAM has been employed by researchers to investigate the consumer adoption of information technologies like e-commerce (Pavlou 2003; Gefen et al. 2003) and instant messaging (Jiang and Deng 2011). Furthermore, TAM has been used to explain technology acceptance in financial settings like mobile payments (Bailey et al. 2017) and recently robo-advisors (Belanche et al. 2019). Some research papers draw from both sources, e.g., for the mobile payment services (Thakur and Srivastava 2014).

Venkatesh et al. 2003 sought to derive a unified theory from the existing IS literature. The constructs of 8 different models were empirically validated: TRA, TAM, motivational model (MM), theory of planned behavior (TPB), a model combining TAM and TPB, the model of PC utilization (MPCU), innovation diffusion theory (IDT), and social cognitive theory (SCT). The final and henceforth standard model includes the following constructs:

- Performance expectancy is defined as "the degree to which an individual believes that using the system will help him or her to attain gains in job performance".
- Effort expectancy is defined as"the degree of ease associated with the use of the system".
- Social influence is defined as "the degree to which an individual perceives that important others believe he or she should use the new system".
- Facilitating conditions are defined as "degree to which an individual believes that an organizational and technical infrastructure exists to support use of the system".

Performance expectancy, effort expectancy, and social influence are the standard constructs to explain behavioral intention to use a technology. Facilitating conditions and behavioral intention to use a technology predict the actual technology usage in the standard model.

In comparison to other models, UTAUT has been shown to possess the highest model fit (Venkatesh et al. 2003). UTAUT has been successfully applied in numerous fields: Venkatesh et al. 2012 employed UTAUT to explain mobile internet adoption. Zhou 2012 showed the applicability of UTAUT in location-based services in China. Yu 2012 demonstrated the applicability of UTAUT to mobile banking adoption in Taiwan. Zhou et al. 2010 explained mobile banking adoption employing UTAUT. Amoroso and Magnier-Watanabe 2012 chose UTAUT for their model on mobile wallet adoption in Japan.

The focus that the information systems literature has put on the technology acceptance models, has received some criticism (Benbasat and Barki 2007). Although they acknowledge the merits of the findings made with these models, they argue that not enough researchers venture to go beyond the established models. Specifically, they propose that researchers identify antecedents of the beliefs in the adoption models to inform practice, i.e., IT design and characteristics. Furthermore, they propose the development and testing of multi-stage models to capture the influence of beliefs at different stages of implementation, ideally with longitudinal studies. This dissertation will address both proposals of Benbasat and Barki 2007.

2.2 Overview of the Robo-Advisory Adoption Literature

Belanche et al. 2019 used a model based on the technology acceptance model (TAM) to investigate attitudes towards robo-advisor adoption of North American, British, and Portuguese participants recruited online, having previous experience with online banking. The dependent variable in their model is the intention to use a robo-advisor. Their hypotheses based on TAM could be confirmed apart from the direct influence of perceived usefulness on the intention to use a robo-advisor. They found that subjective norms composed of interpersonal influence and external influence had a positive impact on intention to use. The effect of subjective norms on intention is stronger when familiarity with robots is lower or participants came from North America or the UK.

Fan and Chatterjee 2020 as well as Todd and Seay 2020 based their research on robo-advisor adoption on the data set of the 2015 state-by-state National Financial Capability Study (NFCS) and Investor Survey (IS). Both studies confined themselves to participants "who reported having investments in non-retirement accounts and who participated in the household financial decision-making process" (Fan and Chatterjee 2020). Thus, their research is restricted to the adoption process of people already invested on the financial markets, i.e., compromising generalizability to people who are not invested on the stock market. The dependent variable is the answer to the question "Have you ever used an automated financial adviser that provides investment advice and makes trades on your behalf?" (Fan and Chatterjee 2020; Todd and Seay 2020), i.e., actual usage of robo-advisors. Although the data basis of Fan and Chatterjee 2020 and Todd and Seay 2020 share a lot of similarities, their research models differ.

Fan and Chatterjee 2020 employ the diffusion of innovations (DOI) model developed by Rogers 1962. The model includes information search sources which are divided into internal (e.g., financial knowledge and risk tolerance) and external sources (e.g., friends and the media), demographic and economic characteristics, and the attitudes of freeing up time as well as receiving more access to investments by using a robo-advisor. They find that the need to free up time, risk tolerance, subjective financial knowledge, young age, participation in investment clubs, researching credit card information, and amounts of investable assets are positively affecting the probability to have used a robo-advisor. Curiously, objective basic and advanced financial knowledge are negatively associated with robo-advisor adoption.

Todd and Seay 2020 base their analysis on the Engel-Blackwell-Miniard model, which is developed from the Engel-Kollat-Blackwell model (Engel et al.

1990; Engel et al. 1978) defining consumer decisions as "(a) problem recognition, (b) information search, (c) evaluation of alternatives, (d) purchase decision and (e) post purchase behaviour" (Mishra and Kumar 2011) concluding that an "information search framework coupled with microeconomic cost-benefit analysis" (Todd and Seay 2020) is best suitable to back up the study theoretically. They concluded that young age, low to middle income, and low financial literacy are positively affecting prior usage of robo-advisory.

Cheng 2021 investigates the antecedents of the continuance intention of robo-advisor users of three financial services companies in Taiwan, thus shifting the focus from the adoption to the continuance of robo-advice. The research model is based on the expectation confirmation model (ECM) and flow theory to investigate fit, network, and psychological factors. Cheng 2021 finds support that the following dependent constructs have an impact on the continuance intention ("defined as the behavior of a user to continue using a service after accepting it" Bhattacherjee 2001):

- Confirmation ("refers to the degree of users' perception of the congruence between the expectation of the IS/IT use and its actual performance" Cheng 2021 based on: Bhattacherjee 2001)
- Flow experience (defined as "the holistic sensation that people feel when they act with total involvement" Csikszentmihalyi 1975)
- Perceived usefulness (defined as "the degree to which a person believes that using a particular system would enhance his/her job performance" Davis 1989)
- Satisfaction (which "refers to a psychological or affective state related to and resulting from a cognitive appraisal of the expectation-performance discrepancy" Cheng 2021 based on: Bhattacherjee 2001)

Cheng 2021 provides evidence that the previously mentioned dependent constructs are impacted by the following independent constructs, which thus have an indirect effect on the continuance intention:

- Task-technology fit ("TTF refers to the degree to which technology assists an individual in performing his or her portfolio of tasks" Cheng 2021 based on: Goodhue and Thompson 1995)
- Perceived network size ("Perceived network size can be used as the proxy for direct network externalities and it refers to the user's perception of the number of other users using the IS/IT" Cheng 2021 based on: Lin and Bhattacherjee 2008; Zhao and Lu 2012; Lin and Huang 2014)

- Perceived complementarity ("Perceived complementarity can be used as the proxy for indirect network externalities and it refers to the user's perception of increased benefits from the complementary products or services provided by the IS/IT providers/vendors to support the IS/IT usage" Cheng 2021 based on: Lin and Bhattacherjee 2008; Lin and Lu 2011; Zhao and Lu 2012)
- Perceived informativeness ("Perceived informativeness refers to the ability of the IS/IT to handle information and make information available" Cheng 2021 based on: Chiang 2013; Chang 2018; Ma et al. 2019; Mouakket 2019; Ray et al. 2019)
- Perceived enjoyment ("Perceived enjoyment refers to the degree to which the activity of using a particular system is perceived to be personally enjoyable in its own right apart from the instrumental value of the specific type of system" Cheng 2021 based on: Davis et al. 1992; Teo et al. 1999; Lee et al. 2005)
- Perceived social influence ("Perceived social influence can be defined as an individual's perception of the opinions of salient social referents about whether he/she should or should not perform the behavior in question" Cheng 2021 based on: Fishbein and Ajzen 1975; Venkatesh et al. 2003)

The most important difference between the approaches presented above and this thesis is to introduce individual path dependence as an explicit factor, which in turn is explained by different financial attitudes. Furthermore, *the intention to use robo-advisor technology (IURA)* and *the intention to invest on the stock markets (IINV)* are modeled as two distinct factors influencing *the intention to invest with a robo-advisor (IIRA)* allowing to disentangle the impact of technology and financial attitudes[1] on adoption intention and behavior.

[1] In this thesis, I employ the term "attitude" to describe all non-demographic drivers of the intention to perform a certain behavior, e.g., to *invest on the stock market (IINV)* or to *use robo-advisor technology (IURA)*. The usage of other authors might differ, e.g., Davis 1985 differentiates between cognitive responses (perceived usefulness and perceived ease of use) influencing the affective response (attitude towards using) to a technology in his first version of the technology acceptance model (TAM).

2.3 Individual Path Dependence and Technology Adoption

Section 2.3 presents the logical relationship between investment on the stock market and investment with a robo-advisor constituting individual path dependence. Furthermore, several examples of other technologies exhibiting individual path dependence are provided.

2.3.1 The Logic Between Investment and Robo-Advisors

In addition to the established relationships posited by the UTAUT and TAM literature, I argue that acceptance and adoption of technology are not entirely explained by the characteristics of the new components of the technology (advanced technology). Robo-advisors employ new technologies to advise people on which assets to invest in and manage the said investments. But the products that are in the scope of the advice are already established on the market (basic technology). Exchange-traded funds (ETFs) have been on the market since 1989 and are used by a variety of investors and institutions (Gastineau 2002). Other assets in the scope of robo-advisory have been on the market for decades (like real estate investment trusts (REITs) created by Eisenhower in 1960 in US Public Law Section 10(a), no. 86–779, 74 Stat. 998, 1003–1008 (Sept. 14, 1960)), or millennia like gold. Hence, it is important to acknowledge that the two steps of technology adoption (basic and advanced) are indeed subject to distinct decisions. Therefore, the technological innovation of robo-advisors consists in the advice delivery and the way that assets are managed, but not the assets themselves.

To clarify the logical relationships in the process of robo-advice, assume that A denotes the usage of the advanced or new technology, i.e., robo-advisor technology, B denotes the usage of the basic technology, i.e., investments on the stock market, and C denotes the usage of the combined technology, i.e., stock market investments using robo-advisors. These technologies fulfill the following logical relationships:

$$A \rightarrow B \tag{2.1}$$

$$\neg B \rightarrow \neg A \tag{2.2}$$

$$B \wedge A \leftrightarrow C \tag{2.3}$$

Relationship 1 indicates that the application of the advanced technology A is sufficient for the application of the basic technology B. Relationship 2 indicates that the application of the basic technology B is a necessary condition for the application of the advanced technology A. Relationship 3 indicates that the usage of the combined technology C is equivalent to the simultaneous usage of the basic technology B and the advanced technology A.

Furthermore, identifying and disentangling different steps of technology adoption (basic, advanced, and combined) by introducing them as distinct constructs will be most beneficial in fields in which the basic technology fulfills two conditions:

1. The basic technology serves a purpose which provides an independent advantage to the customer or user.
2. The basic technology is not adopted by a vast majority of the population.

These conditions serve as a heuristic to disentangle different steps of technology adoption when customers have an incentive to adopt it on its own. If the basic technology serves no independent purpose, it is likely that the basic technology is only adopted to enable the advanced and combined technology. The second condition makes sure that the adoption of the basic technology is not self-evident, e.g., electricity is a basic technology for practically all information technologies, but it is treated as a given by most people in developed countries. Therefore, measuring the adoption or adoption intention of electricity will provide no further insights and might confuse study participants.

To provide an example illustrating the above arguments, modern smartphones (or other devices) with NFC-technology have an independent benefit for their users by allowing them to surf online with their phones, make calls, or use apps (condition 1), but are not adopted by the entire population of most countries (condition 2). Furthermore, mobile payment by phone fulfills the logical conditions to provide a case which might necessitate a differentiation between basic and advanced technologies. In this case mobile payment without bank or credit cards would be the advanced technology (A), modern smartphones with NFC-technology would be the basic technology (B), and mobile payment using an NFC-enabled smartphone (or other device) would be the combined technology (C) fulfilling the logical relationships posited above. It is possible that one basic technology enables multiple advanced technologies or that one advanced technology requires several basic technologies. While NFC-enabled smartphones are the basic technology for mobile payment, they also act as a basic technology for digital identity cards (IDs) in Germany but require a special software (advanced technology) to use them.

Another example is the gaming industry in which specific games need specific equipment from a specific generation. The gaming industry example fulfills condition 1 as customers can play different games using their equipment apart from the game in question, but gaming equipment is by no means adopted by the entire population (condition 2).

As a counter example, while the widespread adoption of electric cars requires a net of specific charging stations to supply electrical power, the charging stations currently serve no independent purpose. Therefore, explicitly modeling the adoption intention for electric charging stations might only provide a limited benefit to explain the adoption intention of all-electric cars, as it violates condition 1.

It is straightforward that these conditions apply to robo-advice. Stock market investment fulfills both conditions posited above for basic technologies, as stock market investment can also be profitable without using robo-advisors (condition 1) and stock market investment is not adopted by a vast majority of the population (condition 2). In Germany, a major part of the population does not invest on the stock market (Balonier et al. 2022 from *Deutsches Aktieninstitut*). The logical relationships between the different adoption steps of robo-advisors are fulfilled with the following technologies: Robo-advisor technology corresponds to the advanced technology (A), stock market investment is the basic technology (B), and stock market investment using robo-advisor technology represents the combined technology (C).

The dependence of one technology on past decision-making is not unique to this scenario nor to the technologies mentioned above. This dependence can also be found in a literature which up until now was often separated from the technology adoption research: the literature of individual path dependence.

2.3.2 Individual Path Dependence

It is a common adage that "history matters." This concept was applied to the evolutionary development of firms' capabilities and behavior in market environments (Nelson and Winter 1982) focusing on self-reinforcing effects (Arthur 1989; Arthur 1996), e.g., technologies exhibiting increasing returns.

The study of self-reinforcing effects led to the concept of path dependence. It was defined and applied to the adoption of QWERTY keyboards, which were adopted more readily and persisted against more efficient versions of keyboards (David 1985). Path dependence was defined by David 1985 as:

> *"A path-dependent sequence of economic changes is one of which important influences upon the eventual outcome can be exerted by temporally remote events, including happenings dominated by chance elements rather than systematic forces. Stochastic processes like that do not converge automatically to a fixed-point distribution of outcomes and are called non-ergodic. In such circumstances "historical accidents" can neither be ignored, nor neatly quarantined for the purpose of economic analysis; the dynamic process itself takes on an essentially historical character."*

As a factor leading to path dependence, consider the network effects described by Arthur 1996:

> *"Many high-tech products need to be compatible with a network of users. Thus, if much downloadable software on the Internet will soon appear as programs written in Sun Microsystems' Java language, users will need Java on their computers to run them."*

Furthermore, another factor leading to path dependence on the individual level is customer groove-in described by Arthur 1996 as:

> *"High tech products are typically difficult to use. They require training. Once users invest in this training—say the maintenance and piloting of Airbus passenger aircraft—they merely need to update these skills for subsequent versions of the product."*

David 2001 has refined his previous definition of path dependence into two definitions. A negative one which defines *"[p]rocesses that are non-ergodic, and thus unable to shake free of their history, are said to yield path dependent outcomes."* His positive definition of path dependence states that *"[a] path dependent stochastic process is one whose asymptotic distribution evolves as a consequence (function of) the process's own history."* This thesis adheres to the positive definition by David 2001 as it is concise, clear, and preserves the spirit of the original definition by David 1985.

This definition can be applied to the adoption of robo-advice: The stochastic process is the adoption of robo-advisory services within a given population, e.g., Germans, US-Americans, or investors and non-investors in Germany or the United States. As I previously argued, the asymptotic distribution of the adoption of robo-advisory services depends on the stock market participation within a given population. Furthermore, stock market participation is a necessary step for the adoption of robo-advisory services, thus, it is part of the history of every robo-advisor adoption process. Therefore, the adoption of robo-advice can be seen as path dependent as per the definition of David 2001. The history of the adoption process, i.e., whether an individual invests on the stock market, directly affects that individual's choice and only indirectly affects the aggregate adoption within a population. Thus, I refer to the adoption of robo-advice as path dependent on the individual level. However, as previously done in this paragraph, that path dependence of robo-advisor adoption can also be described and measured on an aggregate level.

Although the concept of path dependence has been mostly applied in the context of capabilities (Nelson and Winter 1982; Cohen and Levinthal 1990), market dominance (Arthur 1989; Arthur 1996; Mueller 1997), or choice (Tang and Ho 2019) and implementation (Rossi et al. 2011; Albrecht et al. 2018) of technological standards of organizations, its mechanisms can also be applied to individuals (Aversi et al. 1999). According to choice theory, individual choice behavior is influenced by experiences shaping memories in turn shaping perceptions, beliefs, motivations, and affects (Ben-Akiva et al. 1999; McFadden 2001) as well as by history shaping perceptions and preferences (Ben-Akiva et al. 2002).

The negligence of the phenomenon of path dependence in the adoption and diffusion of IT was pointed out by Lyytinen and Damsgaard 2001. Different approaches to incorporate it were presented in the literature, but they almost exclusively focus on path dependence in an institutional setting. Technologies considered in this regard include electronic data interchange (EDI) (Lyytinen and Damsgaard 2001), OpenOffice (Rossi et al. 2011), blockchain use cases in the energy sector (Albrecht et al. 2018) and the Internet of Things (Tang and Ho 2019).

2.3.2.1 Alternative Definitions of Path Dependence

Some definitions of path dependence differ from David's concept (David 1985 and David 2001). I choose to present selected definitions to highlight the diversity of concepts. However, I do not necessarily endorse them.

Liebowitz and Margolis 1995 aim to prevent a transfer of the plausibility of *"the empirical and logical support"* for weaker forms of path dependence (first- and second-degree) to third-degree path dependence, which posits inefficiency.

They define three different degrees of path dependence:

- First-degree path dependence: *"[S]ensitivity to starting points exists but has no implied inefficiency first-degree path dependence."* The decision for a system to power a plant is an example cited by Liebowitz and Margolis 1995, which might have long-lasting effects. They argue that these effects might be fully taken into account by decision-makers.

- Second-degree path dependence: *"[S]ensitive dependence on initial conditions leads to outcomes that are regrettable and costly to change."* Decisions subjected to second-degree path dependence might be inferior in hindsight.
- Third-degree path dependence: *"[S]ensitive dependence on initial conditions leads to an outcome that is inefficient—but in this case the outcome is also remediable."* In this scenario, a better outcome could have been derived, as there is or was the possibility to recognize and realize the negative effect of the initial conditions. Nevertheless, the better outcome is not reached.

Barnes et al. 2004 use the term *"behavioral lock-in"* to *"stress and develop David's concept of 'irreversibility due to learning and habituation.'"* (David 1985). They elaborate that *"[b]ehavioral lock-in occurs when the behavior of the agent (consumer or producer) is 'stuck' in some sort of inefficiency or sub-optimality due to habit, organizational learning, or culture."*. The concept of behavioral lock-in might explain the reluctance of Germans to adopt stocks, as the German pension system relies predominantly on defined benefit plans, often mandated (Deutsche Rentenversicherung) or supported by the German government (Riester-Rente). Thus, they can be considered as "stuck" due to habits formed by culture and institutional settings.

Vergne and Durand 2010 define path dependence *"as a property of a stochastic process which obtains under two conditions (contingency and self-reinforcement) and causes lock-in in the absence of exogenous shock."* in an effort to narrow the scope of the concept of path dependence. They define contingency as *"unpredictable, non-purposive, and somewhat random events"*. They clarify this statement by giving the example that *"a first mover advantage is rarely contingent: firms strategically plan to enter first in markets when they know it can be beneficial. Therefore, a persisting market domination explained by first mover advantage would not qualify for a path dependence explanation."*. To substantiate the necessity of self-reinforcement for path dependence, they stipulate that path dependence requires *"a mechanism that decreases the relative attractiveness of alternatives"*. An example is the QWERTY keyboard for which learning how to operate the keyboard (constituting increasing returns resulting in self-reinforcement) not only makes it more attractive, but also alternatives less attractive due to the time it would take to use the alternative system efficiently. Vergne and Durand 2010 define lock-in as a *"state of equilibrium with a very low potential for endogenous change—put simply, lock-in is a hard-to-escape situation."*.

Although these alternative concepts and definitions have their merits, they have a more particular and context-specific view on path dependence than the general definition by David 2001. Thus, this thesis is guided by the general definition by David 2001, while acknowledging that the alternative definitions might be applicable in specific contexts.

2.3.3 Individual Path Dependence and Robo-Advice

Robo-advisory services—as defined in this thesis—are used to allocate financial resources among stocks, bonds, and other assets. Thus, the investment on the stock market is a necessary condition for the adoption of robo-advice and fulfills the two conditions of Section 2.3.1 for modeling the effect of the basic technology on the new technology. The timing of the decision to invest on the stock market can principally be differentiated by taking the decision

a. **before** the adoption of robo-advisor technology.
b. **during** the adoption of robo-advisor technology.

From the point of view of an investigation of robo-advisor adoption, the difference between people adopting stock market investment before or during the adoption of robo-advisor technology equals the difference between investors and non-investors in this investigation. I will use these terms in the remainder of the thesis.

Investors and non-investors can be considered as having different histories regarding the robo-advisor adoption process. To illustrate this statement, consider the example of a person evaluating investments to prepare for retirement. Investments on the stock market are one option for private investment which requires specific learning costs. These learning costs can be assumed to equal a positive value x and might include finding a broker, defining an investment strategy, choosing the right assets, etc. Hence, experience with investments on the stock market leads to a customer groove-in, as described by Arthur 1996 cited in Section 2.3.2 causing path dependence.

Investing on the stock market using robo-advisor technology also involves learning or setup costs, e.g., for choosing a supplier, for filling in the necessary questionnaires, etc. As the investment with a robo-advisor always entails the investment on the stock market, the learning costs of using a robo-advisor for non-investors can be thought of as a combination of x (the learning costs for investing on the stock market) and y (the specific contribution of robo-advisory services to the learning costs). As robo-advisors provide a service that might make investments easier, y might be negative. Thus, the learning costs for investing on the stock market using a robo-advisor are $x + y$ for non-investors and y for investors. As x is positive, the learning costs for non-investors are always higher than for investors driving the individual path dependence of decision making, as it will influence the asymptotic distribution of robo-advisor-acceptance by investors and non-investors.

The exact size of the learning costs is an empirical question that depends on factors as the country and population in question. This example illustrates which mechanisms can cause individual path dependence. This thesis concentrates on the effects that these mechanisms have for technology adoption. Hence, the exact size of x and y is neither investigated nor quantified.

Learning how to invest on the stock market or in real estate might also influence the attitudes towards technologies. When a person has experience with investments on the stock market, the person might be better able to judge how much the service of a robo-advisor facilitates the choice of an investment strategy and appropriate assets. Furthermore, the person might already be acquainted with the companies offering robo-advisory services as a huge proportion of robo-advisors are also online brokers, e.g., Scalable Capital.

The author is not aware of any paper investigating path dependence of past technology choices on the individual level.[2] In the following, I am going to extend the UTAUT model to incorporate path dependent effects of any nature and point out technologies for which this model might be applicable.

2.4 The PDA-UTAUT Model

In this section, I propose how to integrate individual path dependence in the form of the adoption of a basic product or technology into the UTAUT model, i.e., the path dependence augmented UTAUT model (PDA-UTAUT model). The resulting model is not specific to robo-advisors and can be generally applied to new technologies which rely on basic technologies. In Chapter 3, I will adjust the PDA-UTAUT model to the technology of robo-advisory services.

[2] The only attempt to consider path dependence on the level of individual decision-making investigates mobile reading (Zhang et al. 2018). Zhang et al. 2018 investigate individual decision making for mobile reading. They define path dependence as "users‘ reliance on the mobile reading apps of smartphone. Once it was used before to reading, it was the first considerable choice next time when users want to read or search for information and relax.". This definition is more closely related to consumer inertia regarding brand or product choice (e.g., Dubé et al. 2010) than to the concept of individual path dependence used in this study.

2.4.1 The UTAUT Model with Exogenous Path Dependence

Including path dependence based on past technological choices, i.e., the adoption of a basic product/technology, in models of technology adoption (UTAUT and TAM) requires the inclusion of an additional construct in the respective model. The basic technology "facilitates" in a certain sense the adoption of the new technology. Nevertheless, it is substantially different from the construct "facilitating conditions" already considered in the classical UTAUT model, defined as "the degree to which an individual believes that an organizational and technical infrastructure exists to support use of the system" (Venkatesh et al. 2003).

Adoption of a basic product/technology has to be treated as a distinct concept from "facilitating conditions" due to the following marked differences:

- "Facilitating conditions" usually reflect the *beliefs* of potential users about conditions in their environment, *do not influence the attitudes towards a technology*, and are treated as *exogenous* (Venkatesh and Zhang 2010; Yu 2012; Venkatesh et al. 2012; Morosan and DeFranco 2016).
- The concept of the adoption of a basic product or technology relies on (past) *behavior* of the users, *has potential effects on their attitudes towards the new technology* (as described later in this section), and can be endogenized as in the next Section 2.4.2.
- In contrast to "facilitating conditions", the adoption of a basic product or technology is often a necessary condition to adopt the new technology.[3]

Some researchers solve the issue of necessary basic products or technologies by excluding the part of the population which does not use the basic technology from their investigation (Venkatesh et al. 2012; Todd and Seay 2020; Fan and Chatterjee 2020; Morosan and DeFranco 2016). This approach comes with some important disadvantages. Firstly, evidently no information can be gathered at the population level. This is important in situations in which people who use or do not use a specific product differ in their attitudes. Secondly, the effect of the usage of the basic product on the attitudes towards the new technology cannot be accounted for. This might potentially lead to an omitted variable bias (Wooldridge

[3] Examples for necessary basic technologies and their respective new technologies include mobile devices and mobile internet (Venkatesh et al. 2012), value-added networks (VAN) or internet service providers (ISP) making electronic data interchange feasible (Lyytinen and Damsgaard 2001), and mobile devices and near field communication mobile payments (NFC-MP) (Morosan and DeFranco 2016).

2019). Thirdly, the population which did not adopt the basic technology might be of special importance to solve the underlying adoption problem. Consider the case of digital micro banking offered in developing countries requiring smartphones. It is hard to argue that those who do not have smartphones are less likely to need financial support.

Nevertheless, there might be other aspects than a specific product or technology in an environment that serve as facilitating conditions. Therefore, including the adoption of a basic technology or product does not mean that the items reflecting the perception of the facilitating conditions, or other measures of facilitating conditions, have to be removed. Furthermore, multiple technologies can constitute basic technologies for one new technology, e.g., programming languages, software products or operating systems for the usage of a new software.

In the following, I explain how to incorporate these ideas into a UTAUT model. The UTAUT model represents the basic scenario explained in *Figure 2.1.* Although Arthur's seminal theories on path dependence (Arthur 1989; Arthur 1996) are derived from a technology and competition economics point of view, I would like to take his examples to illustrate how to integrate path dependence into UTAUT models.

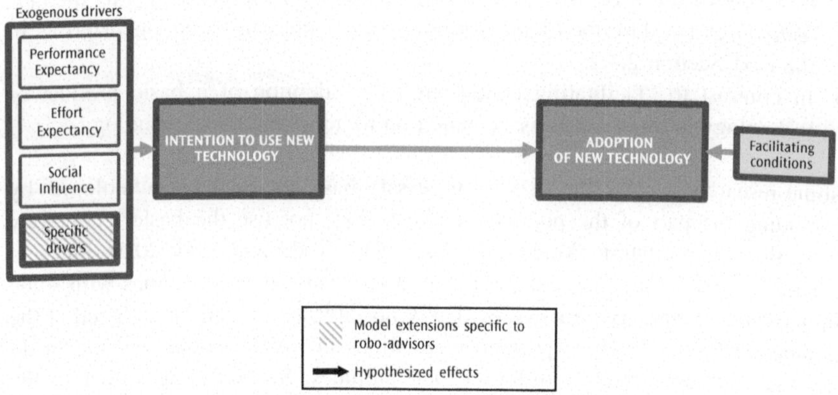

Figure 2.1 Classical UTAUT model

Arthur uses the example of different versions of a high-tech product like planes to describe the specific abilities acquired by an individual by the usage of another technology. A similar "groove-in" can also be expected when using different products of the same product family. An example could be products of a company using an operating system sharing similar properties of the user interface. Another example could be cars from the same producer sharing properties like the location of the parking brake. In cases like these, I expect people to find it easier to use these products, as they have used products with a similar logic before.

To account for these effects, I propose to include a construct dubbed "adoption of basic product/technology" into the model with a direct effect on the adoption of the new technology (see *Figure 2.2*). I refer to the established technology (e.g., the last version of an aircraft) as the basic product as it provides the experience, knowledge, or infrastructural basis for the new product (e.g., the latest aircraft from this specific provider). Contrarily, the new technology can be seen as an "add-on to the existing technology base" as Lyytinen and Damsgaard 2001 put it for the case of electronic data interchange (EDI).

It is not necessary that only one basic product is included in the model of technology adoption to account for path dependence effects. To take Arthur's example of the Java language necessary to use certain programs, it is easy to imagine that a user needs two (or more) languages, operating systems, or software products to use another program. The number of basic products included in the specific model should be limited by practical reasons and plausibility of influencing effects.

To take the idea of experience with the basic product further, it is possible that usage of the basic products influences the exogenous constructs of the new technology (potentially causing an omitted-variable bias when not included in the model as mentioned above). I do not claim that these effects exist for all technologies nor that they have a specific direction a priori. Consider the example of the programming language Java for illustrative purposes: Having experiences with this language might give an individual a clear idea of what to expect from the software which was programmed using this language. If the individual has experienced that using Java is a very useful tool to program a variety of helpful programs, but lacks behind in its ease of use, the individual might have a higher "performance expectancy" and a lower "effort expectancy" compared to an individual who has not made these experiences. When using this model, researchers should judge which effects from the adoption of the basic idea to the exogenous drivers are plausible and worth investigating.

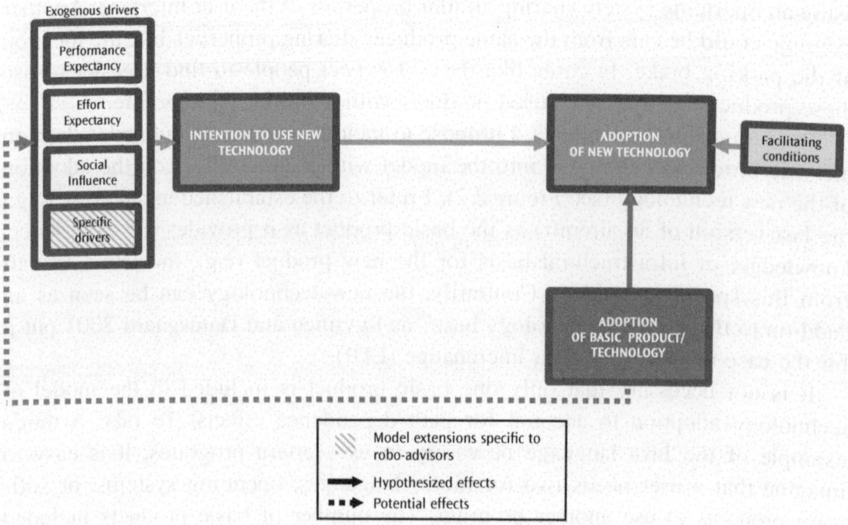

Figure 2.2 UTAUT model with exogenous path dependence

2.4.2 Endogenizing the Basic Product Adoption

In Section 2.4.1, the adoption of the basic product has been treated as not necessary for the adoption of the new product. This contrasts with the logical relationship of adoption that I have provided above for new technologies that require the basic technology to function, as robo-advisors do. In the next paragraphs, I will describe the difference between basic products that are necessary to implement the new technology and basic products that are not. Furthermore, I will discuss how to incorporate necessary basic products in technology acceptance models. The resulting model is referred to as the path dependence augmented UTAUT model (PDA-UTAUT model).

Consider the two examples from Arthur 1996. Knowing previous versions of an aircraft might give an individual an advantage in using new versions and require less training and investment, but it is not a necessary condition. Thus, it is possible for a new pilot to fly with the new aircraft without ever having used the older version. If you consider Java, which is necessary to run certain programs, the case is different. If I do not adopt or use Java, I cannot use the programs. Thus, the adoption of the basic product is a necessary condition to use the new program. This role as a necessary condition of the adoption of basic technology for the adoption of the new technology can be found for different technologies: mobile devices for NFC technology (Morosan and DeFranco 2016), specific game consoles for the usage of virtual reality (VR) equipment, smartphone usage for the adoption of digital micro banking as development aid, etc.

Therefore, I argue that the adoption of the basic product can be modeled as an endogenous construct. Thus, the basic technology is explained by exogenous drivers. In the case of technologies, the constructs of technology adoption models can be applied. If the basic technology should be of a non-technological nature (more about this below), other constructs should be considered. This has an influence on the intention constructs. While the traditional UTAUT model has only one intention construct (for the new technology) and this remains sufficient for cases where the basic product is not necessary to use the new technology, this changes when the basic technology becomes an endogenous construct.

One might be tempted to consider that path dependence could be modeled as a moderating variable, analogously to the variable "previous experience" or "familiarity", which is often included in UTAUT and TAM models as a moderating variable (Venkatesh et al. 2003; Venkatesh et al. 2012; Belanche et al. 2019). Nevertheless, the content of the two concepts is distinct. Experience or familiarity relates to the target technology itself and was initially operationalized as the passage of time since a person was introduced to a system (Venkatesh et al. 2003). Path dependence on the other hand relates to the impact that the adoption of another technology has on the adoption of the new technology. Especially, if the basic technology is a necessary condition, a specification as a moderating effect is necessarily flawed: If the basic technology is not adopted, the new technology cannot be adopted until the basic technology is adopted together with it. On the other hand, even though no previous experience is necessary to adopt a technology, it can influence how the attitudes towards a technology influence the usage intention.

Thus, path dependence is modeled as a construct with a direct effect on the adoption of robo-advice and not as a moderating effect for the following reasons:

- The adoption of the basic technology is a necessary condition in some cases, e.g., in the case of robo-advice. Moderating factors are usually not factors that contain necessary conditions, e.g., although gender might moderate the effect of certain attitudes on robo-advisor adoption, it is never a prohibiting factor.
- The adoption of the basic technology can directly influence the attitudes towards the new technology, as it influences the experiences of a person assessing a new technology.

- The construct "facilitating conditions" in the UTAUT model directly influences the adoption of the new technology, as its importance is beyond influencing the mere intention to use the new technology. As the adoption of the basic technology also "facilitates" in some sense the adoption of the new technology, its influence on the adoption of the new technology is modeled in the same way. Nevertheless, the adoption of the basic technology is distinct from the construct "facilitating conditions" of the UTAUT model as discussed in Section 2.4.1.

I argue that it is useful to differentiate three constructs: The intention to use the basic product, the intention to use the new technology, and the intention to use the basic product/technology with the new technology. This differentiation is useful to identify the individual effects of the adoption intentions of the new and the basic technology. The three intentions can be categorized in the following way:

- The intention to use the basic product/technology: This intention only relates to the basic product/technology without any interaction with attitudes towards the new technology. Applied to the case of robo-advice and stock market investment, this construct would relate to the intention to invest on the stock market irrespective of the attitudes towards robo-advice or even knowledge about the existence of robo-advice.
- The intention to use the new technology: This intention exclusively concerns the new technology without a direct effect of the basic technology and possibly without the knowledge that the adoption of the basic technology is necessary. Applied to the case of robo-advice and stock market investment, this construct describes the intention to use robo-advisor technology without considering that this constitutes a stock market investment and possibly without the participant's knowledge that a stock market investment is necessary to use the new technology. One might correctly argue that a lack of awareness of stock market investment might only apply to very naïve individuals in the case of robo-advice. Nevertheless, when considering other technologies, this might be an important factor. Consider the case of a program which requires Java to work on a computer. The potential user might form opinions on the program, based on reviews from colleagues, suggestions on the internet, etc., without knowing that he/she requires the basic technology (Java) to use it, and he/she

might only learn about the requirement of Java when trying to install the new program.

- The intention to use the basic product/technology with the new technology: This intention relates to the combination of both the new and basic technology, i.e., the intention to use the new product is formed in the full knowledge that the basic product has to be used. Applied to the case of robo-advice and stock market investment, the construct represents the idea that an individual has formed the idea to adopt robo-advice being fully aware that this entails an investment on the stock market.

The inclusion of the third intention construct, i.e., the intention to use the basic product/technology with the new technology, is of further theoretical relevance: As some models in the technology acceptance literature do not include the adoption but only focus on intention to use, e.g., Belanche et al. 2019, this construct allows to consistently disentangle the influence of the attitudes towards the new technology and the basic product technology in these cases.

If there would be no such construct, researchers who choose to investigate the intention instead of adoption behavior would not be able to differentiate the effects of the independent factors of the intention to use the new and basic technology or would have to assume a direct effect of the intention to use the basic technology on the intention to use the new technology. Thus, they could only investigate a new technology, which is necessarily dependent on the attitudes towards the basic technology. To reconsider the example of the new program requiring Java, intentions would be modeled in a way that the intention to use the new program would necessarily depend on the intention to use Java. As argued above, potential users might not even be aware that they have to install Java before installing the new technology.

Finally, the question whether a differentiation between *the intention to use the new technology* and *the intention to use the basic product/technology with the new technology* is useful remains an empirical question. It might be answered differently depending on the technologies and populations under investigation.[4]

See *Figure 2.3* for the PDA-UTAUT model.

[4] This question will be addressed for robo-advisors in Germany and the USA in Section 4.2.1 as part of the empirical investigation of the PDA-UTAUT model.

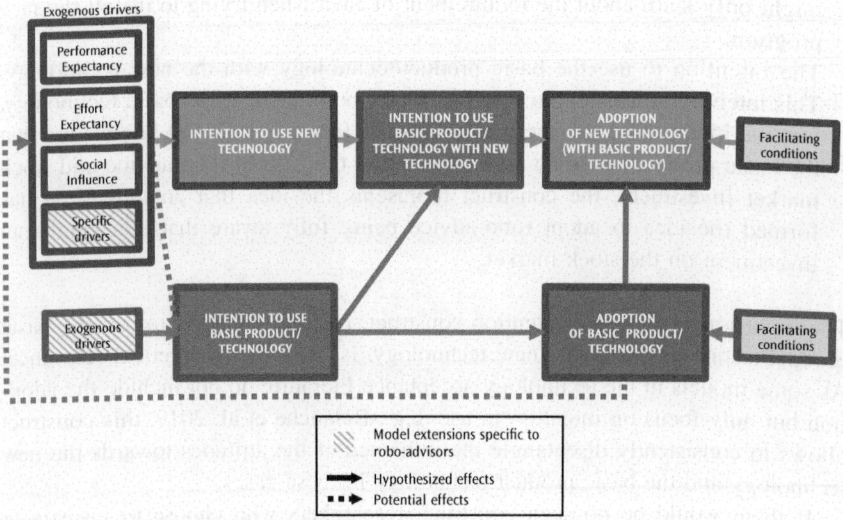

Figure 2.3 PDA-UTAUT model

By incorporating the concept of individual path dependence, the PDA-UTAUT model is an answer to Benbasat and Barki's 2007 call for a multi-stage model of technology adoption applicable to technologies which rely on a basic technology.

3 Adapting the Model to Robo-Advice

In this chapter, I will explain how to adapt the PDA-UTAUT model to the case of robo-advisory. As already mentioned above, investment in assets on the stock market is a necessary condition to be able to invest with robo-advisors. Therefore, I conclude that a PDA-model, which treats the basic product as an endogenous construct, is the most appropriate one to investigate the adoption of robo-advisors. Furthermore, investment on the stock market corresponds rather to an investment product with its own adoption literature than a technology. Thus, the adoption of investment on the stock market is not treated as a technology explained by the exogenous variables of a technology acceptance model (e.g., UTAUT), but with the drivers established in the academic literature and explained below.

To enhance clarity, I will derive the PDA-UTAUT model applied to robo-advisors in three steps, which will be theoretically derived and analyzed in different sections of this thesis, but are an integral part of one cohesive model:

1. The "classical UTAUT model part" of the PDA-UTAUT model applied to robo-advisors describes the effects of the classical drivers of the UTAUT model and the specific drivers on *the intention to use robo-advisor technology (IURA)*. This step does not yet incorporate path dependence. It is theoretically derived in the Section 3.1 for the classical drivers of the UTAUT model and in Section 3.2 for the drivers which are specific to robo-advisor technology. The results are presented in Section 4.3.1.
2. The "exogenous path dependence part" of the PDA-UTAUT model applied to robo-advisors contains the effect of the adoption of the basic technology, i.e., the investment on the stock market, on the investment with a robo-advisor and the attitudes towards robo-advisor technology. The theoretical reasonings

M. Horn, *Technology Acceptance, Path Dependence, and the Demand for Robo-Advisory Services*, Forschung zur Digitalisierung der Wirtschaft | Advanced Studies in Business Digitization, https://doi.org/10.1007/978-3-658-44679-6_3

behind the "exogenous path dependence part" are presented in Section 3.3. Section 4.3.2 presents the empirical results.
3. The "endogenous path dependence part" of the PDA-UTAUT model applied to robo-advisors presents the drivers of the adoption of the basic technology, i.e., the investment on the stock market, and incorporates the differentiation between *the intention to invest with a robo-advisor (IIRA)*, *the intention to use robo-advisor technology (IURA)*, and *the intention to invest (IINV)*. While Section 3.4 details the theory behind the "endogenous path dependence part", Section 4.3.3 presents its empirical results.

However, these three steps belong to one common PDA-UTAUT model applied to robo-advisors. Hence, the empirical results *in Section 4.3* are obtained in *one common model* involving all three steps. Thus, they have to be considered as a unity, which reflects the theory of path dependence and technology acceptance models applied to robo-advisors. For a concise presentation, I will refer to the steps of the model in some instances without explicity mentioning that they belong to "the complete PDA-UTAUT model applied to robo-advisors".

3.1 The Constructs of the Traditional UTAUT Model

As already noted, the UTAUT model was established to investigate the adoption of technology. Therefore, the factors described in this section are associated with the technological step of robo-advisor adoption, i.e., the intention to use robo-advisor technology.

3.1.1 Performance Expectancy

Venkatesh et al. 2003 define performance expectancy as the degree to which an individual believes that using the system will help him or her to attain gains in job performance. Performance expectancy has proven to be the strongest predictor of behavioral intention to use technologies in a plethora of studies (Compeau and Higgins 1995 (computer use in Canada); Davis et al. 1992 (computer use in the workplace); Taylor and Todd 1995a (computer resource center by business students); Venkatesh and Davis 2000 (in four organizations, two with mandatory and two with optional usage of the technology)).

Belanche et al. 2019 found the direct effect of perceived usefulness (the corresponding construct from TAM to performance expectancy in UTAUT) on intention to use a robo-advisor not to be significant. But they found a significant positive effect on attitude (explained by the two constructs perceived usefulness and perceived ease of use), which in turn had a significant influence on intention to use.

3.1.2 Effort Expectancy

Venkatesh et al. 2003 define effort expectancy as the degree of ease associated with the use of a technology. Davis et al. 1989 demonstrated the positive effect of perceived ease of use (equivalent terminology from TAM) of a word processing program among American MBA students.[1] Effort expectancy is shown to be of importance for technology adoption in various contexts, but its importance diminishes when familiarity increases (Thompson et al. 1991; Thompson et al. 1994; Agarwal and Prasad 1997; Agarwal and Prasad 1998).

No direct effect of effort expectancy on performance expectancy is included in the model. The original idea behind the inclusion of this effect in the technology acceptance model (TAM) was in the words of Davis 1985:

> *"Given that a non-trivial fraction of a user's total job content is devoted to physically using the system per se, if the user becomes more productive in that fraction of his or her job via greater ease of use, then he or she becomes more productive overall."*

Thus, an effect of perceived ease of use (PEOU) on perceived usefulness (PU) was hypothesized because the technologies in question were used on the job with a substantial amount of time spent on them. This condition is not met by robo-advisors: Their purpose is to automate investment and, thus, render the time spent with them trivial.

3.1.3 Interpersonal and External Influence

I follow Bhattacherjee's concept of subjective norms, which are defined as "perceptions about social forces influencing a behavior" (Bhattacherjee 2000).

---

[1] Belanche et al. 2019 showed that perceived ease of use has an impact on the behavioral intention to use a robo-advisor through the variable of attitude (explained by perceived usefulness and perceived ease of use) among British, American, and Portuguese web survey participants.

According to Karahanna et al. 1999, social influence consists both of informational influence and normative influence. Informational influence is exerted when individuals accept information as evidence of reality. Normative influence is exerted when individuals conform to others' expectations. This distinction is consistent with the communication channels described in Rogers 1962 proposing that two sources of information are considered to judge an innovation.

Interpersonal influence describes word-of-mouth influence by friends, colleagues, superiors, and other prior adopters in the social environment of the test subject and represents the normative influence of social norms. The concept of interpersonal influence shares a strong overlap with the definition of social influence as "the degree to which an individual perceives that important others believe he or she should use the new system" by Venkatesh et al. 2003.

The importance of social influence has been demonstrated in different applicable fields: Brancheau and Wetherbe 1990 found, contrary to their own hypothesis coming from a perspective of the innovation diffusion theory (IDT), that interpersonal communication was the dominant factor of the adoption decision making of spreadsheet software of 500 professionals in 18 distinct businesses. Experienced voluntariness had a negative influence on world wide web adoption among business school students according to the study of Agarwal and Prasad 1997 showcasing the influence of normative influence. Therefore, the interpersonal influence part of subjective norms is represented by the construct of social influence established throughout the UTAUT literature.

External influence, which describes nonpersonal information, is considered by decision makers to make a "rational" decision. External influence includes media reports, expert opinions, and other nonpersonal information and corresponds to the information influence. Thus, external influence will be measured by a distinct construct to account for the influence of modern media.

Belanche et al. 2019 found an effect of subjective norms measured by interpersonal (i.e., social influence) and external influence on the behavioral intention of study participants in the UK, Portugal, and in the USA to use a robo-advisor. Herr et al. 1991 demonstrated the effect of word-of-mouth on the product evaluations of students on personal computers and automobiles from a marketing perspective.

3.1.4 Facilitating Conditions

Facilitating conditions were originally defined as "the degree to which an individual believes that an organizational and technical infrastructure exists to support use of the system" (Venkatesh et al. 2003), while it later was defined as "consumers' perceptions of the resources and support available to perform a behavior" to adapt it to consumers (Venkatesh et al. 2012).

Facilitating conditions are theorized to predict actual usage of a technology alongside the behavioral intention to use a technology in the UTAUT model (Venkatesh et al. 2003). The items to measure them are usually beliefs (Venkatesh and Zhang 2010; Yu 2012; Venkatesh et al. 2012; Morosan and DeFranco 2016). Nevertheless, for the operationalization of facilitating conditions, I choose the objective feature household wealth, as it makes investment with a robo-advisor (and on the stock market in general) easier.[2]

In the context of this study, household wealth can be seen as an objective factor that makes an act easy to do as it enables the investment in stocks with or without a robo-advisor. The positive impact of household wealth on stock market participation was demonstrated in the major European economies of France, Germany, Italy, the Netherlands, Sweden, and the UK (Guiso et al. 2003) as well as the USA (Bertaut 1998), thus, it can be considered as established for the countries in focus (Germany and the USA). Furthermore, it constitutes an objective measure potentially increasing the comparability of German and American results. Therefore, household wealth is assumed to predict actual investment behavior, i.e., the factors "investment using robo-advisor technology" and, if the basic product is endogenized as in Section 3.4, "investment in stocks" in the research model.

Household wealth might not be the only facilitating condition applicable in this situation. Another evident facilitating condition is access to the internet. Nevertheless, the population of the countries in focus had an individual internet participation rate of 91% in the USA and 90% in Germany in 2020[3]. Furthermore, internet availability cannot be measured in the scope of this investigation as participation required access to the internet, as data are collected via online surveys (see Section 4.1). This reduces generalizability in the countries in question and should be considered by researchers investigating robo-advisor adoption in countries with a lower individual internet participation rate.

---

[2] Thus, I follow the definition of one of the root constructs of "facilitating conditions" in the UTAUT model, which is derived from the model of PC utilization (MPCU): "Objective factors in the environment that observers agree make an act easy to accomplish." (Thompson et al. 1991).

[3] According to data from the International Communication Union endorsed by the World Bank n.d.

3.1.5 Control and Moderator Variables

Demographic variables play an established role in the models of technology acceptance UTAUT and TAM as control and moderator variables because they have proven significant in various studies with diverse technologies:

- While younger age was associated with a higher importance placed on performance expectancy (Venkatesh et al. 2003), higher age exhibited the tendency to strengthen gender differences (Morris et al. 2005).
- Familiarity with AI and robots was shown to have a moderating role such that participants with a lower level of familiarity are more influenced by opinions of others or mass media (Belanche et al. 2019).
- Gender was confirmed to influence the role of others' opinions on the adoption decision (Venkatesh et al. 2003).
- Income uncertainty was shown to increase risk aversion (Guiso and Paiella 2008).
- Education was confirmed to have a positive impact on stock market participation (Guiso et al. 2003; Van Rooij et al. 2011; Yoong 2011).

Accounting for path dependence introduces many modifications to the UTAUT model. Thus, it is plausible that the role of demographic variables might be different from past studies. Therefore, this study focuses on the direct role of path dependence and treats the demographic variables as control factors. These control factors are controlled for ex-post. The following demographic and financial variables are included in the survey: age, familiarity, gender, income, and education. The effects of familiarity (with the use of robots) are only checked for those paths in which the dependent construct is a construct relating to the adoption of or attitudes towards robo-advisor technology as the construct itself directly relates to robots.[4] Special attention during the analysis is paid to those effects that emerge in both the German and American sample and, thus, show consistency.

[4] In the empirical analysis, the effects of the control and moderator variables are analyzed at every step of the model.

3.2 Personal Factors Extending the UTAUT Model

Section 3.2 extends the original UTAUT model by Venkatesh et al. 2003 by factors which adapt it to robo-advisor technology. Furthermore, I hypothesize regarding the effects that these factors have on the intention to use robo-advisor technology based on established research.

3.2.1 Perceived Privacy Risk

Different concepts of risk attitude can be found in the literature. The expected utility theory based on Arrow 1971 and Pratt 1964 defines risk attitude by the shape of the utility function determining the choices that people take in risky situations. The common metric of risk attitude in this context is absolute risk aversion.[5] Depending on the absolute risk aversion, people can be categorized as risk averse, risk neutral or risk seeking.

The prospect theory based on Kahneman and Tversky 1979 adds to this literature by including different factors mostly from psychology as the endowment effect, i.e., the loss felt by losing an item is perceived more strongly than winning the same item. Furthermore, the certainty effect (Tversky and Kahneman 1992), which states that a reduction in probability of positive outcomes from certainty to high probability (e.g., 99 %), creates a steeper decline in pleasure than predicted by expected utility theory, i.e., people attribute a high importance to the unlikely event of losses.

These definitions mostly apply to financial risks and are usually measured by lotteries. Different risk factors have been shown to influence consumers' decision making (Featherman and Pavlou 2003). Among them are financial, performance, social, psychological, privacy/security, and time-loss risks. In the context of the investment tool robo-advisor privacy/ data security risks as well as financial risks are the most salient and, therefore, are included in my model. Consequently, a broader definition of risk attitude is chosen. The risk attitude is determined in a psychological risk-return formula by Weber et al. 2002:

$$Preference(x) = a * (expected\ benefit(x)) + b * (perceived\ risk(x)) \tag{3.1}$$

[5] Absolute risk aversion is commonly measured by the Arrow-Pratt measure (Arrow 1971; Pratt 1964), which depends on the shape of a person's utility function: Absolute risk aversion = - u''(x)/u'(x), with u' and u'' denoting the first and second derivative of the utility function, respectively.

In this conceptualization expected benefit and perceived risk are thought to be specific to option x and the situation. Therefore, the specific perceptions of risks and benefits play a central role. This can account for different risk assessments of managers in private and business situations (MacCrimmock and Wehrung 1990). The coefficients a and b specify which utility a person can derive from the expected benefit and risk. b is termed the perceived risk attitude and denotes a preference towards risk which is either risk averse, risk neutral or risk seeking, depending on the sign of b. The assumption is that perceived risk attitude is relatively stable across situations, while the perceived risk is varying; empirical evidence is provided in Weber and Milliman 1997.

The differentiation between perceived risk of an option and the attitude towards that risk has brought some interesting insights. Weber and Hsee 1998 demonstrated that the major differences between students in the USA, Germany, Poland, and China in the risk assessment and resulting willingness to pay could be attributed mostly to differences in how they perceived risks, instead of differing attitudes towards the risks that they perceived.

Apart from the more general risk definition by Weber et al. 2002, privacy risk as per Featherman and Pavlou 2003 covers especially "potential loss of control over personal information, such as when information about you is used without your knowledge or permission." Security and privacy risks include fraud or hacking of an online user's account and phishing of data (Reavley 2005). Moreover, many consumers of online banking are afraid of identity theft (Littler and Melanthiou 2006).

Lee 2009 found a direct impact of perceived privacy risk on the intention to adopt online banking in Taiwan. Lu et al. 2011 demonstrated the negative impact of perceived risk (scales for privacy risk were used) on the behavioral impact to use mobile payment of Chinese speaking users of AliPay.

The General Data Protection Regulation and the right to be forgotten applicable in the EU are anecdotal evidence of the value that EU citizens and especially Germans ascribe to data privacy and security. A company study by Morey et al. 2015 published in the Harvard Business Review indicates that representative citizens of Germany, USA, UK, China, and India would pay significantly different amounts of money to keep their data secret in different settings. German citizens would on average pay the highest amounts of money for their data privacy, British and American citizens rank in the middle, while Chinese and Indian citizens would pay the lowest amounts for their privacy.

I hypothesize based on the evidence:

Hypothesis 1: Perceived privacy risk negatively affects the behavioral intention to use robo-advisor technology.

3.2.2 Personal Innovativeness

Agarwal and Prasad 1998 conceptualized the construct of personal innovativeness in the domain of information technology to describe the willingness of an individual to try out any new information technologies. The construct has been included in different papers in various TAM and UTAUT models. Agarwal and Karahanna 2000 found an effect of personal innovativeness on perceived usefulness and perceived ease of use through the psychological variable cognitive absorption for the internet usage of American students. Yang et al. 2012 demonstrated the positive effect of personal innovativeness on behavioral intention to use (or continue to use) mobile payment in China. Thakur and Srivastava 2014 found an impact of personal innovativeness on the behavioral intention to use mobile payment in India. Furthermore, the direct effect of personal innovativeness on innovation adoption could be replicated in various contexts like online shopping and usage of digital assistants (Yi et al. 2006) as well as adoption and ease of use perception of online shopping of Spanish consumers (Bigné-Alcañiz et al. 2008).

Although anecdotal evidence suggesting that Americans show a fast pace of product adoption is plentiful, direct comparisons of measures of personal innovativeness in research between Germany and the USA are scarce. Proxies suggest that Americans show a higher personal innovativeness compared to Germans. A study by Mocker and Chapman 2017 from *Nesta* conducted in 2016 among 9,000 European adults shows that Germany is the least open out of nine countries to new or emerging technologies, e.g., driverless cars and robots. A study for the year 2019 by Fisher 2020 from *eMarketer* indicates that 29% of American smartphone users have used mobile payment in the 6 months before the study, but only 12.5% of the Germans did. Kennedy and Funk 2016 from the *PEW Research Center* present the results of a study conducted in 2014 among 2840 American adults suggests that as many as 28% are early technology adopters.

I hypothesize based on established research:

Hypothesis 2a: Personal innovativeness positively affects performance expectancy of robo-advisor technology.

Hypothesis 2b: Personal innovativeness positively affects effort expectancy of robo-advisor technology.

Hypothesis 2c: Personal innovativeness positively affects the behavioral intention to use robo-advisor technology.

3.2.3 Financial Literacy

According to a definition study by Remund, "financial literacy is a measure of the degree to which one understands key financial concepts and possesses the ability and confidence to manage personal finances through appropriate, short-term decision-making and sound, long-range financial planning, while mindful of life events and changing economic conditions" (Remund 2010).

I decided for a single factor of financial literacy as the differentiation of these two concepts has little theoretical impact on the question at hand and literature showed that the effects of basic and advanced financial literacy have the same direction (Van Rooij et al. 2011; Fan and Chatterjee 2020; Todd and Seay 2020), but the content of both factors is relevant for potential customers' understanding of advantages and disadvantages of robo-advisors. Furthermore, the number of potential indicators measuring advanced financial literacy surpasses the scope of this investigation (Van Rooij et al. 2011). Therefore, financial literacy is included as a single factor incorporating aspects of basic and advanced financial literacy as defined by Van Rooij et al. 2011. Van Rooij et al.'s classification of basic financial literacy covers "interest rates and interest compounding to the effect of inflation, discounting, and nominal versus real values" (Van Rooij et al. 2011) and advanced financial literacy includes knowledge on "topics such as the difference between stocks and bonds, the function of the stock market, the workings of risk diversification, and the relationship between bond prices and interest rates" (Van Rooij et al. 2011).

The items associated with basic financial literacy were adopted from Lusardi and Mitchell 2008, 2011a, and 2014. The items were originally employed to show the positive impact of financial literacy on retirement by reducing old-age poverty. Older Americans, especially women, minorities and less educated participants exhibited a lower level of financial literacy. Financial literacy correlated with a stronger reliance on formal retirement planning as calculators, seminars, or financial advisors than on information from personal relations. The items associated with advanced financial literacy were a reduced form of the questionnaire from Van Rooij et al. 2011 and were further reduced after comprehension issues were detected during the pre-study.

Lusardi and Mitchell 2011b found that financial literacy is relatively low across different developed and developing markets such as Germany, Japan, the United States, and Russia. The share of respondents who could answer all three questions of basic financial literacy correctly ranged from 57% in Germany to only 3% in Russia. Across markets male gender and a high level of education were positively correlated with financial literacy.

As already noted, Fan and Chatterjee 2020 and Todd and Seay 2020 found a negative effect of objective basic and advanced financial literacy on robo-advisor adoption. Fan and Chatterjee 2020 as well as Todd and Seay 2020 provide similar potential reasons for the negative relationship between objective financial literacy noting that more knowledgeable investors may not need support in their investment-decision making. On the other hand, more knowledgeable investors may resort to human investment advice because they realize that they need more sophisticated support.

Another aspect can be added when considering the two-dimensional approach taken in this study. A negative relationship between financial literacy and robo-advisor adoption contrasts to a certain degree with past literature predicting that financial literacy has a positive effect on stock market participation (Yoong 2011; Van Rooij et al. 2011). Thus, it is reasonable to attribute the negative relationship between financial literacy and robo-advisor adoption established by Fan and Chatterjee 2020 and Todd and Seay 2020 to effects that regard the robo-advisor as a technology. Meanwhile the positive relationship between financial literacy and stock market participation should also hold in this study as it concerns the investment dimension of the research model, which will be discussed later.

Based on the evidence presented above, I hypothesize:

Hypothesis 3a: Financial literacy negatively affects the intention to use robo-advisor technology.

Consider *Figure 3.1* for an overview of the "classical UTAUT model part" of the PDA-UTAUT model applied to robo-advisors.

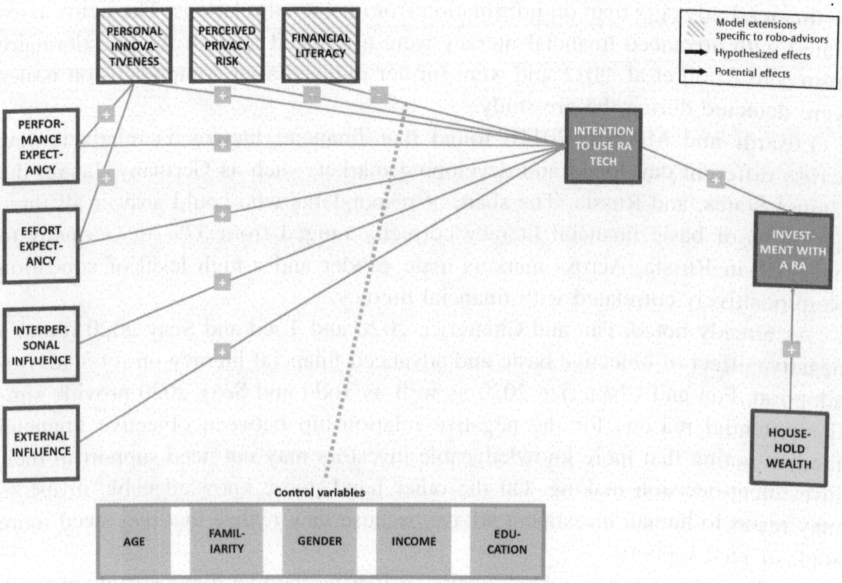

Figure 3.1 "Classical UTAUT model part" of the PDA-UTAUT model applied to RA

3.3 The Inclusion of Path Dependence Into the Model

The basic technology in the context of robo-advice is investment on the stock market as robo-advisor technology serves to manage stock market investment. I assume a direct and positive relationship between the adoption of the basic technology and the adoption of the advanced technology. In this section, analogous to Section 2.4.1, path dependence is introduced into the model without explicit exogenous constructs. However, unlike Section 2.4.1, this only constitutes an intermediate step to the PDA-UTAUT model applied to robo-advisors to be completed in Section 3.4.

I argue that the adoption of the investment on the stock market might have an influence on some of the exogenous drivers of the intention to use robo-advisor technology. I do not refer to this connection as a hypothesis as it is not clear whether the influence should be positive, negative, or existing at all. These effects are merely plausible and, thus, worth to be investigated. I assume that the adoption of investment on the stock market might influence performance expectancy, effort expectancy, external influence, and perceived privacy risk. Performance expectancy could be influenced because investors already have a certain knowledge about investments and, therefore, might be better informed to pass judgment on how much an investment advisor will help them. Consumers with some level of experience with online banking are conceptualized as potential users of robo-advisors (Belanche et al. 2019). Indeed, it is possible that they have a better understanding on how easy or difficult the usage of robo-advisors is (effort expectancy), as robo-advice also constitutes an online service and many robo-advisors are offered by companies which also provide an online broker. Furthermore, similar effects might also be applicable to perceived privacy risk. Investors might lose their reservations against dealing with stock investments online or increase their reservations because they have suffered from a data incident with their online broker.

Streaming platforms like Netflix or video platforms such as YouTube are highly demand driven, i.e., consumers choose the content displayed to them. This is reinforced by marketing targeted at consumers with a high likelihood of interest in the specific product or service. Therefore, it is possible that consumers already invested in stocks and exhibiting interest towards the stock market both consume more content on investments and are more often targeted by advertisements for investment products or services. Therefore, a higher exposure to content on robo-advice could lead to different perceptions of external influence of investors compared to non-investors. *Figure 3.2* gives an overview of the "exogenous path dependence part" of the PDA-UTAUT model applied to robo-advisors.

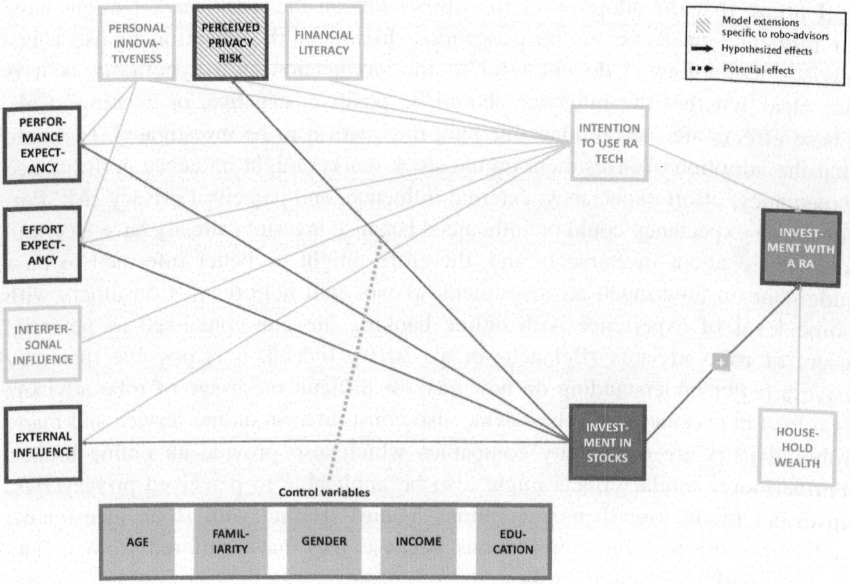

Figure 3.2 "Exogenous path dependence part" of the PDA-UTAUT model applied to RA

3.4 Endogenizing the Basic Technology

The investment on the stock market is not the adoption of one specific technology, but of a class of basic products. Moreover, it is a necessary condition to be able to use robo-advisors. Thus, as argued above, the adoption of the (class of) basic product(s) should be endogenized. As stock market participation is investigated in its own strand of literature and constitutes rather an adoption of a class of basic products than of a technology, the literature on stock market participation is considered in the following, instead of concentrating on the classical UTAUT drivers.

3.4.1 Financial Literacy

Van Rooij et al. 2011 employing a data set of over 2,000 households as part of the De Nederlandsche Bank (DNB) Household Survey found an effect of financial literacy on stock market participation. Most respondents demonstrated command of basic concepts as inflation and interest compounding, but only few participants could tell the difference between stocks and bonds or the fundamentals of risk diversification. Van Rooij et al. 2011 conclude that advanced financial literacy has an effect above and beyond traditional determinants of stock market participation even after controlling for basic financial literacy, education in economics, and usage of economic understanding in daily life.

Yoong 2011 demonstrated with a sample of 533 participants from the RAND American Life Panel (ALP) that stock market investment knowledge had a significant positive impact on stock market participation. The finding is especially interesting as the participant pool exhibited higher levels of income, education, financial literacy, and stock market participation than the American average. The study suggests that increasing financial knowledge and familiarity with finance will increase wealth accumulation capabilities.

Based on the above arguments, I hypothesize:

Hypothesis 3b: Financial literacy positively affects the intention to invest on the stock market.

3.4.2 Ethical Stance Towards the Stock Market

Keller and Siegrist 2006 demonstrated the effect that a negative ethical stance towards the stock market, understood as the view that profiting from the market is unethical or unfair, negatively affects stock market participation. The investigation relies on the concept that people view money as good or evil (Tang 1993). Webley et al. 2001 demonstrated that investors' ethical concerns play a role in investment decisions at the stock market by showing that "ethical" investors are willing to hold their assets chosen for ethical concerns even if they exhibited a bad performance.

Keller and Siegrist 2006 gathered data from over 1,500 study participants in German- and French-speaking Switzerland. They identified financial risk attitude and negative ethical stance toward the stock market as factors predicting the willingness to invest in stocks. According to Keller and Siegrist 2006, a negative ethical stance towards stocks was rooted in the view that profits from stocks are not acquired by work and achievement.

This approach offers interesting insights in the scope of this study, as it directly focuses on the moral attitudes towards the stock market and the products invested in. Following this approach can elicit the moral judgment that potential investors have towards the stock market irrespective of their decision whether to invest on their own or use a robo-advisor. While this factor has not been investigated in depth on an international scale, as per the author's knowledge, investigation on the relationship between moral and religious beliefs and economic behavior can be found in sociology research with a prominent example of Weber's 1905 research on the relationship between Protestantism and modern capitalism.

Conducting the study both in Germany and the USA could answer the question whether the ethical stance towards the stock market can account for the tendency in Germany to invest relatively less on the stock market and in the USA to invest relatively more. This tendency is reflected in an average (mean) wealth of $217,000 in Germany versus $432,000 in USA per adult (Global Wealth Report 2020 by Shorrocks et al. 2020 from *Crédit Suisse*). The lacking investment on the financial markets is showcased by the low share of equity capital of 14% in Germany (European Asset Allocation Survey 2020 by Scott and Watson 2020 from the management consultancy *Mercer*).

Based on the evidence, I hypothesize:

Hypothesis 4: A negative ethical stance towards the stock market negatively affects the behavioral intention to invest on the stock market.

3.4.3 Financial Risk Attitude

As individual stocks and the overall stock market are volatile, an investment in stocks entails financial risks.[6] Therefore, a negative impact of a negative financial risk attitude on the intention to invest on the stock market is straightforward and has been shown in different studies.[7] Keller and Siegrist 2006 demonstrated that financial risk attitude was a good predictor of the willingness to invest in stocks among their Swiss participants. Dimmock and Kouwenberg 2010 found that loss-aversion reduced household participation in equity markets, based on data from the Dutch CentERdata DNB Household Survey.

Financial risk attitude can be conceptualized as a psychometric or a lottery-based measure. Faff et al. 2008 found that the two concepts are closely aligned. The findings of Pennings and Smidts 2000 are very interesting in this context as their comparison of the two risk attitude measures show some degree of convergent validity, but that both measures had a higher predictive power on

[6] See Section 3.2.1 on "Perceived privacy risk" for a definition of risk attitude in this thesis.
[7] Risk attitude also influences the investment characteristics of investors, e.g., their trading behavior and investment horizon. Less risk averse investors trade more and invest on a more short-term basis (Wood and Zaichkowsky 2004).

different attitudes and behaviors. While the psychometric measure was correlated with self-reported attitude and intention measures, e.g., innovativeness and market-orientation, the lottery-based expected utility measure was correlated with behavior. As risk attitude in the context of this model predicts intention, the items of the psychometric measure are adapted from Pennings and Smidts 2000. Furthermore, these items promise a higher discriminant validity from "behavioral intention to invest on the stock market" than the items developed in Weber et al. 2002 based on Weber and Milliman and 1997 as well as Weber and Hsee 1998.

Based on the arguments presented above, I hypothesize:

Hypothesis 5: The financial risk attitude positively affects the behavioral intention to invest on the stock market.

The "endogenous path dependence part" of the PDA-UTAUT model applied to robo-advisors is provided in *Figure 3.3*, while *Figure 3.4* presents the complete PDA-UTAUT model applied to robo-advisors.

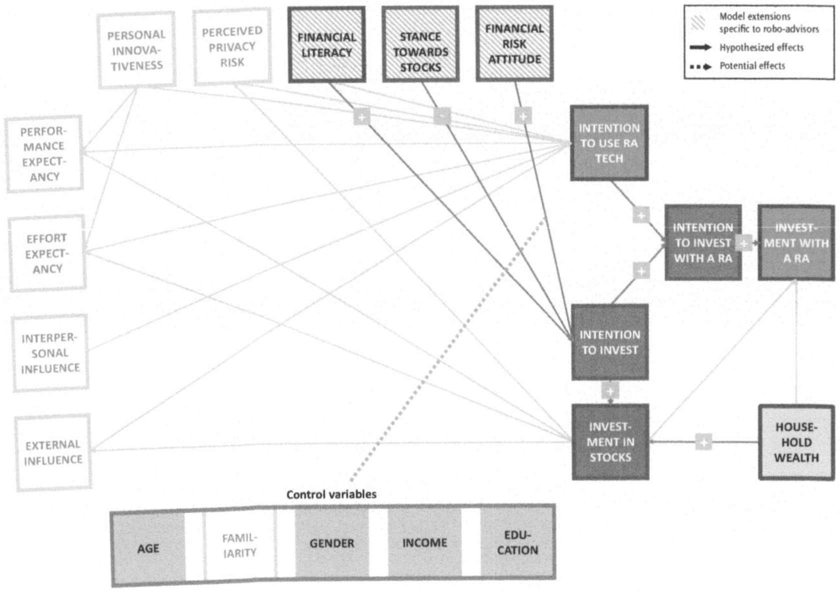

Figure 3.3 "Endogenous path dependence part" of the PDA-UTAUT model applied to RA

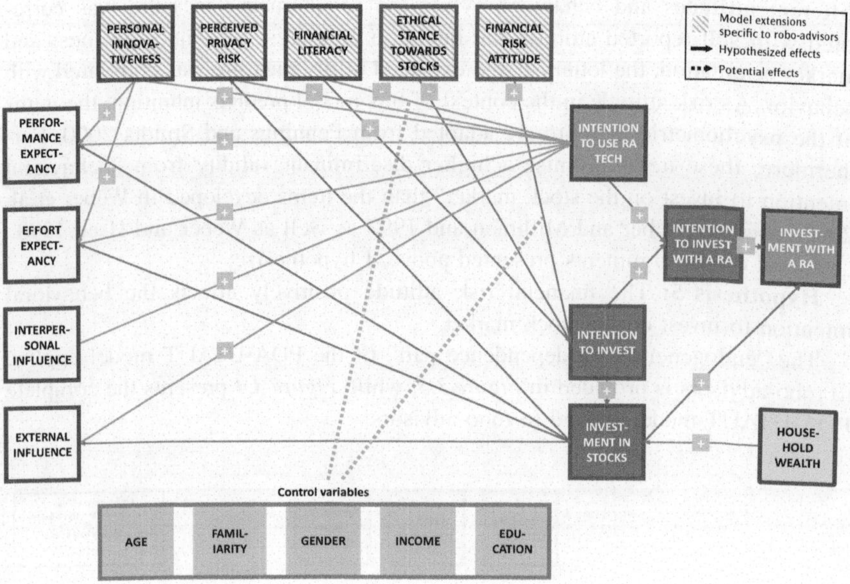

Figure 3.4 Complete PDA-UTAUT model applied to robo-advisors

Empirical Evaluation of the PDA-UTAUT Model Adapted to Robo-Advisors

4

This chapter tests the research model from Chapter 3, analyzes the results, and draws conclusions. This chapter is divided into the following sections: In Section 4.1, I will elaborate the empirical methodology employed, especially the online survey to collect the data. The German and American measurement and structural models will be estimated using SmartPLS 3, as well as adapted and evaluated drawing on the relevant literature in Section 4.2, with the aim of explaining structures in the data. I will test the hypotheses derived in Chapter 3 in Section 4.3 finding support for most hypothesized effects and specifically for the impact of path dependence based on the adoption of stock market investment on the adoption of robo-advice. The differences between the German and American participant samples as well as between the stock market investors and non-investors within the German and American samples will be determined using multi-group analyses in Section 4.4. In Section 4.5, I will summarize the empirical findings and draw theoretical and practical conclusions finding support for the importance of path dependence for the adoption of robo-advice.

Supplementary Information The online version contains supplementary material available at https://doi.org/10.1007/978-3-658-44679-6_4.

M. Horn, *Technology Acceptance, Path Dependence, and the Demand for Robo-Advisory Services*, Forschung zur Digitalisierung der Wirtschaft | Advanced Studies in Business Digitization, https://doi.org/10.1007/978-3-658-44679-6_4

4.1 Empirical Methodology

4.1.1 Online Survey

Data for the American sample were collected employing an online survey conducted on Amazon Mechanical Turk with a sample size of 1093 participants between June 30 and July 1, 2021. German participants for the online survey were recruited on Clickworker with an overall sample size of 1102 between July 2–7, 2021. Both samples constitute convenience samples, as they do not contain any information on non-respondents.

The description of robo-advisors utilized in the online survey is provided in the Appendix A4.1.1 in the Electronic Supplementary Material. The latent constructs are measured using indicators derived from the literature presented in the Appendix A4.1.1 including the literature from which the indicators are derived. Psychometric indicators were measured using a 7-step Likert-scale ranging from "Strongly disagree" to "Strongly agree". Control variable measurements are listed in the Appendix A4.1.1 as well.

4.1.2 Survey Data Quality Control

Online surveys provide a powerful tool to gather data from test subjects in different geographic locations and from diverse demographic groups. Therefore, results derived from online surveys and specifically the ones undertaken on larger platforms like Amazon Mechanical Turk might be even more generalizable than data gathered through surveys at universities only including students (Paolacci et al. 2010). But the risk of non-serious answering behavior might increase noise and decrease statistical power (Oppenheimer et al. 2009). Different reasons can lead to non-serious answering behavior. Firstly, respondents of online surveys are typically incentivized by money, which might lead to time minimizing answering behavior to maximize monetary rewards. Secondly, respondents might try to minimize cognitive effort, as cognitive resources are limited and, therefore, satisfice by finding the first solution that comes to mind and not the optimal one (Krosnick 1991; Anduiza and Galais 2017).

A two-stage process was employed to ensure that respondents' answers are both serious and answered with an adequate degree of diligence as more checks are shown to increase data validity (Berinsky et al. 2014). Oppenheimer et al. 2009 found that an instructional manipulation check (IMC) can increase statistical power of tests already established in psychological literature. The instructional manipulation check involves instructions to press a specific screen button instead of filling in the Likert-scale, as described by Oppenheimer et al. 2009. The purpose of the test is to find out whether the respondents read and understand all the instructions before answering.

According to Oppenheimer et al. 2009, a sizable part of the study participants is not able to answer the IMC correctly during the first trial (46 % of their study cohort). People who failed in the IMC were not significantly different considering demographic factors as age, gender, or the motivation to participate in the test (course credit versus monetary incentive). The exclusion of those respondents increased the statistical power of the established studies. Including an IMC in the beginning and only allowing the participants to proceed when they answered the question correctly made the differences in answering behavior disappear showing that this process increased the concentration of participants who had failed to concentrate adequately before.

To attain a maximum sample size and the opportunity to compare the group not passing the IMC to the group passing the IMC, a simple version of an IMC was included at the end of the surveys and participants were allowed to continue to answer even if they answered the IMC incorrectly. The instructional manipulation check used in the survey is provided in the Appendix A4.1.2 in the Electronic Supplementary Material. 28 American and 19 German participants were excluded from further analysis as they failed the IMC.

Aust et al. 2013 found that including a seriousness check at the end of the questionnaire asking the respondent whether the answers were serious, led to a higher data quality, while only excluding 3.2% of the respondents. Aust et al. 2013 demonstrated that the impact on data quality was superior to excluding participants with a short answering time. 66 American participants and 24 German participants were excluded from further analysis as they reported to not have taken enough time to take their results seriously for academic analysis.

Additionally, one American participant was excluded for stating an impossible age. This was interpreted as lacking attention in the answering behavior. See *Table 4.1* for an overview of the key demographic data of the samples. The descriptive characteristics of this sample, however, do corroborate the stylized facts on investment behavior and wealth in the US and Germany outlined above.

Table 4.1 Sample description

Sample	Sample size	Mean age	% of women	% of investors using a robo-advisor
Germany	1059	37.8	 44.5	 4.8
USA	998	37.8	 39.9	 44.5

4.2 Results and Model Evaluation

Data were analyzed using partial least squares regressions (PLS regressions) with the software SmartPLS 3 (Ringle et al. 2015) as this method allows to test complex models containing multiple interaction terms. My study fulfills the following conditions of Sarstedt et al. 2021's recommendation on the usage of PLS: it has a complex model with a high number of constructs and indicators, contains formatively measured constructs, and has a rather high sample size. PLS's higher statistical power makes it suitable for exploratory research (Sarstedt et al. 2021), fitting this study's use of an established model with new features.

German and American data were assessed in country specific models to account for their heterogeneity. The country specific data analysis was conducted in the following way: 1. Measurement models were adapted to the specificities of the German and American samples. 2. The structural models were adapted to the specific samples by including the control variables and their possible moderating effects. 3. The hypotheses were tested with the German and American samples, and the adjusted R^2-values of the full model are compared to restraint models not accounting for path dependence. 4. Multi-group analyses between different potential customer groups according to their current investment behavior, i.e., their current path, were run to derive which adoption factors show specific importance for these groups. 5. A model incorporating all constructs of the German and the American model was used to compare the German and American sample using a multi-group analysis to derive insights on path coefficients of the different factors.

The analysis of the data generally follows the recommendations of Benitez et al. 2020 and Sarstedt et al. 2021. I follow Sarstedt et al.'s 2021 assessment not to provide goodness-of-fit measures like the standardized root mean square residual (SRMR) in the following statistical evaluation as the relevance of these measures can be questioned. The PLS algorithm, unlike factor-based SEM, does not explicitly minimize the discrepancy between the empirical and model-implied covariance matrices serving as the basis for the fit indices, but provides it as a byproduct (Hair et al. 2017; Lohmöller 1989). As this goodness-of-fit measure is not optimized, it should not be used to judge models (Lohmöller 1989).

4.2.1 Measurement Model Adaptation and Evaluation

The model was measured using the PLS algorithm with additional analyses conducted with the PLS bootstrapping with 5000 subsamples. The traditional PLS algorithm as opposed to the consistent version is chosen as the model contains the formative construct of financial literacy. The consistent PLS algorithm was found to show more pronounced biases for composite models than the PLS algorithm for common factor models (Sarstedt et al. 2016). All constructs were measured using the standard default settings: The reflective constructs were estimated using correlation weights (Mode A in PLS-SEM) and the formatively specified construct financial literacy was estimated with regression weights (Mode B in PLS-SEM).[1] Furthermore, all indicators of financial literacy were assigned with the predefined weight of 1 as all its components are assumed to have equal importance. The results of the measurement models are presented in *Table 4.2* and *Table 4.3* and are analyzed in the following.

Germany

As all constructs except financial literacy are modeled as reflective constructs, rho_alpha, average variance extracted (AVE), factor loadings, and discriminant validity are the decisive criteria for the measurement model (Benitez et al. 2020).

Table 4.2 German measurement model results

Construct	Indicator	rho_a	AVE	VIF	Weight	Loading
Effort expectancy (EE)		0.907	0.770			
	EE_1				0.259***	0.856***
	EE_2				0.277***	0.876***
	EE_3				0.280***	0.892***
	EE_4				0.323***	0.886***

(continued)

[1] See Sarstedt et al. 2021, p. 11.

Table 4.2 (continued)

Construct	Indicator	rho_a	AVE	VIF	Weight	Loading
Ethical stance (ESSM)		0.837	0.666			
	ESSM_1				0.287***	0.831***
	ESSM_2				0.309***	0.867***
	ESSM_3				0.367***	0.750***
	ESSM_4				0.269***	0.812***
External influence (EI)		0.718	0.634			
	EI_1				0.434***	0.828***
	EI_2				0.364***	0.768***
	EI_3				0.457***	0.792***
Familiarity (FAM)		0.863	0.779			
	FAM_1				0.343***	0.866***
	FAM_2				0.397***	0.909***
	FAM_3				0.393***	0.873***
Financial literacy (FL)		1				
	FL_A_1			1.122	0.211***	0.552***
	FL_A_2			1.200	0.211***	0.598***
	FL_A_3			1.285	0.211***	0.573***
	FL_A_4			1.887	0.211***	0.647***
	FL_A_5			1.231	0.211***	0.594***
	FL_B_1			1.459	0.211***	0.554***
	FL_B_2			1.337	0.211***	0.636***
	FL_B_3			1.584	0.211***	0.589***
Financial risk (FR)		0.941	0.889			
	FR_1				0.361***	0.956***
	FR_2				0.331***	0.916***
	FR_3				0.368***	0.955***

(continued)

Table 4.2 (continued)

Construct	Indicator	rho_a	AVE	VIF	Weight	Loading
Intention to invest on the stock market (IINV)		0.959	0.923			
	IInv_1				0.339***	0.953***
	IInv_2				0.354***	0.970***
	IInv_3				0.347***	0.959***
Intention to invest with a robo-advisor (IIRA)		0.950	0.909			
	IIRA_1				0.354***	0.950***
	IIRA_2				0.345***	0.954***
	IIRA_3				0.350***	0.955***
Intention to use robo-advisor technology (IURA)		0.949	0.907			
	IURA_1				0.347***	0.952***
	IURA_2				0.348***	0.952***
	IURA_3				0.355***	0.953***
Interpersonal influence (II)		0.939	0.890			
	II_1				0.362***	0.953***
	II_2				0.341***	0.929***
	II_3				0.357***	0.947***
Perceived privacy risk (PPR)		0.889	0.802			
	PPR_1				0.332***	0.885***
	PPR_2				0.366***	0.886***
	PPR_3				0.417***	0.915***
Performance expectancy (PE)		0.907	0.820			
	PE_1				0.417***	0.923***
	PE_2				0.317***	0.876***
	PE_3				0.367***	0.918***
Personal innovativeness (PI)		0.899	0.815			
	PI_1				0.386***	0.925***
	PI_3				0.320***	0.864***
	PI_4				0.400***	0.917***

Note: * $p < 0.05$, ** $p < 0.01$, *** $p < 0.001$.

In the German sample, rho_alpha providing information on composite reliability is consistently above the 0.707 threshold indicating that more than 50% of the variance of the construct scores are accounted for by the latent variable (Benitez et al. 2020; Dijkstra and Henseler 2015; Nunnally and Bernstein 1994). The AVE is used to assess convergent validity providing information on how much of the indicators' variance is accounted for by the latent variable. The threshold of 0.5 indicates that half of the variance of the indicators is explained by their latent variable, thus, more than by all other latent variables of the model together (Fornell and Larcker 1981). All AVE-measures in the German sample are above 0.5. PI_2 was removed due to a very low factor loading of 0.589. This low factor loading may be attributed to the reverse coding of the indicator.

Discriminant validity is measured by the heterotrait-monotrait ratio (HTMT) (Henseler et al. 2015), which has a recommended conservative threshold of 0.85 (Voorhees et al. 2016) or lenient threshold of 0.9 (Henseler et al. 2015). Values ranging from 0.001 to 0.74 (performance expectancy on IURA) indicate discriminant validity for all factors. See Appendix A4.2.1 in the Electronic Supplementary Material for the complete list of HTMT values.

According to Benitez et al. 2020, composite constructs as financial literacy should be analyzed for multicollinearity, weights, composite loadings, and the significances of weights and loadings. In the German model, all indicators of financial literacy have variance inflation factor (VIF) values well below 5, indicating an absence of collinearity problems. According to Cenfetelli and Bassellier 2009, loadings show the absolute and weights the relative contribution of an indicator to its respective construct. The weights and loadings of all indicators are highly significant and show the expected sign. Thus, there is no requirement to delete further indicators.

USA

The American model consistently fulfills the recommended threshold of 0.707 for rho_alpha indicating composite reliability by showing that 50% of the indicators' variance is explained by the latent variable (Benitez et al. 2020; Dijkstra and Henseler 2015; Nunnally and Bernstein 1994). Convergent validity's measure AVE of at least 0.5 is fulfilled by all constructs (Fornell and Larcker 1981).

Table 4.3 American measurement model results

Construct	Indicator	rho_a	AVE	VIF	Weight	Loading
Effort expectancy (EE)		0.865	0.708			
	EE_1				0.276***	0.839***
	EE_2				0.312***	0.844***
	EE_3				0.287***	0.838***
	EE_4				0.312***	0.845***
Ethical stance (ESSM)		0.976	0.790			
	ESSM_1				0.150	0.793***
	ESSM_2				0.473***	0.939***
	ESSM_4				0.471***	0.926***
External influence (EI)		0.841	0.750			
	EI_1				0.391***	0.880***
	EI_2				0.348***	0.825***
	EI_3				0.414***	0.892***
Familiarity (FAM)		0.747	0.793			
	FAM_1				0.596***	0.905***
	FAM_2				0.526***	0.876***
Financial literacy (FL)		1				
	FL_A_1			1.122	0.203***	0.480***
	FL_A_2			1.200	0.203***	0.560***
	FL_A_3			1.285	0.203***	0.616***
	FL_A_4			1.887	0.203***	0.756***
	FL_A_5			1.231	0.203***	0.558***
	FL_B_1			1.459	0.203***	0.645***
	FL_B_2			1.337	0.203***	0.614***
	FL_B_3			1.584	0.203***	0.706***
Financial risk (FR)		0.930	0.877			
	FR_1				0.361***	0.945***
	FR_2				0.353***	0.925***
	FR_3				0.354***	0.939***

(continued)

Table 4.3 (continued)

Construct	Indicator	rho_a	AVE	VIF	Weight	Loading
Intention to invest on the stock market (IINV)		0.872	0.780			
	IInv_1				0.324***	0.836***
	IInv_2				0.394***	0.904***
	IInv_3				0.411***	0.908***
Intention to invest with a robo-advisor (IIRA)		0.926	0.870			
	IIRA_1				0.349***	0.926***
	IIRA_2				0.362***	0.934***
	IIRA_3				0.361***	0.937***
Intention to use robo-advisor technology (IURA)		0.930	0.877			
	IURA_1				0.355***	0.933***
	IURA_2				0.359***	0.937***
	IURA_3				0.354***	0.940***
Interpersonal influence (II)		0.940	0.892			
	II_1				0.355***	0.945***
	II_2				0.352***	0.944***
	II_3				0.352***	0.945***
Perceived privacy risk (PPR)		0.915	0.790			
	PPR_1				0.328***	0.887***
	PPR_2				0.473***	0.901***
	PPR_3				0.321***	0.878***
Performance expectancy (PE)		0.874	0.794			
	PE_1				0.401***	0.897***
	PE_2				0.354***	0.887***
	PE_3				0.367***	0.889***

(continued)

Table 4.3 (continued)

Construct	Indicator	rho_a	AVE	VIF	Weight	Loading
Personal innovativeness (PI)		0.851	0.766			
	PI_1				0.396***	0.897***
	PI_3				0.393***	0.875***
	PI_4				0.353***	0.853***

Note: * $p < 0.05$, ** $p < 0.01$, *** $p < 0.001$.

Three construct pairs of the American model surpass the conservative HTMT threshold of 0.85:

- Intention to use robo-advisor technology (IURA) → intention to invest using a robo-advisor (IIRA)
- Interpersonal influence → intention to invest using a robo-advisor (IIRA)
- Performance expectancy → intention to use robo-advisor technology (IURA)

One of these construct pairs exceeded the more lenient threshold of 0.9, while the 95%-two-sided confidence interval does not cover 1 for either of them (Voorhees et al. 2016):

- Intention to use robo-advisor technology (IURA) → intention to invest using a robo-advisor (IIRA)

The high HTMT of *the intention to use robo-advisor technology (IURA)* on *the intention to invest using a robo-advisor (IIRA)* might be explained by the similarity of the concepts. Both *the intention to invest with a robo-advisor (IIRA)* and *the intention to use robo-advisor technology (IURA)* remained in the model as the high HTMT between them was the only irregularity observed, while both constructs reached convergent validity and composite reliability. Nevertheless, the results indicate that the differentiation between IIRA and IURA is not vital in the American model. See *Table A4.2* and *Table A4.3* in Appendix A4.2.1 in the Electronic Supplementary Material for the complete list of HTMT values.

The factor loading criterion was met by all constructs apart from personal innovativeness, ethical stance towards the stock market, and intention to invest on the stock market. PI_2 was removed due to a very low factor loading of −0.227. Its deletion increased composite reliability of personal innovativeness considerably. As noted above for the German model, PI_2 was reverse coded, which might have been ignored by participants. ESSM_3 was deleted as its factor loading of 0.444 was below the threshold and its deletion increased AVE considerably. FAM_3's outer loading is at the limit of acceptability, slightly above or below it, depending on the model specifications that were chosen to analyze the effects of the control variables. It was deleted as its deletion increases AVE considerably to 0.793. The indicators of the formative construct of financial literacy show healthy VIF-values and their weights as well as loadings are highly significant showing no issues with multicollinearity and no requirement for indicator deletion for financial literacy. Indicators and constructs loadings and crossloadings are presented in *Table A4.4* and *Table A4.5* in Appendix A4.2.1 in the Electronic Supplementary Material.

4.2.2 Structural Model Adaptation

The possible direct and moderating effects of age, familiarity, gender, education, and income on *the intention to use robo-advisor technology (IURA)* were examined to identify significant relationships, i.e., the "classical UTAUT model part" of the PDA-UTAUT model applied to robo-advisors. The same investigation was applied to the effects of *investment on the stock market (INV)* on the independent factors of *the intention to use robo-advisor technology (IURA)*, i.e., the "exogenous path dependence part". Furthermore, all possible direct and moderating effects—except for familiarity with the use of robots, as this construct does not relate to financial decision making—on *the intention to invest on the stock market (IINV)* were analyzed, i.e., the "endogenous path dependence part".

The simultaneous inclusion of all potential control variables and moderating effects is not yet possible in SmartPLS 3 considering the number of connections to analyze. Therefore, the direct effects with their respective moderating effects were included to the model sequentially and retained when significance was reached at the $p < 0.05$ level. Finally, all remaining effects of the sequential tests were tested together and all effects that did not reach the $p < 0.05$ significance level were removed. Please consider the Appendix A4.2.2 in the Electronic Supplementary Material for a full overview of the construct correlation matrices of the final German and American models.

4.2.3 Structural Model Summary

See *Table 4.4* and *Table 4.5* for the complete German and American path coefficient results.

German model

Table 4.4 Path coefficients results German structural model

	Path coefficient	Standard deviation	95%-Confidence intervall	t-statistic	p-value	Cohen's f^2
Age → IINV	−0.116	0.023	[−0.162, −0.072]	5.103	0.000***	0.026
Age → IURA	0.040	0.021	[0.000, 0.082]	1.889	0.058	0.003
Age → Perceived privacy risk	0.125	0.031	[0.063, 0.183]	4.079	0.000***	0.016
Age → Performance expectancy	−0.087	0.032	[−0.147, −0.022]	2.726	0.006**	0.008
Age on financial risk → IINV	0.083	0.022	[0.039, 0.124]	3.842	0.000***	0.014
Age on perceived privacy risk → IURA	−0.051	0.021	[−0.094, −0.010]	2.431	0.015*	0.006
Education → IINV	0.087	0.021	[0.045, 0.128]	4.129	0.000***	0.015
Education → IURA	−0.017	0.022	[−0.062, 0.024]	0.768	0.443	0.001
Education on personal innovativeness → IURA	0.056	0.027	[0.004, 0.108]	2.106	0.035*	0.007
Effort expectancy → IURA	0.096	0.030	[0.037, 0.154]	3.181	0.001**	0.014
Ethical stance → IINV	−0.306	0.025	[−0.355, −0.257]	12.437	0.000***	0.165
External influence → IURA	0.039	0.026	[−0.010, 0.089]	1.530	0.126	0.002

(continued)

Table 4.4 (continued)

	Path coefficient	Standard deviation	95%-Confidence intervall	t-statistic	p-value	Cohen's f^2
Familiarity → Effort expectancy	0.266	0.034	[0.200, 0.332]	7.874	0.000***	0.073
Familiarity → External influence	0.274	0.032	[0.211, 0.336]	8.551	0.000***	0.081
Familiarity → Performance expectancy	0.013	0.037	[0.028, 0.175]	2.761	0.006**	0.010
Financial literacy → IINV	0.174	0.024	[0.129, 0.221]	7.248	0.000***	0.050
Financial literacy → IURA	−0.118	0.023	[−0.165, −0.075]	5.178	0.000***	0.024
Financial risk → IINV	0.438	0.023	[0.391, 0.482]	18.817	0.000***	0.341
Gender → IINV	0.062	0.023	[0.017, 0.108]	2.676	0.007**	0.007
Gender → IURA	−0.081	0.022	[−0.125, −0.038]	3.702	0.000***	0.013
Gender → Perceived privacy risk	−0.083	0.031	[−0.147, −0.022]	2.642	0.008**	0.007
Gender on financial literacy → IURA	−0.072	0.022	[−0.116, −0.030]	3.318	0.001**	0.011
Gender on financial risk → IINV	−0.044	0.022	[−0.085, 0.000]	2.016	0.044*	0.004
IINV → IIRA	0.343	0.022	[0.298, 0.387]	15.441	0.000***	0.270
IINV → INV	0.601	0.020	[0.561, 0.638]	30.336	0.000***	0.597
IIRA → IWRA	0.283	0.029	[0.223, 0.339]	9.772	0.000***	0.091

(continued)

Table 4.4 (continued)

	Path coefficient	Standard deviation	95%-Confidence intervall	t-statistic	p-value	Cohen's f^2
IURA → IIRA	0.655	0.020	[0.615, 0.693]	33.159	0.000***	0.984
Income → IURA	0.001	0.021	[−0.040, 0.042]	0.029	0.977	0.000
Income → Perceived privacy risk	−0.105	0.031	[−0.167, −0.044]	3.343	0.001**	0.010
Income on personal innovativeness → IURA	−0.053	0.021	[−0.097, −0.012]	2.490	0.013*	0.006
Interpersonal influence → IURA	0.202	0.031	[0.144, 0.264]	6.589	0.000***	0.066
INV → Effort expectancy	0.104	0.027	[0.050, 0.156]	3.802	0.000***	0.013
INV → External influence	0.106	0.031	[0.047, 0.165]	3.470	0.001**	0.012
INV → IWRA	0.160	0.022	[0.115, 0.202]	7.320	0.000***	0.026
INV → Perceived privacy risk	−0.113	0.031	[−0.174, −0.050]	3.586	0.000***	0.012
INV → Performance expectancy	−0.045	0.029	[−0.101, 0.012]	1.535	0.125	0.002
Perceived privacy risk → IURA	−0.089	0.025	[−0.140, −0.041]	3.529	0.000***	0.016
Performance expectancy → IURA	0.533	0.030	[0.475, 0.590]	17.740	0.000***	0.422
Personal innovativeness → Effort expectancy	0.232	0.034	[0.165, 0.298]	6.781	0.000***	0.054
Personal innovativeness → IURA	−0.015	0.026	[−0.066, 0.036]	0.567	0.571	0.000

(continued)

Table 4.4 (continued)

	Path coefficient	Standard deviation	95%-Confidence intervall	t-statistic	p-value	Cohen's f^2
Personal innovativeness → Performance expectancy	0.243	0.038	[0.168, 0.315]	6.458	0.000***	0.052
Wealth → INV	0.167	0.025	[0.118, 0.216]	6.675	0.000***	0.046
Wealth → IWRA	0.069	0.033	[0.000, 0.131]	2.067	0.039*	0.005

Note: * p < 0.05, ** p < 0.01, *** p < 0.001.

American model

Table 4.5 Path coefficients results American structural model

	Path coefficient	Standard deviation	95%-Confidence intervall	t-statistic	p-value	Cohen's f^2
Age → IINV	−0.003	0.025	[−0.052, 0.047]	0.112	0.911	0.000
Age on financial literacy → IINV	−0.062	0.028	[−0.116, −0.004]	2.175	0.030*	0.006
Education → External influence	0.075	0.030	[0.014, 0.132]	2.510	0.012*	0.009
Education → IINV	0.104	0.035	[0.036, 0.173]	2.983	0.003**	0.014
Education → Perceived privacy risk	0.108	0.033	[0.042, 0.172]	3.235	0.001**	0.012
Education → Performance expectancy	0.081	0.030	[0.021, 0.138]	2.736	0.006**	0.009
Effort expectancy → IURA	−0.017	0.028	[−0.071, 0.040]	0.598	0.550	0.001

(continued)

Table 4.5 (continued)

	Path coefficient	Standard deviation	95%-Confidence intervall	t-statistic	p-value	Cohen's f^2
Ethical stance → IINV	−0.086	0.038	[−0.155, −0.004]	2.257	0.024*	0.006
External influence → IURA	0.107	0.038	[0.034, 0.183]	2.827	0.005**	0.017
Familiarity → Effort expectancy	0.196	0.041	[0.116, 0.275]	4.839	0.000***	0.040
Familiarity → External influence	0.610	0.025	[0.560, 0.659]	24.375	0.000***	0.582
Familiarity → Perceived privacy risk	0.277	0.039	[0.200, 0.355]	7.035	0.000***	0.077
Familiarity → Performance expectancy	0.246	0.040	[0.171, 0.326]	6.167	0.000***	0.062
Familiarity on INV → External influence	0.088	0.029	[0.033, 0.143]	3.074	0.002**	0.014
Familiarity on INV → Perceived privacy risk	0.151	0.036	[0.079, 0.222]	4.167	0.000***	0.027
Financial literacy → IINV	0.133	0.039	[0.058, 0.210]	3.424	0.001**	0.015
Financial literacy → IURA	−0.099	0.023	[−0.145, −0.055]	4.320	0.000***	0.024
Financial risk → IINV	0.578	0.034	[0.510, 0.643]	16.838	0.000***	0.351
Gender → IURA	−0.046	0.016	[−0.076, −0.015]	2.916	0.004**	0.008
Gender → Performance expectancy	−0.081	0.024	[−0.125, −0.033]	3.411	0.001**	0.010

(continued)

Table 4.5 (continued)

	Path coefficient	Standard deviation	95%-Confidence intervall	t-statistic	p-value	Cohen's f^2
IINV → IIRA	0.206	0.031	[0.150, 0.268]	6.744	0.000***	0.173
IINV → INV	0.473	0.029	[0.416, 0.527]	16.517	0.000***	0.287
IIRA → IWRA	0.430	0.021	[0.386, 0.470]	20.198	0.000***	0.265
IURA → IIRA	0.791	0.023	[0.742, 0.833]	34.350	0.000***	2.545
Income → Effort expectancy	0.031	0.029	[−0.027, 0.089]	1.046	0.296	0.001
Income → IINV	0.097	0.029	[0.038, 0.155]	3.298	0.001**	0.012
Income → IURA	−0.034	0.017	[−0.067, −0.003]	2.056	0.040*	0.005
Income on financial literacy → IINV	0.092	0.029	[0.035, 0.148]	3.139	0.002**	0.013
Income on INV → Effort expectancy	0.064	0.029	[0.008, 0.120]	2.250	0.024*	0.007
Income on perceived privacy risk → IURA	0.051	0.020	[0.013, 0.092]	2.501	0.012*	0.011
Interpersonal influence → IURA	0.364	0.041	[0.287, 0.444]	8.951	0.000***	0.170
INV → Effort expectancy	0.072	0.033	[0.008, 0.136]	2.213	0.027*	0.007
INV → External influence	0.119	0.030	[0.061, 0.178]	4.016	0.000***	0.020
INV → IWRA	0.321	0.023	[0.274, 0.368]	13.669	0.000***	0.142
INV → Perceived privacy risk	0.088	0.033	[0.024, 0.154]	2.693	0.007**	0.007
INV → Performance expectancy	0.020	0.030	[−0.036, 0.079]	0.666	0.505	0.001

(continued)

Table 4.5 (continued)

	Path coefficient	Standard deviation	95%-Confidence intervall	t-statistic	p-value	Cohen's f^2
Perceived privacy risk → IURA	−0.089	0.022	[−0.132, −0.046]	4.046	0.000***	0.025
Performance expectancy → IURA	0.404	0.037	[0.331, 0.477]	10.860	0.000***	0.254
Personal innovativeness → Effort expectancy	0.434	0.047	[0.341, 0.523]	9.277	0.000***	0.202
Personal innovativeness → IURA	0.091	0.026	[0.039, 0.141]	3.457	0.001**	0.020
Personal innovativeness → Performance expectancy	0.400	0.042	[0.317, 0.483]	9.607	0.000***	0.176
Wealth → INV	0.100	0.028	[0.045, 0.154]	3.627	0.000***	0.013
Wealth → IWRA	−0.041	0.024	[−0.089, 0.006]	1.724	0.085	0.003

Note: * $p < 0.05$, ** $p < 0.01$, *** $p < 0.001$.

4.2.4 Model Evaluation

As all data analyzed in this study are self-reported, common method bias is a potential pitfall. VIF-values of the latent variables of below 2.0 indicate that common method bias was not a severe issue in the German sample. The VIF-values of the latent variables in the American sample are all within the conservative threshold of 3.3 possibly indicating that collinearity was not a critical issue (Kock 2015; Kock and Lynn 2012).

In order to analyze the effect of incorporating path dependence into the UTAUT model, three different models are compared by their adjusted R^2 values: the classical UTAUT model for robo-advisors in which all constructs related to the concept of path dependence are deleted[2], the UTAUT model with exogenous path dependence in which the basic technology investment is not explained endogenously[3], and the full PDA-UTAUT model[4].

The data show that both in Germany and the USA the adjusted R^2 of investment with a robo-advisor (IWRA) reaches the highest value in the complete PDA-UTAUT model and the lowest in the classical UTAUT model. This supports the idea that the PDA-UTAUT model is indeed able to capture the path dependence in the adoption of robo-advisor technology. See *Table 4.6* and *Table 4.7* for an overview of the adjusted R^2 results.

Table 4.6 Adjusted R^2 results German model

Endogenous variable	**Adjusted R^2**		
Model	**Classical UTAUT**	**UTAUT model with exogenous path dependence**	**PDA-UTAUT**
Effort expectancy (EE)	0.132	0.202	0.202
External influence (EI)	N/A	0.093	0.093
Intention to invest on the stock market (IINV)	N/A	N/A	0.527
Intention to invest with a robo-advisor (IIRA)	N/A	N/A	0.564
Intention to use robo-advisor technology (IURA)	0.549	0.548	0.558
Investment on the stock market (INV)	N/A	N/A	0.444
Investment with a robo-advisor (IWRA)	0.049	0.086	0.128
Perceived privacy risk (PPR)	N/A	0.052	0.052
Performance expectancy (PE)	0.086	0.102	0.102

2 *Figure 3.1* in Section 3.2.3 illustrates this model.

3 *Figure 3.2* in Section 3.3 depicts the extension added to the model in *Figure 3.1*.

4 *Figure 3.4* in Section 3.4.3 gives an overview of the full PDA-UTAUT model.

Table 4.7 Adjusted R^2 results American model

Endogenous variable	Adjusted R^2		
Model	**Classical UTAUT**	**UTAUT model with exogenous path dependence**	**PDA-UTAUT**
Effort expectancy (EE)	0.296	0.332	0.332
External influence (EI)	N/A	0.440	0.440
Intention to invest on the stock market (IINV)	N/A	N/A	0.353
Intention to invest with a robo-advisor (IIRA)	N/A	N/A	0.785
Intention to use robo-advisor technology (IURA)	0.755	0.755	0.755
Investment on the stock market (INV)	N/A	N/A	0.252
Investment with a robo-advisor (IWRA)	0.223	0.339	0.361
Perceived privacy risk (PPR)	N/A	0.124	0.124
Performance expectancy (PE)	0.287	0.353	0.353

4.3 Hypothesis Testing

As the models are quite complex, their results are presented in several steps. As described in the introduction to Chapter 3, I will start with the "classical UTAUT model part" in Section 4.3.1, continue with "exogenous path dependence part" in Section 4.3.2, and will finally discuss the "exogenous path dependence part" of the PDA-UTAUT model applied to robo-advisors in Section 4.3.3. Please consider that the path coefficients shown in the subparts of the model are measured as part of the full model. Effect sizes are measured using Cohen's f^2. Values above 0.02 indicate a small, above 0.15 a medium and above 0.35 a large effect size (Cohen 1988; Benitez et al. 2020; Sarstedt et al. 2021). Values under 0.02 are negligible. The control and moderating effects will be discussed in their respective part of the model. The effect sizes of control and moderating effects are small or negligible unless mentioned explicitly.

4.3.1 The classical UTAUT Model with Additional Drivers

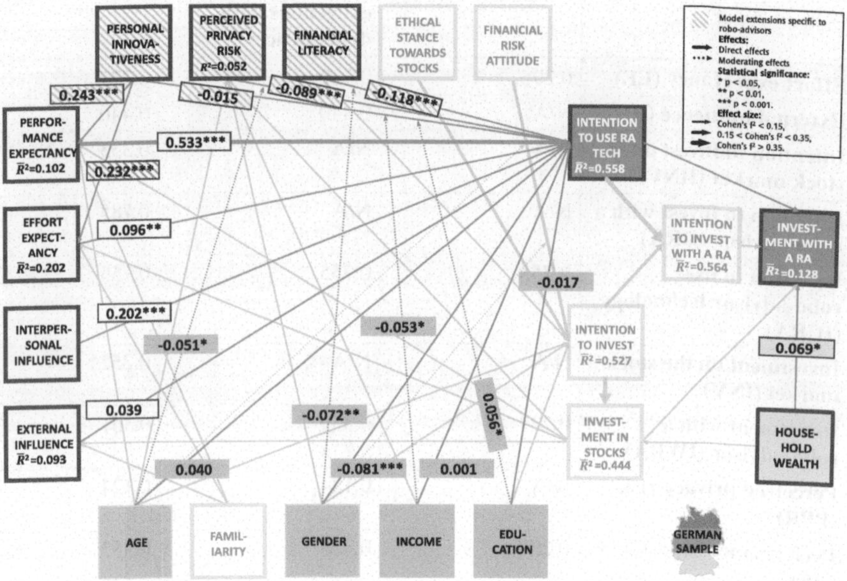

Figure 4.1 "Classical UTAUT model part" results—German sample

Figure 4.1 and *Figure 4.2* give an overview of the results of the "classical UTAUT model part" of the PDA-UTAUT model applied to robo-advisors. See Appendix A4.3.2 in the Electronic Supplementary Material for an overview of all results of the PDA-UTAUT model applied to robo-advisors.

Performance expectancy is significantly positive both in the German as well as the American sample with a large effect size in Germany and a medium effect size in the American sample. Effort expectancy is positively significant on the intention to use robo-advisor technology in Germany with a negligible effect size. Effort expectancy has no significant effect in the American sample. The missing significance of effort expectancy is not new in the technology acceptance literature: Subramanian 1994 found that perceived ease of use (the equivalent of effort expectancy in TAM) had no significant effect on predicted future usage for voice mail and customer dial up systems. He attributed the missing significance to the easy-to-use nature of the technologies at hand and the exposure of users

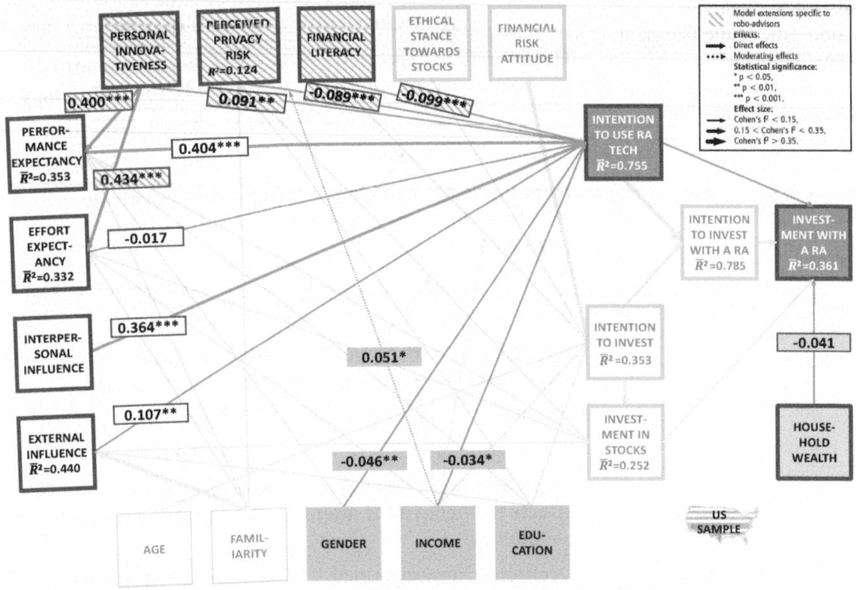

Figure 4.2 "Classical UTAUT model part" results—American sample

to the system as perceived ease of use matters most at the early stages of use. Robo-advisors could be seen as quite easy to use and the American sample has a high ratio of 44.5% of participants with experience with robo-advisors.

Interpersonal influence has a significant and small positive effect in Germany on the intention to use robo-advisor technology (IURA). In the American sample, the significant positive effect of interpersonal influence on the intention to use robo-advisor technology (IURA) has a medium effect size. In the German and American sample, external influence has a positive significant effect on the intention to use robo-advisor technology with a negligible effect size. Wealth has a significant, but negligible effect on robo-advisor adoption in the German sample and no significant effect in the American sample.

Table 4.8 summarizes the results of the hypothesis tests for the "classical UTAUT model part" of the PDA-UTAUT model applied to robo-advisors for the German and American samples.

Table 4.8 Tested hypotheses of the classical UTAUT model section—German and American sample

	German sample	US sample
Hypothesis 1: Perceived privacy risk negatively affects the behavioral intention to use robo-advisor technology.		
Decision	supported ($p < 0.001$)	supported ($p < 0.001$)
Effect size	negligible	small
Hypothesis 2a: Personal innovativeness positively affects performance expectancy of robo-advisor technology.		
Decision	supported ($p < 0.001$)	supported ($p < 0.001$)
Effect size	small	medium
Hypothesis 2b: Personal innovativeness positively affects effort expectancy of robo-advisor technology.		
Decision	supported ($p < 0.001$)	supported ($p < 0.001$)
Effect size	small	medium
Hypothesis 2c: Personal innovativeness positively affects the behavioral intention to use robo-advisor technology.		
Decision	not supported	supported ($p < 0.01$)
Effect size	negligible	small
Hypothesis 3a: Financial literacy negatively affects the intention to use robo-advisor technology.		
Decision	supported ($p < 0.001$)	supported ($p < 0.001$)
Effect size	small	negligible

Hypothesis 1 that perceived privacy risk negatively affects the intention to use robo-advisor technology is supported by both the German and the American sample at the $p < 0.001$ level. The effect size of perceived privacy risk on the intention to use robo-advisor technology can be characterized as small but significant in the American sample, while it is negligible in the German sample. Age has a negative moderating effect on the relationship between perceived privacy risk and the intention to use robo-advisor technology in Germany, which leads to the inclusion of the non-significant direct effect of age on intention to use robo-advisor technology. Income has a positive moderating effect on the relationship between perceived privacy risk and the intention to use robo-advisor technology in the USA.

Hypothesis 2a that personal innovativeness has a positive effect on performance expectancy is supported in the German sample with a significant effect to the $p < 0.001$ level and a small effect size. Hypothesis 2b that personal innovativeness has a positive effect on effort expectancy is supported in the German sample at the $p < 0.001$ level with a small effect size. Hypothesis 2c that personal innovativeness has a positive effect on the intention to use robo-advisor technology finds no support in the German sample with a slightly negative path coefficient, although values in its 95%-confidence interval range from negative to positive.

In the American sample hypothesis 2a-b are supported at the $p < 0.001$ level, while 2c is supported at the $p < 0.01$ level. Effect sizes of hypothesis 2a-b are medium and 2c small. Thus, personal innovativeness can explain performance and effort expectancy to some degree, but it is less useful in directly explaining the intention to use robo-advisor technology.

Income has a negative moderating effect on the relationship between personal innovativeness and the intention to use robo-advisor technology in Germany, which leads to the inclusion of a non-significant direct effect of income on the intention to use robo-advisor technology. Education has a positive moderating effect on the relationship between personal innovativeness and the intention to use robo-advisor technology, which leads to the inclusion of the non-significant direct effect of education on the intention to use robo-advisor technology in Germany.

Hypothesis 3a that financial literacy has a negative effect on the intention to use robo-advisor technology is supported at the $p < 0.001$ level with a small effect size in the German sample. Likewise, the negative effect of financial literacy on the intention to use robo-advisor technology is supported at the $p < 0.001$ level with a negligible effect size in the American sample. Male identity has a negative influence on the relationship between financial literacy and the intention to use robo-advisor technology in Germany.

In the American sample identifying as male and income has a negative impact on the intention to use robo-advisor technology.

4.3.2 The Addition of path Dependence to the Model

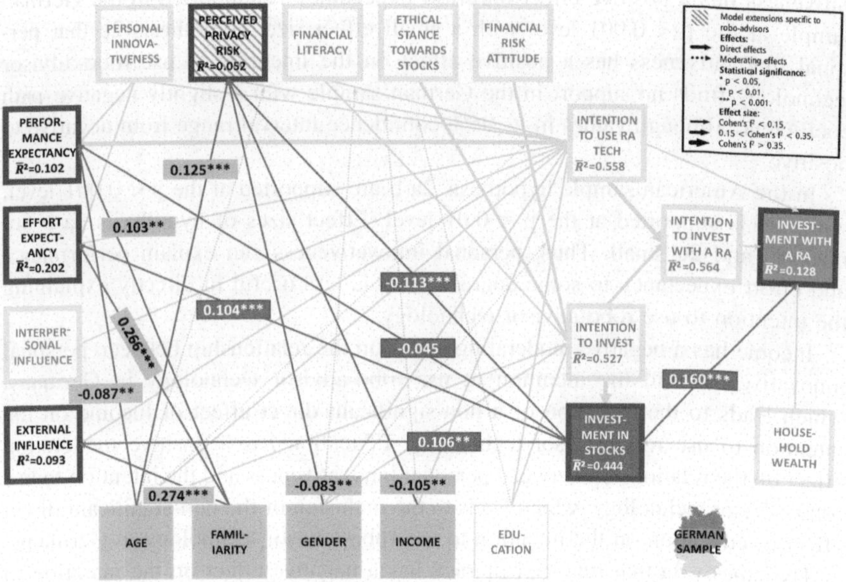

Figure 4.3 "Exogenous path dependence part" results—German sample

See *Figure 4.3* and *Figure 4.4* for a summary of the "exogenous path dependence part" of the PDA-UTAUT model applied to robo-advisors. In the German sample investment on the stock market has a significantly positive influence on investment with a robo-advisor with a small effect size. Investment on the stock market has a significantly positive effect on effort expectancy and external influence, while it has a significantly negative effect on perceived privacy risk. All effect sizes are negligible. Age has a significantly positive influence on perceived privacy risk in the German sample, while income and an identification as male had a negative influence. Investment on the stock market has no significant effect on performance expectancy, while age shows a significantly negative effect on performance expectancy. Familiarity with robots has a positive influence on performance expectancy, effort expectancy, and external influence in the German sample.

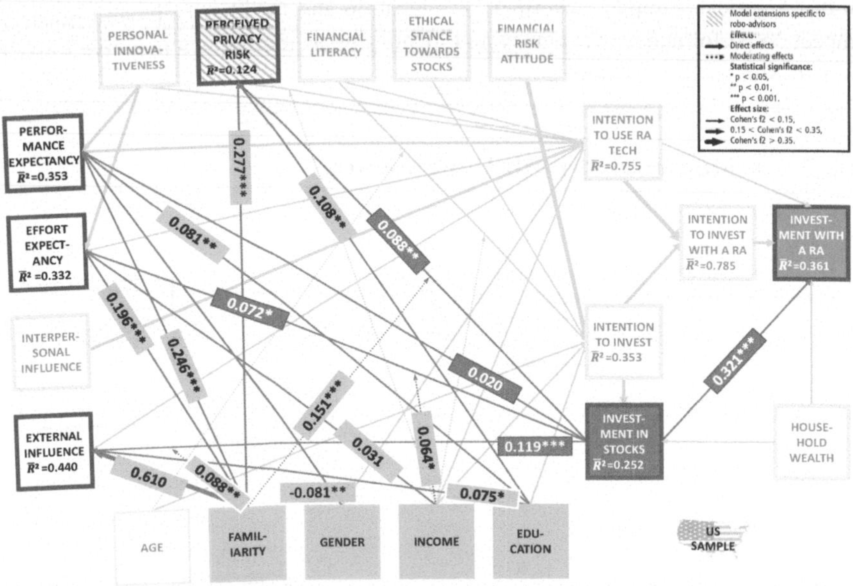

Figure 4.4 "Exogenous path dependence part" results—American sample

In the American model investment on the stock market has a significant impact on investment with a robo-advisor with a small effect size supporting the path dependence model. Furthermore, investment on the stock market has a significantly positive influence on effort expectancy (negligible effect size), external influence (small effect size), and perceived privacy risk (negligible effect size). Familiarity has a positive effect on effort expectancy. Income has a positive moderating effect on the relationship between investment on the stock market and effort expectancy leading to the inclusion of income with no significant effect on effort expectancy. Education has a positive effect on external influence. Familiarity has a positive effect with a large effect size on external influence and a moderating effect on the relationship between investment on the stock market and external influence. The positive effect on perceived privacy risk is especially interesting, as the effect is opposite to the one found in the German sample. Education and familiarity have a positive impact on perceived privacy risk. Furthermore, familiarity has a positive moderating effect on the relationship between investment on the stock market and perceived privacy risk. No significant effect could be found between investment on the stock market and performance expectancy in the American sample. Nevertheless, education and familiarity have a positive impact on performance expectancy and identifying as male has a negative impact on performance expectancy.

4.3.3 Endogenizing path Dependence

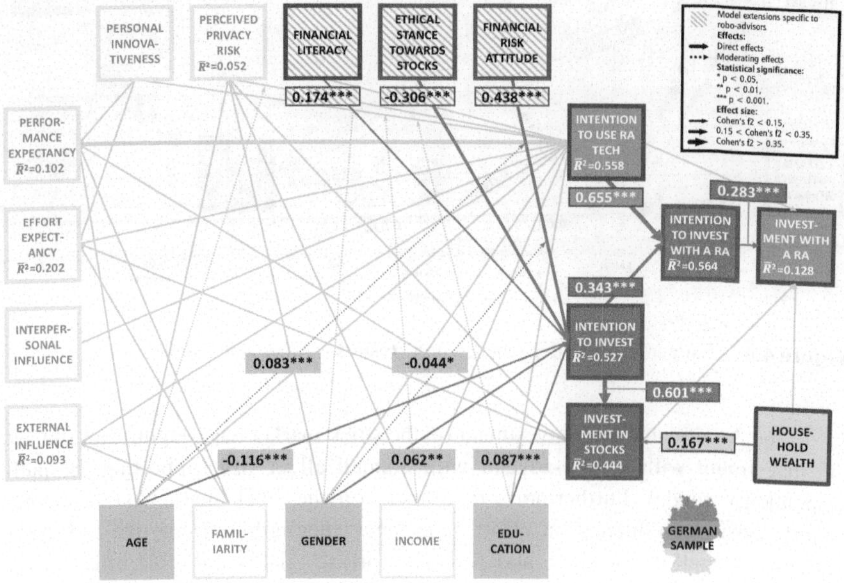

Figure 4.5 "Endogenous path dependence part" results—German sample

Figure 4.5 and *Figure 4.6* summarize the "endogenous path dependence part" of the PDA-UTAUT model applied to robo-advisors. In the German sample both the intention to use robo-advisor technology and the intention to invest have a significantly positive influence on the intention to invest with a robo-advisor. While the effect size of the first effect is large, the second one is medium. The intention to invest with a robo-advisor has a significant effect on the actual investment with a robo-advisor with a small effect size, possibly an effect of the small sample size of German users of robo-advisors (n = 51).

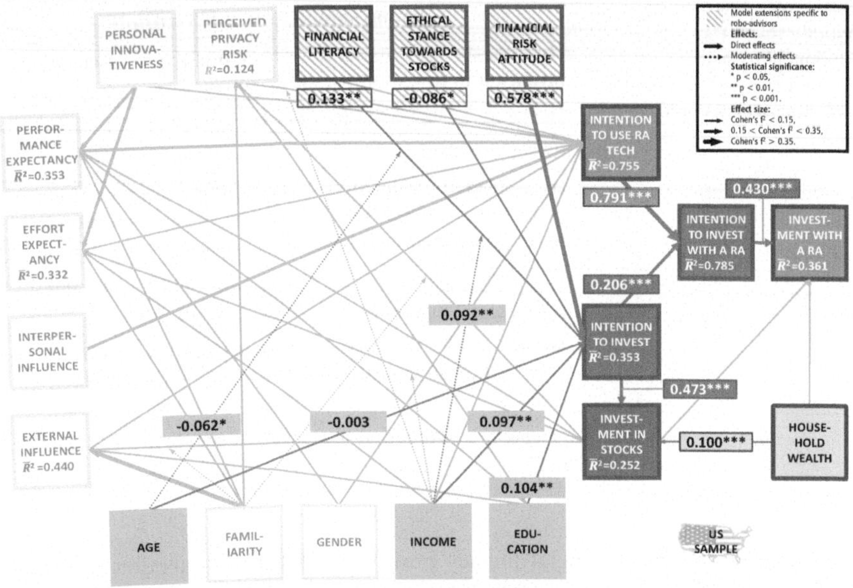

Figure 4.6 "Endogenous path dependence part" results—American sample

In the American sample, both the intention to use robo-advisor technology with a large effect size and the intention to invest with a medium effect size have a significant positive effect on the intention to invest with a robo-advisor. The intention to invest with a robo-advisor has a significant influence with a medium effect size on the investment with a robo-advisor.

The intention to invest has a significant effect on investment on the stock market in the German sample with a large effect size showing that behavioral intention constructs can predict behavior towards non-technological products. In the American sample, the intention to invest has a significant effect with a medium effect size on investment on the stock market. Wealth has a significantly positive influence on the investment on the stock market with a negligible effect size in both the German and the American sample.

See *Table 4.9* for an overview of the hypothesis tests for the path dependence augmented UTAUT model section for the German and American samples.

Table 4.9 Tested hypotheses of the "endogenous path dependence part"—German and American sample

	German sample	US sample
Hypothesis 3b: Financial literacy positively affects the intention to invest on the stock market.		
Decision	supported ($p < 0.001$)	supported ($p < 0.01$)
Effect size	small	limited
Hypothesis 4: A negative ethical stance towards the stock market negatively affects the behavioral intention to invest on the stock market.		
Decision	supported ($p < 0.001$)	supported ($p < 0.05$)
Effect size	medium	negligible
Hypothesis 5: The financial risk attitude positively affects the behavioral intention to invest on the stock market.		
Decision	supported ($p < 0.001$)	supported ($p < 0.001$)
Effect size	medium	large

Hypothesis 3b that financial literacy positively affects the intention to invest on the stock market is supported by the German sample with a small effect size and the American sample with a limited effect size, i.e., the diverging effects of financial literacy could be found in both samples. Income has a positive moderating effect on the relationship between financial literacy and the intention to invest in the American sample.

Hypothesis 4 posits a negative effect of a negative ethical stance towards the stock market on the intention to invest on the stock market. The hypothesis could be supported both in the German sample to the $p < 0.001$ level with a medium effect size and to the $p < 0.05$ level with a negligible effect size in the American sample.

Hypothesis 5 that financial risk has a positive influence on the intention to invest is supported with a medium effect size in the German sample and large effect size in the American sample. Age has a positive influence on the relationship between financial risk and the intention to invest in the German population. Being male has a negative moderating effect on the relationship between financial risk and the intention to invest.

Age has a negative impact and education a positive influence on the intention to invest in the German population. Identifying as a man has a positive impact on the intention to invest and a negative impact on the intention to use robo-advisor technology. Age has a positive moderating effect on the relationship between financial literacy and the intention to invest in the American sample leading to the addition of age with no significant effect on the intention to invest. In the American sample income and education have a positive influence on the intention to invest.

4.4 Subgroup Analyses

According to the theory presented in Chapter 2 and Chapter 3, the adoption of robo-advisor technology to invest on the stock market involves two central steps: the adoption of the new technology (i.e., robo-advisor technology) and basic technology (i.e., investment on the stock market). Following this logic, it is interesting to compare the adoption factors of groups which are on different steps of the adoption process of robo-advisors and, therefore, have taken different paths in the past: Investors not using robo-advisors (INRA) and non-investors (NI). They are compared using a multi-group analysis in SmartPLS 3, which estimates the samples in their respective models separately, i.e., the German and American model, to compare significant differences in the path coefficients. Thus, the multi-group analysis treats the attribute which differentiates the different samples as a moderator of the effects in the model.

The subgroup of those that have already adopted robo-advisors are not studied using subgroup analyses, as this would require a different research model. When the customers have already adopted robo-advisors, the important question shifts from the adoption or adoption intention to the intention to continue to use the robo-advisory service. I refer to the model developed by Cheng 2021 based on the expectation confirmation model and flow theory showing that task-technology fit, network factors, and psychological factors have a significant impact on the dependent variable of end-users' continuance intention. Similar models investigating continuance have been applied to cloud enterprise resource planning (ERP) (Cheng 2018; Cheng 2019b) and e-learning (Cheng 2014a, b; Cheng 2019a).

Furthermore, the American and German samples are also analyzed in one common model to identify differences between the countries.

4.4.1 Subgroup Analysis Between INRA and NI

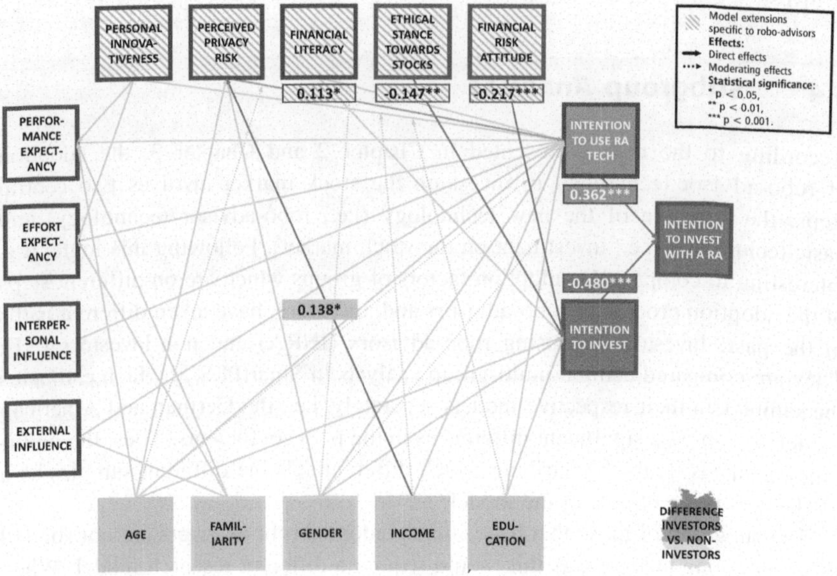

Figure 4.7 Path coefficient differences (INRA-NI)—German sample

The significant differences between German investors who do not invest with robo-advisors and non-investors are depicted in *Figure 4.7*. See Appendix A4.4.1 in the Electronic Supplementary Material for the complete set of estimates.

The most notable difference between the two samples consists in the significant difference of the path coefficients between *the intention to invest (IINV)* and *the intention to use robo-advisor technology (IURA)* on *the intention to invest using robo-advisor technology (IIRA)*. Aligned with the theory presented in this thesis, people already invested on the stock market put a higher importance on their assessment of robo-advisor technology (IURA) than people who are not invested on the stock market. Thus, a differentiation between basic technology, i.e., stocks, and additional technology, i.e., robo-advisory, allows to understand the adoption behavior of the subgroups in a more differentiated manner.

Furthermore, it is noticeable that risk (perceived privacy risk and financial risk) plays a larger role in the non-invested group. While perceived privacy risk

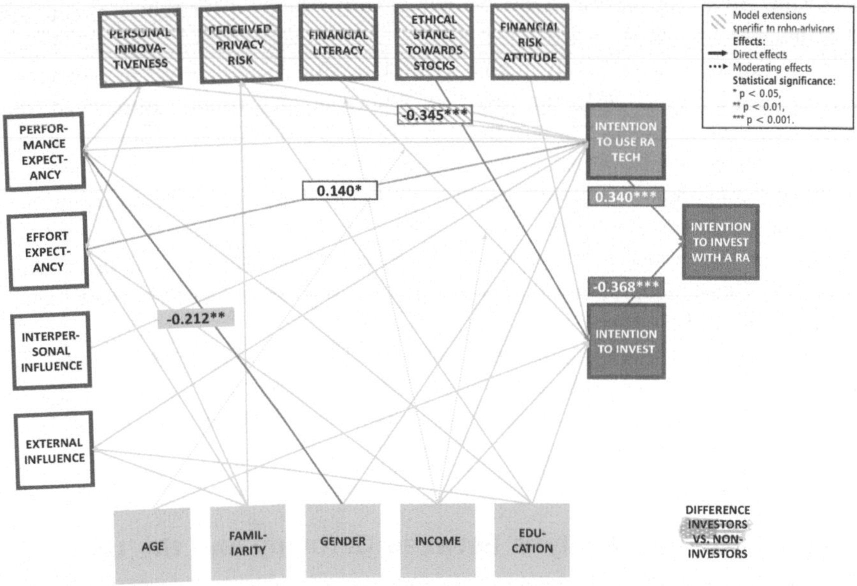

Figure 4.8 Path coefficient differences (INRA-NI)—American sample

is not even a significant factor among the investors, it is highly significant for the non-investors. This finding relates to the literature (Keller and Siegrist 2006; Dimmock and Kouwenberg 2010) showing that less risk averse people are more likely to invest on the stock market. Furthermore, income has a negative effect on perceived privacy risk only in the non-investor group. This might be indicative that for people who can afford investments (see the positive relationship between wealth and investment on the stock market) risk concerns play a major role.

Another notable difference between the invested and the non-invested German sample consists in the influence of ethical stance on the intention to invest. Although this factor is highly significant in both samples, the path coefficient in the invested sample is significantly larger. This finding is indicative of ethics playing an important role for investment decisions in Germany and especially for those already invested.

Another notable difference between the groups is that income has a negative effect on perceived privacy risk only in the non-investor group.

The significant differences between the American investors who do not invest with robo-advisors and non-investors are depicted in *Figure 4.8.* See

Appendix A4.4.1 in the Electronic Supplementary Material for the complete set of estimates.

The pattern of a relatively higher importance of *the intention to use robo-advisor technology (IURA)* for investors and relatively higher impact of *the intention to invest (IINV)* for non-investors, which was already observed in the German sample, is also found in the American one.

As in the German sample, the impact of ethical stance is significantly higher in the invested than in the non-invested sample in the USA. Ethical stance alone is not a significant factor for non-invested Americans, although it is significant in Germany. This finding shows that ethical considerations are an important factor for investors in the USA.

Effort expectancy has a significantly different effect between invested and non-invested Americans. In both samples the path coefficients are negative, but not significant. Nevertheless, the negative effect is more significantly pronounced in the non-invested sample.

4.4.2 Subgroup Analysis Between Germany and the USA

As different models were built for the German and American sample, the samples are compared in a common model, which includes all constructs of both the German and the American models. The significant differences between the German and American participants are depicted in *Figure 4.9*. See Appendix A4.4.2 in the Electronic Supplementary Material for the complete data set.

The path coefficients of the moderating effects and control variables showed significant differences between the German and the American samples. This can be explained by the fact that they were individually introduced to each model to account for the effects of the specific samples.

The behavioral intention to invest (IINV) had a higher path coefficient on *the behavioral intention to invest with a robo-advisor (IIRA)* and *the investment on the stock market (INV)* in Germany than in the USA, while the behavioral intention to use robo-advisor technology had a higher path coefficient on the behavioral intention to invest with a robo-advisor in the USA than in Germany. This result can be seen in the light of the distribution among the different investor subgroups. In the German sample, 542 participants belong to the subgroup of non-investors and 466 to the subgroup of investors who do not use robo-advisors. In the American sample, 217 belong to the subgroup of non-investors and 337 to the subgroup of investors who do not use robo-advisors. The subgroup of non-investors showed higher path coefficients for IINV on IIRA both in the German and the American

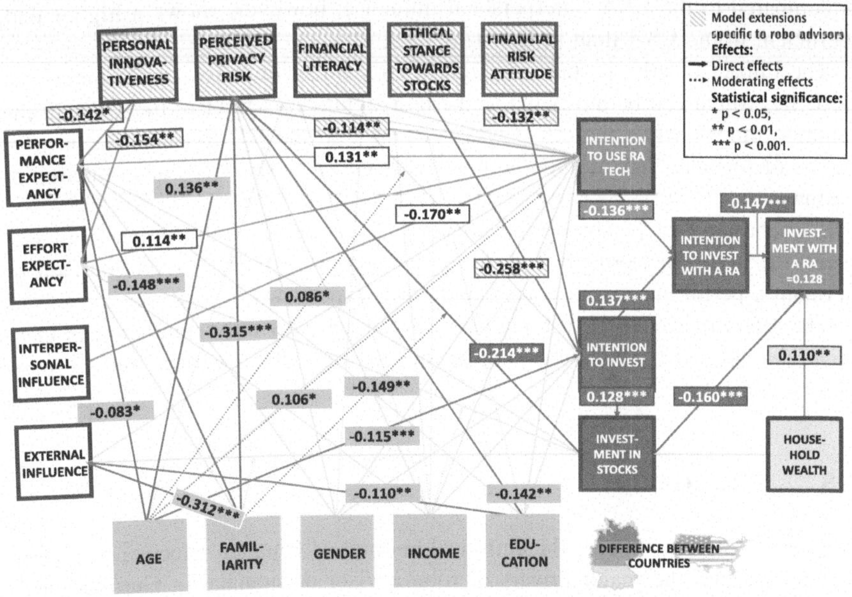

Figure 4.9 Path coefficient differences between Germany and the USA

samples than the investors who do not use robo-advisors. The path coefficient from intention to invest with a robo-advisor to the adoption of robo-advisors is significantly higher in the USA as opposed to Germany, possibly due to a much higher market penetration in the USA than in Germany.

The American and the German samples diverge in the path coefficient of investment on the stock market on investment with a robo-advisor while being significant in both samples. The American sample shows a higher path coefficient for this key construct of path dependence.

Investment has an interesting diverging effect on perceived privacy risk. While investment significantly increases perceived privacy risk, it reduces perceived privacy risk significantly in the German sample.

Effort expectancy has a significantly higher path coefficient in Germany than in the USA, which can be partly attributed to the significantly positive result in Germany and the non-significant negative result in the USA. Similarly, the path coefficient for performance expectancy was significantly higher in Germany as compared to the USA. Interpersonal influence, however, shows a higher path coefficient in the USA than in Germany.

The impact of ethical stance is significantly different between Germany and the USA, which can be attributed to the non-significant effect in the USA in the common model, while the effect was noticeable in the US model. The positive impact of financial risk attitude is more pronounced in the USA as compared to Germany.

The construct of personal innovativeness has a consistently higher influence in the USA than in Germany concerning its impact on IURA (not significant in Germany), performance expectancy, and effort expectancy.

The effect of wealth on robo-advisor investment was only significant in Germany and, therefore, constitutes a difference between the American and German path coefficients.

4.5 Discussion

In Section 4.5, I summarize the empirical findings of Chapter 4 focusing on path dependence and the major drivers of robo-advisor acceptance in Germany and the USA. Practical implications are drawn from these findings, while limitations and future research opportunities are outlined.

4.5.1 Empirical Findings

This section is structured into evidence on the impact of path dependence on robo-advisor adoption in Section 4.5.1.1 and into findings on the major drivers of robo-advisor acceptance in Germany and the USA in 4.5.1.2.

4.5.1.1 The Empirical Evidence of path Dependence

To establish whether path dependence is a vital factor for the adoption of robo-advice, several analyses were conducted: Firstly, the advantage of a model that accounts for path dependence (PDA-UTAUT model) over a model that does not (traditional UTAUT model) in explaining the variation of the adoption of robo-advice was quantified using goodness-of-fit measures. Secondly, the role of investment on the stock market for the adoption of robo-advice was investigated establishing that the basic technology (of stock market investment) plays a facilitating role in the adoption of robo-advice. The impact of investment on the stock market on the attitudes towards robo-advice was confirmed constituting a further aspect of the influence of individual path dependence. Thirdly, the significance of endogenizing stock market investment confirmed its status as a necessary condition for robo-advice. Fourthly, the double role of financial literacy and demographical variables for the adoption of robo-advice underlined the advantages of using the PDA-UTAUT model.

4.5.1.1.1 The Goodness-of-fit of PDA-UTAUT Models

The PDA-UTAUT model achieves a higher goodness-of-fit measure than the traditional UTAUT model and higher adjusted R^2 values of the dependent variable investment with a robo-advisor both in the German and the American sample. Hence, the PDA-UTAUT model with its independent variables explains a higher proportion of the variation of robo-advisor adoption than the traditional UTAUT model substantiating the advantage of modeling path dependence explicitly. Similarly, the PDA-UTAUT model, which treats the stock market investment as a necessary condition for the adoption of robo-advice, i.e., endogenizes stock market investment, exhibits a better goodness-of-fit than the UTAUT model with exogenous path dependence that treats stock market investment as an exogenous variable. See Section 4.2.4 for further details. These findings affirm my assessment of stock market investment as a necessary condition presented in Chapter 2.

4.5.1.1.2 The Role of Stock Market Investment for the Adoption of and Attitudes Towards Robo-advice

The theory of individual path dependence, derived in Chapter 2 and Chapter 3, predicts that the acceptance of the basic technology, i.e., stock market investment, directly affects the acceptance of the new technology, i.e., the investment with a robo-advisor. The PDA-UTAUT model allows to investigate whether this prediction holds true for robo-advisors.

Model estimates revealed the major drivers of investment with a robo-advisor in the German sample:

- The intention to invest with a robo-advisor has a positive effect on the investment with a robo-advisor with a small effect size.
- The investment on the stock market has a positive effect on the investment with a robo-advisor with a small effect size.

In the American sample, the major drivers of investment with a robo-advisor are:

- The intention to invest with a robo-advisor has a positive effect on the investment with a robo-advisor with a medium effect size.
- The investment on the stock market has a positive effect on the investment with a robo-advisor with a small effect size.

Thus, the findings provide clear evidence for individual path dependence in the case of robo-advisor adoption. Nevertheless, the data confirm the suitability of UTAUT models for the study of the adoption of robo-advice as the intention to invest with a robo-advisor, i.e., an intention construct established in UTAUT models, is the most dominant driver of robo-advisor adoption.

According to the theory of individual path dependence for the adoption of technologies presented in Chapter 2 and Chapter 3, the basic product, i.e., stock market investment, should not only affect the final decision to adopt a new technology, but also the attitudes towards the new technology. The theory is substantiated by the influence of investment on the stock market (INV) on the attitudes towards robo-advice.

INV significantly affects the attitudes towards robo-advisors in Germany in the following way:

- INV has a positive effect on effort expectancy.
- INV has a positive effect on external influence.
- INV has a negative effect on perceived privacy risk.

In the US, similar effects of INV are observed, except for perceived privacy risk:

- INV has a positive effect on effort expectancy.
- INV has a positive effect on external influence.
- INV has a positive effect on perceived privacy risk.

Thus, this study demonstrates that the adoption of the basic technology has an impact on the factors explaining the intention to use the new technology, i.e., path dependence influences the attitudes towards the new technology directly. This constitutes further corroboration of path dependence.

The finding that INV has the opposite effect on perceived privacy risk in the German and the American sample demonstrates that the effect of the basic technologies on the attitudes towards the new technology is sample specific. This can be attributed to different experiences (or assessments of these experiences) that customers in Germany and the USA have made with stock market investments.

4.5.1.1.3 Endogenizing Stock Market Investment

Considering investment on the stock market as a necessary condition for the acceptance of robo-advice, I applied the PDA-UTAUT model to robo-advisor technology. The PDA-UTAUT model endogenizes the basic technology, i.e., stock market investment. The endogenization is achieved by adding *the intention to invest (IINV)* construct, which explains both *investment on the stock market (INV)* and *the intention to invest with a robo-advisor (IIRA)*. Hence, I was able to investigate whether endogenizing stock market investment is instrumental in explaining robo-advisor adoption.

The data confirmed IINV to influence the investment on the stock market with a large effect size in Germany and a medium effect size in the USA.

Concerning IIRA, model estimations identified two major drivers in Germany:

- The intention to use robo-advisor technology has a positive effect on IIRA with a large effect size.
- The intention to invest has a positive effect on IIRA with a medium effect size.

IIRA was found to be influenced by two major drivers in the USA:

- The intention to use robo-advisor technology has a positive effect on IIRA with a large effect size.
- The intention to invest has a positive effect on IIRA with a medium effect size.

Thus, while the intention to use robo-advisor technology is the most important driver of the intention to invest with a robo-advisor both in Germany and the USA, the effect of the intention to invest is considerable, i.e., path dependence also explains the adoption intention.

Additionally, path dependence consistently shapes the preferences of customer groups on the same level of path dependence both in Germany and the USA: While investors who do not use robo-advisors base their adoption decision relatively more on their attitudes towards robo-advisor technology, non-investors are rather influenced by their attitudes towards investing. Similarly, ethical stance towards the stock market was a more important factor for investors who do not use robo-advisors as compared to non-investors in both Germany and the USA.

Hence, differences in robo-advisor adoption between Germany and the USA can partly be explained by the countries' respective composition of investors who do not use robo-advisors and non-investors, as *Table 4.10* shows. The higher proportion of investors who do not use robo-advisors equals a higher importance of the technical side (*intention to use robo-advisor technology*) in the more mature American market as compared to the German market with a relatively higher importance on the financial side (*intention to invest*). Thus, the PDA-UTAUT model can account for the varying influence of salient beliefs during different stages of technology adoption (Benbasat and Barki 2007) for path dependent technologies.

Table 4.10 Revealed investment behavior in the German and American sample

Sample	Sample size	% of investors using a robo-advisor	% of investors who do not use robo-advisors	% of non-investors
Germany	1059	 4.8	 44.0	 51.2
USA	998	 44.5	 33.8	 21.7

4.5.1.1.4 The Disentanglement of Diverging Effects: a Further Advantage of Accounting for path Dependence

Apart from the evidence for the importance of individual path dependence for the adoption of robo-advice, there is another advantage that underlines the merits of the PDA-UTAUT model: The disentanglement of factors influencing both the basic and advanced technology allows an analysis of opposing effects of independent factors on the adoption of the advanced and the basic technology. An analysis of these effects would have been impossible without disentangling the effects of attitudes towards the technology from the attitudes towards the stock market. The fact that more than one construct or variable exhibits opposing effects on *the intention to invest on the stock market* and *the intention to use robo-advisor technology* underscores in how many cases opposing effects might be present:

1. The double role of financial literacy on robo-advisor adoption, i.e., a negative effect on *the intention to use robo-advisor technology* and a positive effect on *the intention to invest on the stock market*, confirms the hypotheses 3a-b and

corroborates findings in different publications, which now can be consistently explained using the PDA-UTAUT model. For example, a positive effect of financial literacy on the intention to invest (Yoong 2011; Van Rooij et al. 2011) and an overall negative effect on the intention to adopt robo-advice (Fan and Chatterjee 2020; Todd and Seay 2020) were found.

2. Income in the USA has a significantly negative effect on the intention to adopt robo-advisor technology, but a positive effect on the intention to invest on the stock market. This finding is consistent with prior research showing that income is positively related to stock market investment (Yoong 2011; Van Rooij et al. 2011). According to the findings, the research of Fan and Chatterjee 2020 as well as Todd and Seay 2020 conducted with participants owning assets outside of their retirement funds found that lower incomes are positively associated with robo-advisor adoption and higher incomes were negatively related to robo-advisor adoption. Todd and Seay 2020 attribute the negative impact of income on the acceptance of robo-advice to the theory of information search, i.e., individuals with higher income have more pronounced planning and information needs, thus, automation is less likely. Fan and Chatterjee 2020 cite a higher risk appetite of high-income individuals in the form of investment in stocks, alternative asset classes, and undiversified investments as a possible reason for their lower propensity to invest with robo-advisors.
3. Being male in Germany is negatively associated with *the intention to adopt robo-advisor technology (IURA)* and, in Germany, is positively associated with *the intention to invest on the stock market (IINV)*. This finding corresponds to Almenberg and Dreber 2015 as well as Van Rooij et al. 2011 observing a higher stock market participation rate of men than of women. Todd and Seay 2020 as well as Fan and Chatterjee 2020 did not find an influence of gender in their samples, which only consisted of investors. The correlation between gender and financial literacy might constitute a further reason for the double role of gender for the adoption of robo-advice, especially as Almenberg and Dreber 2015 attribute a large part of the gender gap in stock market participation to different levels of financial literacy between men and women. Several studies find that financial literacy is higher for men than for women across different countries including Germany, Japan, and the Unites States (Lusardi and Mitchell 2014; Lusardi and Mitchell 2011b; Van Rooij et al. 2011; Lusardi and Mitchell 2008). See *Table 4.11* for the average results of German men and women in this study; we observe a significant correlation between male gender and higher financial literacy. However, gender exhibits a significant independent effect beyond financial literacy on *the intention to adopt robo-advisor technology* and *the intention to invest on the stock market* both in the German and American sample.

Table 4.11 Financial literacy test scores—German sample

	Financial literacy score	
	Women	Men
Subsample size	471	584
Average	0.722	0.853
Median	0.750	0.875
SD	0.250	0.203
p-value of two-tailed unequal variances t-test	0.000***	

Note: * $p < 0.05$, ** $p < 0.01$, *** $p < 0.001$.

Summing up, the following empirical findings substantiate path dependence as modeled in the PDA-UTAUT model for the adoption of robo-advice:

- A PDA-UTAUT model explains a higher proportion of the variation of robo-advisor adoption than a traditional UTAUT model, even when the higher parameterization is accounted for.
- Stock market investment is a major driver of the investment with a robo-advisor.
- Stock market investment has an impact on the attitudes towards robo-advisor technology.
- *The intention to invest* is a major driver of *the intention to invest using a robo-advisor.*
- The disentanglement of the *intention to invest* and *the intention to use robo-advisor technology* allows to analyze opposing effects of drivers of robo-advisor acceptance.

4.5.1.2 Major Drivers of Robo-advisor Acceptance in Germany and the USA

This section summarizes the major drivers of the intention constructs of robo-advisor acceptance, *the intention to use robo-advisor technology (IURA)* in Section 4.5.1.2.1 and *the intention to invest (IINV)* in Section 4.5.1.2.2. The results are discussed in the light of recent empirical research on robo-advisor acceptance, which focuses on IURA as it does not account for path dependence.

4.5.1.2.1 The Intention to use Robo-advisor Technology (IURA)

The intention to use robo-advisor technology (IURA) corresponds to the traditional intention to use construct in UTAUT models, i.e., it directly relates to the new technology. IURA is the dominant factor in driving the intention to invest with a robo-advisor confirming its importance for the final decision.

As per the findings of this study, the intention to use robo-advisor technology (IURA) in Germany is driven by:

- Performance expectancy has a positive effect on IURA with a large effect size.
- Interpersonal influence has a positive effect on IURA with a small effect size.
- Financial literacy has a negative effect on IURA with a small effect size.

IURA in the USA has a higher number of major drivers as compared to Germany:

- Performance expectancy has a positive effect on IURA with a medium effect size.
- Interpersonal influence has a positive effect on IURA with a medium effect size.
- Perceived privacy risk has a negative effect on IURA with a small effect size.
- Financial literacy has a negative effect on IURA with a small effect size.
- Personal innovativeness has a positive effect on IURA with a small effect size.

According to the findings of this study, performance expectancy has a positive effect on the intention to use a robo-advisor in Germany and the USA. This corresponds to the recent findings of other researchers. Specifically, perceived usefulness significantly impacts the intention to use a robo-advisor. In Germany, a study involving 96 participants, recruited from an unspecified source, supports this conclusion (Seiler and Fanenbruck 2021). Similarly, in the USA, research with 404 participants recruited via an online survey, who represent a sample with properties akin to the general population, confirms the same trend (Flavián et al. 2022). Furthermore, perceived usefulness was shown to have a positive effect on the attitude towards use among 214 members of the University of Perugia in Italy (Figà-Talamanca et al. 2022).

I found effort expectancy to have a positive effect on the intention to use robo-advisor technology in Germany and no demonstrable effect in the USA. Interestingly, a positive effect of perceived ease of use was found in the USA (Flavián et al. 2022), but not in Germany (Seiler and Fanenbruck 2021). I derive that the effect of effort expectancy is sample specific due to its limited effect on the adoption of robo-advisor technology.

Personal innovativeness only affects the intention to use robo-advisor technology in the USA, but not in Germany as per my findings. Nevertheless, Flavián et al. 2022 found no effect of personal innovativeness on the intention to use robo-advisor technology in the USA. Hence, personal innovativeness can be considered as sample specific due to its limited effect size.

This study demonstrated financial literacy to have a negative effect on the intention to use robo-advisor technology in Germany and the USA. In contrast, financial literacy did not show an effect on the intention to use robo-advisor technology in Germany (Seiler and Fanenbruck 2021). This might be attributed to the fact that Seiler and Fanenbruck 2021 did not account for path dependence. Hence, the negative effect of financial literacy on *the intention to use robo-advisor technology* might have cancelled out with the positive effect of financial literacy on *the intention to invest* in their study.

Perceived privacy risk was confirmed to have a negative effect on the intention to use robo-advisor technology in Germany and the USA. While the positively framed perceived privacy was shown to have a positive effect in Germany (Seiler and Fanenbruck 2021), the negatively framed perceived risk was found to have a negative effect (Seiler and Fanenbruck 2021). Thus, other research confirmed the findings of this study.

Female gender was found to positively influence the intention to use robo-advisor technology (IURA) in Germany and the USA. A potential reason for that might be higher values of financial literacy found for men than for women as discussed and presented in Section 4.5.1.1.4 and found in the literature (Lusardi and Mitchell 2014; Lusardi and Mitchell 2011b; Van Rooij et al. 2011; Lusardi and Mitchell 2008), although gender shows an independent effect on the intention to use robo-advisor technology in this study in both Germany and the USA. Nevertheless, Todd and Seay 2020 as well as Fan and Chatterjee 2020 did not find an influence of gender in their samples, which only consisted of investors. Furthermore, the effect of gender could not be reestablished at a German medium-sized university with 231 undergraduate business students (Oehler et al. 2022). The absence of the effect of gender in these studies could be explained by the specific properties of the samples obtained by Todd and Seay 2020, Fan and Chatterjee 2020 as well as Oehler et al. 2022 and their lack of accounting for individual path dependence. The lack of individual path dependence in their models might be especially important as gender in the German model and financial literacy—shown to correlate with gender—in both the German and the American model have a diverging effect on *the intention to use robo-advisor technology (IURA)* and *the intention to invest (IINV)*, as presented in Section 4.5.1.1.4. Thus, the disentanglement of the adoption intention of the new and basic technology that the PDA-UTAUT model offers might have enabled the detection of the effect of gender on the adoption of robo-advice.

In this study, age did not show a significant effect on the intention to use robo-advisor technology in Germany and the USA, while Flavián et al. 2022 found a negative effect in the USA. This could potentially be attributed to their missing account of path dependence, as this study found a negative effect of age on the intention to invest in Germany.

In summary, the data reemphasize the value of the established constructs of the UTAUT model (performance expectancy and interpersonal influence), but also underline the importance of financial literacy in both samples when analyzing the intention to use robo-advisor technology.

4.5.1.2.2 The Intention to Invest (IINV)

The addition of the intention to invest (IINV) construct endogenizes the investment on the stock market. Hence, it accounts for the status of the investment on the stock market as a necessary condition for the acceptance of robo-advice. As shown above, its influence is especially important for non-investors both in Germany and the USA. Thus, the integration of non-investors on the stock market critically hinges on the construct.

In Germany, IINV is influenced by the following major drivers:

- Financial risk attitude has a positive effect on IINV with a medium effect size.
- Ethical stance towards the stock market has a negative effect on IINV with a medium effect size.
- Financial literacy has a positive effect on IINV with a small effect size.
- Age has a negative effect on IINV with a small effect size.

In the USA, only one major driver affects IINV:

- Financial risk attitude has a positive effect on IINV with a large effect size.

According to the data, financial risk attitude was found to have a positive effect on *the intention to invest (IINV)* and, thus, on *the intention to invest with a robo-advisor (IIRA)*. This effect was confirmed by a positive effect of risk attitude in the financial domain in Germany (Oehler et al. 2022).

Interestingly, ethical stance has quite a large effect in Germany as compared to the USA. Furthermore, the number of drivers with significant effect sizes on the technical and financial side vary considerably between Germany and the USA.

The results show that data privacy and security concerns can have an impact on the adoption of robo-advisor technology, e.g., the investment of financial resources with a robo-advisor poses potential threats of theft by hacking. In Germany, the difference between investors who have not adopted robo-advisors and non-investors in perceived privacy risk shows that risk averse people might choose less often to invest on the stock market, which is aligned to established literature (Keller and Siegrist 2006; Dimmock and Kouwenberg 2010).

While the direct impact of personal innovativeness on the intention to adopt robo-advisor technology is limited (especially in Germany), the impact on performance and effort expectancy is considerable. This indicates that the innovative part of the population might be more easily convinced of the advantages of robo-advisor technology. Furthermore, this reinforces that performance and effort expectations are not solely based on the features of the technology in question, but also on the attitudes of potential consumers.

This investigation reaffirms the link between ethical stance and intention to invest on the stock market, which to the author's knowledge has been understudied since its introduction by Keller and Siegrist 2006. Interestingly, the effect of the ethical stance is found to be stronger for investors than for non-investors and for German participants stronger than for American ones. This finding makes ethical questions a perpetual subject for suppliers of financial services.

Education was the only control variable showing a consistent positive impact on the intention to invest on the stock market (IINV) both in Germany and the USA. This finding is highly consistent with past research showing that education has a positive impact on stock market participation (Guiso et al. 2003; Van Rooij et al. 2011; Yoong 2011). Potential reasons for the correlation between education and stock market participation include a reduction of the information costs necessary to participate in the stock market (Guiso et al. 2003) and a correlation of education and financial literacy (Van Rooij et al. 2011).

4.5.2 Practical Implications Based on the Empirical Findings

The results of this chapter have implications for both the suppliers of robo-advisory services and the promotion of stock market participation by governmental institutions.

The data provide evidence that path dependence, in this case the investment on the stock market, has an impact on technology acceptance and the attitudes towards that technology, in this case of robo-advisors. In the case of robo-advice, path dependence influences the weighting of the technological and financial side of the adoption decision. While non-investors focus relatively more on the financial side, stock market investors focus relatively more on the technological side. This differentiation could provide a starting point for a market segmentation to target specific niches of the markets. While suppliers of robo-advisory services might focus relatively more on influencing the technological attitudes of their target group when catering to investors, they might focus relatively more on the financial attitudes when developing a product for current non-investors. How to influence these attitudes cannot be answered with the data at hand. Nevertheless, I will investigate in Chapter 7 how product attributes can influence customers' attitudes towards the robo-advisor technology.

Different demographical groups, in this study Americans and Germans, show distinct patterns of robo-advisor adoption. I conclude that irrespective of the maturity level of the market, i.e., of the share of customers already invested on the stock market (basic technology), a market segmentation according to the subgroup analyses seems worthwhile for suppliers of robo-advisory services. As the results indicate: The acceptance of the technology is expected to have a higher importance for the invested part of the population, while the focus for the other part is to accept the basic technology first, i.e., invest in stocks. Furthermore, the acceptance of stock market investment is a necessary condition for non-investors to be able to invest with robo-advisors.

Moreover, the results indicate that ethical stance has a higher impact for people already invested on the stock market both in Germany and the USA, i.e., the mature market segment. In Germany, the perceived privacy risks showed a greater impact for non-investors than for investors. Thus, suppliers of robo-advisory services in Germany targeting non-investors might investigate features and communication strategies that allow a reduction in their perceived privacy risk.

From the point of view of a governmental institution trying to increase the share of stockholders in the population, the finding that path dependence is a driver of the acceptance of and attitudes towards robo-advice and that non-investors put relatively more emphasis on the investment decision means that the impact of robo-advisor technology might be limited. One major purpose of robo-advisor technology—allowing non-investors an access to the stock market—presents itself as a potential obstacle for the adoption of robo-advice. At least in Germany, the expectation that current non-investors might be encouraged to invest by robo-advisor technology might be more often fulfilled for women than for men, as they have a higher tendency to *intend to adopt robo-advisor technology*, although they are less likely to *intend to invest on the stock marke*t.

Nevertheless, this study has identified drivers to influence the intention to invest on the stock market: financial literacy, education, the ethical stance towards stocks, and the financial risk attitude. The ethical stance towards stocks and the financial risk might also represent cultural values that might exhibit a degree of idiosyncrasy, education and financial literacy are objective measures of competence. Hence, they can be influenced by governmental institutions using education programs to increase the measures of competence. The knowledge included in the concept of financial literacy could be taught in schools in subjects as economics and other social sciences or as examples in mathematics to guarantee that every person has the opportunity to understand core financial concepts.

4.5.3 Limitations

The data gathered from the participants in Germany and the USA might not be representative for the respective countries, as data were collected by the means of an online survey, thus, they constitute a convenience sample. Studies relying on convenience samples are standard in the technology acceptance literature (Davis 1989; Venkatesh et al. 2003; Venkatesh et al. 2012; Oehler et al. 2022). They allow researchers to collect data without requiring the financial resources that usually only major governmental institutions have at their disposal.

However, the samples from Germany and the USA were similar in some major characteristics (see *Table 4.1* in Section 4.1.2). This similarity of major demographic characteristics enhances the author's trust in the comparison between the two countries. The analysis of the countries has shown that important path coefficients between these groups are relatively homogeneous, and most hypotheses hold in both samples. However, to predict the adoption behavior of every subgroup in detail requires a specific study representative of that subgroup.

4.5.4 Future Research

To counter the lack of generalizability of this study, future research could analyze the PDA-UTAUT model with a representative sample. Moreover, a replication in other countries than Germany or the USA would be interesting to verify whether the findings on path dependence and robo-advisor adoption hold true in other cultures.

Future research might study in more detail the impact of path dependence and specifically the PDA-UTAUT model on technology acceptance in other fields than robo-advisory to elicit further which impact can be attributed to path dependence in different settings. Technologies potentially being impacted by path dependence include gaming, mobile payment, and digital identity cards.

Investigating the previously ignored factor of ethical stance could prove interesting for future research, as ethical considerations currently gain momentum in public discussions and might experience an even greater impact in the future. Research on this topic seems especially relevant in Germany, as ethical stance is one of the major drivers of the intention to invest.

5 Incorporating the Supply Side: Product Features of Robo-Advisors

In earlier chapters, I explored how path dependence influences the adoption of robo-advisors. I did this by distinguishing between basic technology (stock market investment) and advanced technology (robo-advisory), and showing how basic technology affects the adoption and perception of new technology. This method enabled us to analyze the varying preferences of non-investors and investors who have not adopted robo-advisors, showing that these two groups follow different paths. While the former group was found to be relatively more influenced by the investment side, the latter group is relatively more concerned with the technology.

Thus, I have focused on the consumer side, i.e., consumers' preferences, intentions, and usage decisions. This approach has provided new insights into why people adopt robo-advisors, insights that can partly apply to other technologies through the concept of individual path dependence in technology acceptance models (PDA-UTAUT). Practitioners can use these insights to target specific customer groups. However, I have not yet explored the main ways suppliers can affect demand: the robo-advisor technology and its pricing.

While the technology of robo-advisory can be defined straightforwardly, e.g., in the description of robo-advisor technology used for the study in Chapter 4, the specificities of the technologies can be manifold such as personal advice, the questions asked to investors to deduct individualized investment strategies, etc. These specificities, which can be perceived as degrees of freedom within the definition of robo-advisor technology, will be described as "features", "characteristics", and "attributes". A concrete definition is presented in Section 5.1. In the

Supplementary Information The online version contains supplementary material available at https://doi.org/10.1007/978-3-658-44679-6_5.

M. Horn, *Technology Acceptance, Path Dependence, and the Demand for Robo-Advisory Services*, Forschung zur Digitalisierung der Wirtschaft | Advanced Studies in Business Digitization, https://doi.org/10.1007/978-3-658-44679-6_5

following, I provide an overview of the current role of robo-advisors' features in the academic literature, the industry literature of wealth management, on websites giving customers advice on robo-advisors, and most importantly of the features that are offered by all German and the most prominent American robo-advisors. The market overview of the features provides a cohesive overview of the robo-advisor industry in two of the most important markets for robo-advice, allowing to deduct major differences.

To understand the current situation and identify which features customers value, I conduct a choice-based conjoint analysis (CBC). This analysis helps determine the absolute and relative importance customers place on these features. Furthermore, customers can be grouped by their preferences and their willingness to pay for features. This methodology expands the literature on robo-advisor adoption (Belanche et al. 2019; Todd and Seay 2020) by examining how features motivate different customer groups. Additionally, comparing the preferences of German and American participants, along with a market overview, can help explain why robo-advice is more popular in the USA than in Germany by revealing possible mismatches between supply and demand. This knowledge can be used by suppliers of robo-advisory services to identify attributes that can be offered at competitive prices and serve the demand of customers.

The adoption of robo-advisors has been studied among other methods using technology acceptance models like TAM, e.g., by Belanche et al. 2019. As the literature review in Chapter 5 will show, the literature on robo-advisor adoption so far lacks a comprehensive investigation of the influence of objective product features on the adoption of robo-advice. Objectivity in this context is defined as not depending on individual attitudes, but measurability and perceptibility, e.g., cost structures and the provision of services. Product features play an important but often forgotten role in technology acceptance. Their importance is underlined by their role in the technology acceptance model (TAM) as proposed by Davis 1985. Following his approach, I compare robo-advisors which have specific features to robo-advisors without those features. The results can shed light on the features' effect on robo-advisor adoption and its drivers. To give a short example: If the introduction of certain features increases the intention to use a robo-advisor and the performance expectancy associated with it, but not other independent constructs in the UTAUT model, I can conclude that this feature influences the intention to use a robo-advisor by giving the participant an increased perception of the robo-advisor's performance. This can expand the literature by providing evidence on how the attitudes towards a technology are shaped by specific features. Furthermore, it provides the opportunity for suppliers of robo-advice to influence customers' attitudes towards a technology in a planful manner by introducing certain product features. In contrast to Chapter 4, the traditional as opposed to the PDA-UTAUT model will be applied, as the attributes can be considered as minor adjustments within the same technological concept, while an impact of attributes on the financial attitudes of a person does not relate to robo-advisor technology whatsoever. Thus, the fact whether a robo-advisor offers a service such as personal advice cannot be expected to influence a person's financial risk attitude, financial literacy, or ethical stance towards the stock market.

The studies conducted in the Chapters 5–7 have their distinct motivations and findings, but they are united by one overarching goal: eliciting the role of features for the choice of robo-advice. To achieve this goal, Chapter 5–7 are structured as follows:

- In Chapter 5, I will examine the current literature on robo-advisors' attributes demonstrating that an incorporation of objective attributes is still missing in the robo-advisor adoption literature. I will continue by creating a list of objective attributes with potential importance to robo-advisory. I will collect, describe, and compare major product features of all 40 existing German robo-advisors and 34 of the most renowned American robo-advisors. Practical implications will be derived from the market overview.
- In Chapter 6, I will describe and apply a framework how to derive features for a conjoint analysis yielding eight attributes. A choice-based conjoint analysis (CBC) will be described and conducted in Germany and the USA. The following methods will be applied to the data:

    - A counts-analysis will confirm the significant importance of all attributes on an aggregate level.
    - A Hierarchical-Bayes-analysis (HB) will determine the importance that the attributes have at the individual level allowing to sort the attributes according to their importance to consumers.
    - A latent class analysis will cluster participants by their preferences into an ex-ante unknown number of groups.
    - A willingness to pay analysis will provide estimates for the value of attribute levels to consumers.

  The results will be examined for theoretical and practical implications for the suppliers of robo-advice, especially considering the findings of Chapter 5.
- In Chapter 7, I will measure the impact of attributes on the intention to use a specific robo-advisor and its drivers from the traditional UTAUT model. Thus,

this study applies the idea behind the original technology acceptance model (TAM) introduced by Davis 1985 to robo-advice. Practical conclusions are deducted from the findings.

This comprehensive approach sheds light on the role of attributes for robo-advice. It draws practical conclusions by providing a market overview of the attributes of German and American robo-advisors (Chapter 5), by eliciting the preferences of Germans and Americans regarding these attributes (Chapter 6), and by examining the impact that these attributes have on robo-advisor adoption and its drivers in the UTAUT model (Chapter 7).

5.1 Overview of the Literature on Robo-Advisors' Attributes

The study of the influence of product features on demand promises actionable insights to inform practice. To assure the actionability of the studies to come, it is important to expand the existing research on perceptions of consumers with properties that can be measured objectively, i.e., attributes or features (Benbasat and Barki 2007). The term "feature" has been more stringently defined than the interchangeably used terms "characteristic" and "attribute". Thus, the definition of the term "feature" is applied to the terms "characteristic" and "attribute" as well. The term "feature" has been defined in various ways in the software development literature[1]. I adhere to the straightforward definition of Kang et al. 1990 to define a feature as "a prominent or distinctive user-visible aspect, quality, or characteristic of a software system or systems".

In partial contrast to the academic literature on product features of robo-advisors (e.g., Wu and Gao 2021), the term feature is understood in an objectifiable manner, i.e., the presence of a feature cannot be left for judgment of the (potential) customers. Thus, the provision of a human advisor as an add-on to the robo-advisor service is considered a feature of the robo-advisor, as every customer can objectively judge whether the robo-advisor offers this service or not.

[1] Definitions of the term "feature" include, e.g., "a structure that extends and modifies the structure of a given program in order to satisfy a stakeholder's requirement, to implement and encapsulate a design decision, and to offer a configuration option" (Apel et al. 2008), "product characteristic from user or customer views, which essentially consists of a cohesive set of individual requirements" (Chen et al. 2005), or "a triplet, $f = (R, W, S)$, where R represents the requirements the feature satisfies, W the assumptions the feature takes about its environment and S its specification" (Classen et al. 2008).

Terms like "word of mouth" defined as "consumer opinions on a firm's product or service reflected in their daily dialogues" (Al-Tamimi 2006; Wu and Gao 2021) are not considered as features as they reflect subjective judgments and perceptions of the consumers. This distinction is especially important in the context of this dissertation, as the focus is on both objective features as well as subjective attitudes to be considered in further studies.

In Section 5.1, I will give an overview of the literature on the features of robo-advisors. This overview has three main motivations:

- To give a synopsis of the current literature on features of robo-advisors.
- To identify open topics regarding features and the acceptance of robo-advice.
- To comprehensively identify features to provide a holistic market overview.

Characteristics and features of robo-advisors have been studied by several authors in various papers and fields. Therefore, I also provide the name of the journals to show which strands of literature have made contributions. The following sections review relevant studies on feature-related topics. The literature has discussed some topics related to the features of robo-advisors in detail: The difference between human and robot financial advisory, humanization of robo-advisors, and its impact on trust is considered by several authors. Some topics have received attention from only a few authors covered in "Overview of other relevant literature", among them the performance-control dilemma for robo-advice as well as business models of robo-advisors and their features. Furthermore, the study of the effect of product features is at the heart of the development of the technology acceptance model (TAM). Some researchers studying the adoption of robo-advice provide recommendations on how to influence the constructs of the technology acceptance models, but without providing empirical support or not relying on objective features. Thus, I highlight the necessity to test the influence of objective product features on the technology acceptance of robo-advisors.

5.1.1 Human Versus Robot Financial Advisors and Trust Mechanisms

Tauchert and Mesbah 2019 (published in the *International Conference on Information Systems (ICIS) 2019 Proceedings*) investigated the advice on stock price predictions from robo-advisors and human advisors. Their study is based on the judge-advisor systems (JAS) (consult Bonaccio and Dalal 2006 for a comprehensive literature review) and task technology fit (TTF) literature (Goodhue and

Thompson 1995; Goodhue 1995). In a sample of 197 participants recruited with a market research company, participants were asked to estimate the performance of a particular stock based on charts provided to them. In a second step, participants were presented with advice framed to either come from a human advisor or an AI. Estimates of both the human and the robo-advisor corresponded to actual data without informing participants about this. In a third step, participants were asked whether they wanted to adjust their estimation based on the advisors' suggestion. Furthermore, questions on the perceived expertise of the advisor, the task-advisor fit ("the fit between task characteristics and an advisor" Tauchert and Mesbah 2019) and participants' trust in the advisor were added. SmartPLS (Ringle et al. 2015) was used for an analysis finding that robo-advice was used more than human advice. Additionally, they found that task-advisor fit significantly impacted advice utilization for both human and robo-advisors. Task-advisor fit was positively influenced by advisor expertise and efficiency enhancement for robo-advisors and by advisor expertise and advisor integrity for human advisors. The integrity of robo-advisors was interestingly rated higher than that of human advisors. Tauchert and Mesbah 2019 found no support for an influence of emotional trust in an advisor on task-advisor fit and perceived user's expertise on advisor expertise. The authors recommend market research to identify the features that influence task-advisor fit. They propose transparency on algorithms, data usage, and past performance to increase perceived expertise and a communication of the efficiency of robo-advice to increase its perceived efficiency. However, Tauchert and Mesbah 2019 do not provide any empirical evidence backing this advice.

Cheng et al. 2019 (published in the open-access journal *Sustainability*) conducted semi-structured interviews of 15 minutes each with 27 investors with an understanding of robo-advice to elicit trust influencing factors. The interviews were transcribed and coded. Constructs were developed based on the frequency of keywords mentioned, finding three categories with in total six factors influencing trust in the interviews: deposition (attitude toward AI), situational normality (reputation, information quality, and service quality), and structural assurance (service commitment and government regulation). A research model to predict "trust in robo-advisor" was developed based on the findings from the interviews. Supervisory control was added as a structural assurance to the model based on literature. Drawing on the mobile commerce research by Siau and Shen 2003, they divided trust in robo-advisors into trust in vendors and trust in technology. This separation into different domains of trust is not unlike the separation into different domains explored in the first part of this paper (financial and technological attitudes). An online study with 230 valid investors were analyzed using SmartPLS

3.0 and SPSS. They found that the trust influencing factors of situational normality (reputation, information quality, and service quality) had a positive impact on trust in vendors, while the structural assurance factors (government regulation and supervisory control) and attitude towards AI had a positive impact on trust in technology. Trust in vendor and trust in technology showed a positive impact on trust in robo-advisor.

Morana et al. 2020 (published in the *Proceedings of the European Conference on Information Systems (ECIS) 2020*) tested the influence of anthropomorphizing a robo-advisor chatbot on trusting beliefs with three different levels of anthropomorphism on 183 German university students in a laboratory experiment. They tested the investment decisions (conducted with fictitious money equivalent to 3 €) of the participants between three companies from the same industry with recommendations given by a robo-advisor chatbot. The robo-advisor chatbot exhibited different levels of anthropomorphism. These levels were set by introducing different social cues such as names, avatars, dynamic response time, a typing indicator, etc. A questionnaire containing questions on the participants' anthropomorphizing, social presence, trusting beliefs, and disposition to trust in technology was presented subsequently. Afterwards, the (randomly chosen) results of the investment decisions were presented by the robo-advisor chatbot. Data were analyzed using Stata version 13.0. Morana et al. 2020 found that anthropomorphizing the robo-advisor led to higher perceived social presence[2], which in turn had a positive effect on trusting beliefs. Trusting beliefs are formed by users' perceived quality of the information provided by an agent[3] and have the dimensions competence, benevolence, and integrity[4]. While trusting beliefs alone had a significant effect on the likeliness to follow the robo-advisor's recommendation, social presence alone had no significant effect on the likeliness to follow a recommendation, but it had a positive indirect effect via trusting beliefs. Thus, the authors recommend using social cues as investigated in their study to ensure an adequate level of social presence to increase customers' trusting beliefs and, therefore, the likeliness to follow advice.

Zhang et al. 2021 (published in the *Journal of Services Marketing*) base their research partly on the existing literature on self-service technologies (SSTs), which found that reliability and perceived fun (Weijters et al. 2007) as well as convenience (Collier and Kimes 2013) play a positive role in the SST adoption.

---

[2] Described by Nass and Moon 2000 as "the more computers present characteristics that are associated with humans, the more likely they are to elicit social behavior".

[3] See Qiu and Benbasat 2009.

[4] See McKnight et al. 2002.

Zhang et al. 2021 investigated the consumers' trust perceptions (measures for cognitive and emotional trust adapted from Komiak and Benbasat 2006), performance expectancy, and intention to hire towards robo-advisors and high/low expertise human financial advisors of 602 participants in three studies recruited on the platforms Amazon MTurk and Prolific. The intention to hire the advisor for the investment of an inheritance of $100,000 was the major dependent variable. High and low expertise advisors were represented in the vignettes, i.e., verbal descriptions, by their certification, work experience, and position within the financial services company. The second study was conducted to control whether a female as opposed to a male advisor (first study) would have an impact, but it found consistent results to the first study. The third study contained multi-dimensional measures for trust and performance expectancy as opposed to the first and second studies. Data were analyzed using MANCOVA. In all three studies, human financial advisors with a high expertise receive more trust, higher performance expectancy and intention to hire than robo-advisors. There was no significant difference between performance expectancy and intention to hire between a human financial advisor with low expertise and a robo-advisor. The results for trust in low-expertise human advisors versus robo-advisors were inconclusive. Zhang et al. 2021 recommend that robo-advisor providers offer hybrid robo-advice to increase consumers' trust by this human interaction. Thus, a human provider of financial advice is advocated to be supported by AI.

Hodge et al. 2021 (published in *Contemporary Accounting Research*) investigated the effect of providing a name for robo-advisors, one example of humanizing them, and human financial advisors in a study with 108 MBA students from a large public university in an undisclosed location. Participants were randomly assigned to a description of their advisor, i.e., human vs. robot and named vs. unnamed, and were presented with data on three different companies suggesting the same value. The advisor recommends investing in one and avoiding investing in the two others due to an alleged over- or undervaluation. After being presented with the advisor's recommendation, participants should rate how likely they are to follow the financial advisor's recommendation and which company they choose to invest in. Data were analyzed using ANOVA. Hodge et al. 2021 found that participants were more likely to rely on advice from an unnamed robo-advisor than from a named one. This result corresponds to the pilot study of Bengtsson et al. 1999, finding that less anthropomorphic computer partners had a higher influence on their test subjects. Nevertheless, human financial advisors' recommendations were followed more often when their name was provided. In a second study with 125 MBA students from a different large public university in an undisclosed location, Hodge et al. 2021 investigated the importance of task complexity. The experiment contained a manipulation for humanization (based on names) and a description of portfolio rebalancing: once framing it as relatively simple and once describing it as difficult. The respondents were asked whether they would use the financial advisor to rebalance their portfolio. Data were analyzed using ANOVA. Hodge et al. 2021 could demonstrate that participants were more likely to rely on a named robo-advisor when the task of robo-advice was primed as being simple and less likely to rely on a named robo-advisor when the task was primed as being complex.

Lourenço et al. 2020 (published in the *Journal of Interactive Marketing*)[5] sought to analyze the effect that firm characteristics have on the acceptance of advice of an online automated tool providing recommendations on pension investments for the retirement with a sample of 1,649 respondents representative for the Dutch population sourced online through a professional panel data firm. The firm characteristics were profit orientation and sales channel. Notably, these characteristics were not introduced as objective features to the participants, but through a description of the company type: For-profit companies that provided investment products were represented by insurance firms, while pension funds stood for not-for-profit firms that provided investment products. Advisor-only firms were privately owned comparison websites in the for-profit case and government-sponsored comparison websites in the not-for-profit case. Lourenço et al. 2020 confirmed with a sample of 201 participants representing the Dutch population that the firms framed as being for-profit were indeed perceived as higher in profit orientation and companies that were implicitly depicted as providing their own products were perceived to provide more of their own products. The main dependent variable was the self-assessed probability that the participants would follow the online advice. Three constructs were hypothesized to mediate the effect of the firm characteristics on the dependent variable:

- Expertise is measured with items like "A firm of type X is skilled in the pension domain".
- Trust is operationalized with items like "When it comes to providing information about pensions and pension products, a firm of type X is honest".
- Satisfaction with online tool is quantified with the single item "overall satisfaction with the online tool".

[5] This paper has reached the author's attention only after conducting the studies described in Chapter 5, Chapter 6, and Chapter 7. Thus, the features investigated by Lourenço et al. 2020 were not considered in these studies.

Expertise, trust, and satisfaction had a significantly positive impact on advice acceptance. The effects of firm characteristics had an indirect impact on advice acceptance through their mediators: expertise, trust, and satisfaction. While the indirect effect of being a product provider is significantly positive, the indirect effect of being a for-profit firm is significantly negative. Moreover, education has a significantly positive direct impact on advice acceptance. The effect of firm characteristics on perceived trust and expertise were as follows:

- **Insurance companies** (for-profit and product provider): Participants perceived these companies to have a high expertise, but they had low trust in them.
- **Pension funds** (not-for-profit and product provider): These companies were seen as trustworthy and competent.
- **Privately-owned comparison websites** (for-profit and advisor-only): Participants did not only perceive these firms as not trustworthy but also as incompetent.
- **Government-sponsored comparison websites** (not-for-profit and advisor only): Although participants had a high degree of trust in these firms, they perceived them to lack expertise.

5.1.2 Robo-Advisor Characteristics and Customer Acceptance

Ruf et al. 2015 (in the Proceedings of the *48th Hawaii International Conference on System Sciences*) investigated the requirements for a mobile financial advisory service (mFAS) enabling the communication between private banking customers and their advisors with a focus on the high-net-worth (HNW) customer segment defined by an investment sum of more than $1M. The requirement elicitation (RE) process included ten semi-structured expert interviews with industry insiders lasting between 45 and 75 minutes, four focus groups with industry experts (projects members, investment advisors, and relationship managers), and a literature review including 14 papers. Ruf et al. 2015 used the requirements data model (RDMod) including a feature-based evaluation and content analysis consolidated in a workshop by three of the authors. The requirements were clustered into customer, process, environment, and bank requirements. Customer requirements consisted of ease of use, access to experts, proactive information, information quality, customer insights, support from organizational tasks, situational use and platform independence, social presence, traceability of decisions and transparency, and mitigation of privacy concerns. Process requirements consisted of the system to guide the financial advisory process and to have powerful backend systems and bulletproof technology. Environment requirements consisted of an e-learning concept as well as bandwidth and performance of devices. Banking related requirements consisted of compliance and red flags as well as integration of customer relationship management (CRM), communication, and research. Compliance and red flags were the only requirements not supported by at least two of the three sources.

Jung et al. 2018 (published in *Electronic Markets*) investigated the design principles to cater robo-advisory products to risk-averse, low-budget customers. They derived 12 meta-requirements clustered by four design principles from seven research papers on user-centric design of robo-advisor solutions, EN ISO norms describing general design requirements for user interface and expert discussions with an unspecified number of industry and academic experts. The following list of design principles and meta-requirements is rendered in detail because it relates to the design and features of robo-advisors:

1. design principle ease of interaction included:
   - Ease of navigation ("How well control elements of the robo-advisor are integrated and how they are perceived by the user"; Korner and Zimmermann 2000; Nueesch et al. 2014; Ruf et al. 2015; Ruf et al. 2016; ISO 9241 (published by Beuth Verlag 2020))
   - Controllability ("Degree to which users have control over dialogues and behaviour of the robo-advisor"; Korner and Zimmermann 2000; Nueesch et al. 2014; Ruf et al. 2016; Nussbaumer et al. 2012a, b; ISO 9241)
   - Structural consistency ("Consistent formal layout and content structure"; Ruf et al. 2016; ISO 9241)
   - Error tolerance ("How well the robo-advisor deals with user- or system-induced errors"; Ruf et al. 2016; ISO 9241)
2. design principle work efficiency consisted of:
   - Effectiveness ("How well the robo-advisor helps users to achieve their goals with a certain accuracy, completeness or reliability"; Moewes et al. 2011; Ruf et al. 2015; ISO 9241),
   - Efficiency ("Reasonable relationship between required effort to use the robo-advisory solution and the accuracy with which user goals are attained"; Ruf et al. 2015; ISO 9241).
3. design principle comprised:
   - Expectation conformity ("How well the user interface relates to the knowledge and experience of the user"; Ruf et al. 2015; Ruf et al. 2016; Nussbaumer et al. 2012a, b; ISO 9241)

  - Ease of understanding ("How much cognitive load is associated with understanding the retrieved information throughout the robo-advisory process"; Ruf et al. 2015; Ruf et al. 2016; ISO 9241)
  - Social presence ("Degree to which the communicators behind the robo-advisor are perceived as being 'present' or 'real'"; Korner and Zimmermann 2000; Ruf et al. 2015; Ruf et al. 2016)
4. design principle encompassed:
  - Cost ("How easily cost / pricing model are found and understood"; Nussbaumer et al. 2012a, b)
  - Process ("Level of following, comprehension of the possible activities and their succession in advisory"; Ruf et al. 2016; Nussbaumer et al. 2012a, b; Kilic et al. 2015)
  - Information ("Ability of the user to monitor and understand information, transparency why certain data is needed from the user, and what happens to the data"; Alt and Puschmann 2012; Moewes et al. 2011; Nussbaumer et al. 2012a, b; Ruf et al. 2016)

Jung et al. 2018 followed an iterative consumer-centric approach to develop and design a robo-advisor for inexperienced, risk-averse, and non-high net-worth consumers in collaboration with an anonymous partner company. The design process was conducted in three design cycles. The first design cycle consisted of providing a proof-of-concept with the goal of evaluating the artifact prototype including expert interviews and focus groups with employees of the partner company. A pre-final version of the robo-advisor was designed and evaluated (screen recording, the think-aloud method, and questionnaires) in a laboratory setting with 11 participants in the second cycle. The live robo-advisor was evaluated in a mixed method usability study (screen recording, the think-aloud method, questionnaires, scenario technique, click-stream analysis, and a risk test) with 19 participants in the third design cycle incorporating the findings from the previous design cycles. 9 out of 19 participants indicated in the second study that they would be willing to invest money and that the website seems trustworthy, which was a significant improvement over the first study. They conclude that design is used by consumers to infer trustworthiness and quality of service. Jung et al. 2018 consider the evaluation of design decisions in real-life settings, i.e., with investment of consumers' own money, as a promising avenue to assess long-term effects.

Jung et al. 2018 developed 12 design decisions to implement the design principles in their mixed-method studies backed by the description of the positive feedback from participants. The first design principle ease of interaction was implemented by 1. changing the menu button for better navigation and orientation, 2. implementing one long scrollable website for easier navigation, and 3. stricter coupling of elements' functionality and their "look and feel". The second design principle work efficiency is implemented by 1. providing access to explanations throughout the advisory process and 2. assisting users in the comparison of multiple investments. The third design principle information processing and cognitive load is implemented by 1. adding photos of the team members to increase social presence, 2. providing short and easy-to-read explanations, and 3. adding explanatory videos in simple language. The fourth design principle advisory transparency is implemented by 1. providing interactive cost calculator, 2. providing information about the business model of the robo-advisor, 3. providing links to reports on the underlying assets of the portfolios.

Many of the design decisions taken by Jung et al. 2018 to enact their design principles can be seen as objective features. Nevertheless, the decision for these specific features is rather arbitrary and not backed by data. Instead, the authors rely on quotes from their study participants to support their design decisions.

Fisch et al. 2019 (posted initially in the *Wharton Pension Research Council Working Papers* and included in the publication *The Disruptive Impact of FinTech on Retirement Systems*) discuss different features of robo-advisors from a regulatory point of view. The authors examine the following characteristics to describe the services of robo-advisors and compare them to human advisors: AuM, advisory fees, minimum assets, provision of understanding of investments, provision of confidence in investments, provision of risk understanding, simplification of investment process, keeping of investors' best interests, investment returns, available countries, and investment instruments. They expect a further sophistication of robo-advisor services in the future, e.g., in the elicitation of risk preferences, and a movement towards hybrid advisory combining some elements of robo-advice with human financial advice.

Wu and Gao 2021 (published in the *HCI (human-computer interaction) International Conferences Proceedings 2021*) investigated the influence of robo-advisor product features on the intention to use robo-advisors with a hierarchical acceptance model. The first level consisted of the product features (not all of them are features according to the definition used in this paper) influencing the second level, i.e., user perceptions of robo-advisors (perceived usefulness, perceived control, perceived risk, and social influence), in turn having an impact on the third level, i.e., the intention to use robo-advisors. Important influencing factors were derived from financial behavior, recommendation agent acceptance, robot and technology acceptance literatures, as Wu and Gao 2021 deem the literature on the acceptance of robo-advisors as limited. The factors were clustered in individual differences, user perceptions, and product features. Eleven interviews of 30 minutes were conducted with participants having experience with investment, but not with robo-advisory to gather further factors influencing robo-advisor acceptance. In an online survey with 207 valid responses from participants with investment experience, Wu and Gao 2021 tested their model having individual factors as control variables and user perceptions and product features as independent variables. The product features were arranged to seven factors using the principal component factor analysis with varimax rotation.

The factor "customization" consisted of recommendation accuracy, preference set, explanation/justification, and robo-autonomy. "Account management" included personal information and personal assets. "Competence" was composed of past performance, relative advantages, timely reaction, and process transparency, while "authority" included cash withdrawals and disinvestment. The features of firm status in industry, expected earnings, and word of mouth could not be attributed to other factors.

The features that Wu and Gao 2021 gathered from the literature are provided in the following:

- Robot autonomy (Rühr et al. 2019; Rühr 2020; Beer et al. 2011) is defined as "the robot's ability to plan and make decisions autonomously".
- Recommendation accuracy (Hu and Pu 2009) is defined as "the degree to which a recommendation meets users' preferences".
- Explanation/justification (Xiao and Benbasat 2007; Ye and Johnson 1995; Yoo and Gretzel 2011) is defined as "the capacity to provide explanation and justification for how the recommendation was generated".
- Relative advantages (Venkatesh et al. 2003; Lee 2009; Al-Jabri and Sohail 2012) is defined as "the degree to which the system is perceived as being better than its predecessor".
- Past performance (Al-Tamimi 2006) is defined as "how something has performed in the past".
- Process transparency (Rühr 2020; Cramer et al. 2008; Hu and Pu 2009; Yoo and Gretzel 2011) is defined as "the degree to which the user understands how the system operates".
- Firm status in industry (Al-Tamimi 2006) is defined as "the firm's position relative to other companies that produce similar products or services".
- Expected earnings (Al-Tamimi 2006) is defined as "the amount of money that is expected to earn by the user".
- Word of mouth (Al-Tamimi 2006) is defined as "consumer opinions on a firm's product or service reflected in their daily dialogues".

The six product features that Wu and Gao 2021 collected in the interviews are provided with their definitions:

- Personal information represents the management of personal information (e.g., "…whether I can set the visible status of my personal information (e.g., public, visible to my friends, or only visible to myself)").
- Personal assets represent the management of personal assets (e.g., "…whether I can manage my assets at any time").
- Cash withdrawals refer to the authority to withdraw cash from a robo-advisor (e.g., "…whether I can withdraw cash from the robo-advisor when I want" and "how much withdrawal fee I should pay").
- Disinvestment refers to the authority of disinvestment from a robo-advisor ("…whether I can cancel an investment decided by the robo-advisor").
- Timely reaction refers to whether a robo-advisor can react to changes in financial markets timely ("…whether the robo-advisor can monitor my invested products and adjust my investment timely according to changes in financial markets").
- Preference set refers to whether users can set their preferences (e.g., "…whether I can set my investment preference in the robo-advisor – for example, a certain stock I prefer to invest in").

In their empirical approach, firstly, the impact of control variables (attitude towards new technology etc.) on the user perceptions (perceived usefulness etc.) were analyzed using hierarchical regressions. Secondly, the impact of features on user perceptions was examined again using hierarchical regressions. Thirdly, multiple linear regressions were used to determine the impact of the user perceptions on the intention to use robo-advisors. Expected earnings and competence had a positive impact on perceived usefulness, competence and customization on perceived risk, account management and authority on perceived control, and word of mouth on social influence. Only the perceptions of perceived control and perceived risk were found to have a significant impact on use intention, while perceived usefulness and social influence had no significant effect.

The study of Wu and Gao 2021 provides an approach to investigating the consumers' preferences for characteristics of their robo-advisors. Nevertheless, the product features listed in their study, at least those derived from literature, are mostly subjective perceptions of the robo-advisor, as the definition of process transparency "the degree to which the user understands how the system operates" (Rühr 2020; Cramer et al. 2008; Hu and Pu 2009; Yoo and Gretzel 2011) shows. This construct measures perceptions that are not only related to the system in question, but also to the respondent's understanding and competency. Therefore, the subjective traits investigated by Wu and Gao 2021 do not correspond to the definition of the term "feature" as it is used in this dissertation. The usage of subjective constructs is not limited to the robo-advisor acceptance literature, but it can be found throughout the entire technology acceptance literature as this literature examines the impact of beliefs, attitudes, and intentions on behavior (Fishbein and Ajzen 1975; Davis 1985; Ajzen 1991; Venkatesh et al. 2003). It has a lot of merits and allowed models like the technology acceptance model (TAM) (Davis 1985) and the unified theory of acceptance and use of technology (UTAUT) (Venkatesh et al. 2003) to be applied to different technologies (Venkatesh et al. 2012; Zhou et al. 2010; Yu 2012). But I follow the argument of Benbasat and Barki 2007 that this subjectivity is not appropriate to inform developers and suppliers of specific technologies on which specific features provide the most pronounced impact on their customers' intentions to use, as these subjective perceptions can, by their very nature, not be applied directly by developers and product designers.

5.1.3 Overview of Other Relevant Literature

This section covers studies with topics that could not be attributed to the Sections 5.1.1 and 5.1.2, but which relate to robo-advisors and their characteristics.

Faloon and Scherer 2017 (published in *The Journal of Wealth Management*) deem the advice given by the robo-advisor industry in the year 2016 as too generic and its quality difficult to assess for clients. They suggest individualization as a future driver of competition, e.g., in the fields of risk-taking capacity, personal balance sheets, and diversification of risk premiums.

Rühr 2020 (published in the *ECIS 2020 Proceedings*) investigated the performance-control dilemma of robo-advisor investment. While the robo-advisor algorithm optimizes the portfolio decision often outperforming human decision makers (Reher and Sun 2016), different factors contribute to a demand for control endangering the advantage that robo-advisor investment can deliver by suboptimal human decisions. Relying on investment advice from a robo-advisor brings the investor in a principal-agent relationship (Akerlof 1970) with the robo-advisor leading to a demand for transparency from investment advisors (Nussbaumer et al. 2012a). Based on users' elevated risk perceptions in cases of very high (Diab et al. 2011) or low (Rühr et al. 2019) levels of automation, an inverse U-shaped effect on the intention to use a robo-advisor is expected. Rühr 2020 conducted a choice-based conjoint analysis (CBC) with the help of Lighthouse Studio from Sawtooth

Software with 148 participants recruited from German universities. Rühr 2020 found support for an inversely U-shaped effect of automation (level of human intervention) and a positive influence of transparency (explanation of data inputs and processes) and control (risk profile and portfolio allocation) on the intention to use. No clear support was found for a moderating effect of transparency on the relationship between control and intention to use.

Metzler et al. 2022 (published in the proceedings of the *17th International Conference on Wirtschaftsinformatik*) investigated the business models of the 15 largest American robo-advisors measured by AuM based on their publicly available information. Data were analyzed with the qualitative content analysis approach by Mayring 2015 and categorized using the Business Model Canvas (BMC) introduced by Osterwalder and Pigneur 2010. The BMC describes business models using four pillars with nine elements: "(1) value propositions (value propositions of products and/or services), (2) customer interface (customer relationships, customer segments, and channels), (3) infrastructure management (key activities, key resources, and key partners), and (4) financial aspects (cost structure and revenue streams)." (Metzler et al. 2022). They differentiated pure and hybrid robo-advisors. Main differentiators between pure and hybrid robo-advisors were lower expenses for staff (cost structure), lower minimum capital requirements (customer segments), no phone channel (channels), and no highly customized and human portfolio advice (value proposition), and only automated communication for the pure robo-advisors (customer relationships). They point out that current successes of specific robo-advisors might only be temporary. Metzler et al. 2022 ascribe competitive advantage to the fact that some of these robo-advisors are subsidiaries of large banks and assume that the robo-advisors backed by large institutions will dominate the robo-advisor industry in the future.

5.1.4 Davis' Perspective on Objective Features

The contributions discussed above show that the literature on the features of robo-advisors does not focus on their impact on the adoption of robo-advice.[6]

[6] The study of Lourenço et al. 2020 can be seen as an exception to this statement, as they investigated the characteristics of profit orientation and sales channel. Nevertheless, they studied these features only indirectly relying on participants to associate certain firm types with these characteristics. Moreover, they did not examine robo-advisor adoption, but the self-assessed likelihood of following advice given to the participants by an online automated tool providing recommendations on pension investments. Thus, Lourenço et al. 2020 did not refer to the literature of technology acceptance.

This is remarkable as the investigation of the effect of objective features on the independent constructs of the technology acceptance model (TAM) has been a major motive to develop the model. The motive as stated by Davis 1985 in his dissertation was: "Further, the present research aims to develop a model of the motivational variables linking system features with actual use, and to develop measures for these variables." (Davis 1985). This motivation can also be found in the academic paper presenting TAM: "A key purpose of TAM, therefore, is to provide a basis for tracing the impact of external factors on internal beliefs, attitudes, and intentions." (Davis et al. 1989 published in *Management Science*). The cognitive responses perceived usefulness (U or PU) and perceived ease of use (EOU or PEOU) were theorized to be influenced by design features and other external variables. Thus, these constructs fulfill the aim of the TAM according to Davis et al. 1989 to provide a common framework to investigate the effect of characteristics on the use of specific systems by end-users. See *Figure 5.1* for the TAM as presented by Davis 1985 illustrating the important role of design features[7].

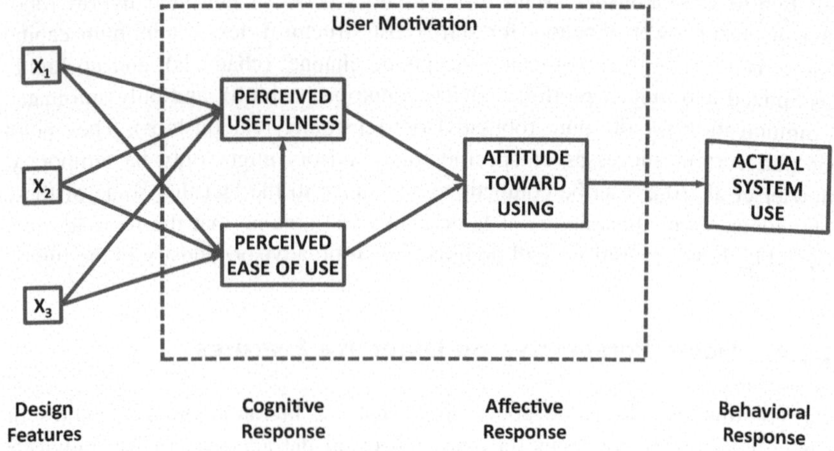

Figure 5.1 The technology acceptance model (TAM), as sketched by Davis 1985 in Figure 1 on page 24

[7] I refer to Chapter 2 for an introduction to the most common technology acceptance models: the unified theory of acceptance and use of technology (UTAUT) and the technology acceptance model (TAM).

The lack of focus of the IS literature after Davis 1985 on the relationship between beliefs and their antecedents does not seem to be limited to the study of robo-advisor acceptance. It has already been voiced by Benbasat and Barki 2007 (published in the *Journal of the Association for Information Systems*) about the technology acceptance literature in general stating that "it would be fruitful to investigate the antecedents of usefulness in order to provide design-oriented advice". Some researchers completely deny a relationship between objective attributes and the independent constructs of the technology acceptance models. For example, Lilienthal et al. 2010 (published in the proceedings of the *21st Australasian Conference for Information Systems*) posit: "The TAM constructs PU [perceived usefulness] and PEOU [perceived ease of use] and their items refer to the technology in general, not to specific products. Therefore there is no reason why the constructs should have any effect on selective stimuli [...]."

Lilienthal et al. 2010 investigated the adoption intention of a web operating system (WebOS) of 412 German consumers. This investigation combined both TAM and choice-based conjoint (CBC) methodologies in one study. As the authors considered it as given that the TAM constructs perceived usefulness (PU) and perceived ease of use (PEOU) correspond to perceptions about the whole technology and not about one product specifically, they did not test the interaction of TAM constructs and the attributes included in the CBC study. Nevertheless, they found a significant negative effect of perceived usefulness (PU) on the utility of the no-choice-option, i.e., the more useful participants assessed WebOS technology, the less they value the option to decide against the WebOS offered hypothetically during the survey. They conclude that a refusal of a technology in general would manifest in TAM constructs, while a refusal of a specific construct would be elicited in the CBC attributes.

The assumption of the independence between TAM constructs and attributes that Lilienthal et al. 2010 establish is not generally accepted in the information systems literature. Benbasat and Barki 2007 encourage researchers to investigate the antecedents of the beliefs in the technology adoption models with a specific focus on IT design. Although Lilienthal et al. 2010 combine a CBC with a TAM study, they avoid a direct test of the interaction between attributes and the constructs of the TAM model by positing that the constructs of the TAM model only relate to the overall technology and not to one specific offer. Thus, I fill this research gap by including attributes and constructs of the UTAUT model, which is closely related to the TAM model, in one study allowing to test Lilienthal et al.'s claim that features do not have an impact on the TAM constructs for the case of robo-advisors.

A lacking investigation of the relationship between objective attributes and the independent constructs of the technology acceptance models combined with an attempt to provide practical advice to industry practitioners has resulted in a contradictory trend. Although some academic papers do not investigate the relationship between objective product features and the constructs of the technology acceptance models, they draw conclusions on how practitioners can influence the independent constructs of technology acceptance models. I would like to give some examples to clarify my position. Note that I do not maintain that the suggested effects of these attributes do not exist. I merely note that these suggestions might be better placed as a topic for future research than as management implications, as the conclusions are not backed by empirical analysis and, hence, are essentially unwarranted:

- Belanche et al. 2019 (published in *Industrial Management & Data Systems*) recommend in their implications for managers and customers:

  "As the main finding, the study reveals that consumer attitudes toward these systems are the key driver of the intention to use them; therefore, the design of an easy to use and useful platform is fundamental to shape users' favorable predisposition toward the use of robo-advisors. In order to increase the number of robo-advisor users, financial companies must be able to assuage customers' doubts and enhance their perceptions of these systems. For this purpose, informing customers about the benefits and profitability of using robo-advisors, allowing them to interact with the robo-advisor platform (even if they do not invest any money or the investment is very low) or including supporting conversational systems (e.g. chatbots or digital assistants that simplify human–machine interactions and improve the interface's interactivity SAP, 2018) could be of help."

  Thus, Belanche et al. 2019 jump from attitudes towards robo-advisors to concrete advice on design without providing support in their own study or academic research. Again, the recommendations are plausible, but not tested directly. Incidentally, I will investigate one of those recommendations ("informing customers about benefits and profitability") in Chapter 7 by investigating the impact of information on past returns of a robo-advisor on the independent constructs of the UTAUT model.
- In their "Implications for Robo-Advisor Design" Wu and Gao 2021 derive several recommendations for the designers of robo-advisors, which I would like to cite in their entirety, as their high level of specificity provide a salient illustration of my point:

  "The findings from this study can help designers to better understand users' perceptions and acceptance of robo-advisors, thereby improving the design to

foster their acceptance and adoption. The acceptance model shows that robo-advisors' competence is helpful to improve perceived usefulness and reduce perceived risk. Therefore, designers should pay attention to enhancing robo-advisors' competence to increase their acceptability. Below are nine suggestions for promoting the competence of robo-advisors.

- *At the beginning of use, inform the user of all steps of the process.*
- *During the process of use, display the current step.*
- *The interface should be clear and readable enough to show the manipulations and information.*
- *Provide simple but effective help and demonstration.*
- *Allow users to view past performance, preferably in the form of graphs.*
- *Summarize the past performance of the portfolio regularly, such as monthly reports.*
- *Display the status of the monitoring market on the interface.*
- *If the portfolio is adjusted due to market changes, inform users of the reasons and how to respond.*
- *Predict future returns and corresponding probabilities when users decide among candidate portfolios."* (Wu and Gao 2021)

Wu and Gao 2021 provide more similar recommendations on the improvement of customization of robo-advisors and the management of personal information and assets. This level of specificity contrasts with the measurement of the features included in their questionnaire. The two examples that Wu and Gao 2021 provide are: "It is important to me that robo-advisors can provide explanation and justification for how they generate recommendation" and "Understanding how robo-advisors operate is important to me". Thus, these items measure whether participants value understanding and transparency, but they cannot clarify which specific features provide a feeling of understanding or transparency to participants. Hence, there is no direct empirical connection between the findings and the recommendations. Interestingly, like Belanche et al. 2019, Wu and Gao 2021 propose a graphical demonstration of the past returns of the robo-advisor, which will be studied in Chapter 7, along with other features.

Thus, this and the next chapters are dedicated to filling the research gap concerning the influence of attributes and features on the attitudes and beliefs expressed in TAM and UTAUT models as proposed by Benbasat and Barki 2007. Potentially important attributes of robo-advisors are derived in the next section to be compared for major suppliers of robo-advisory services in Germany and the USA. Major attributes featured in the market overview of German and American robo-advisors are selected to compare their importance to customers in Chapter 6 using a choice-based conjoint analysis (CBC). The attributes which show the highest importance to customers are subsequently analyzed for their effect on the constructs of the UTAUT model in Chapter 7.

5.2 Empirical Methodology

In this section, I outline the literature and sources used to derive features of robo-advisors which have a potential impact on the robo-advisor market in Germany and the USA. These features are included in the market overview in Section 5.3.

5.2.1 Robo-Advisor Features in Germany and the USA

As the research on the effect of features on customers' attitudes towards a technology is still at an early stage, the decision which features to include in the analysis should only be partly drawn from existing academic literature. Promising candidates also include features derived from industry practice. Following this logic, the question arises: Which features should be considered to compare the German and American robo-advisor markets?

The potential variables are collected from three different types of sources:

1. The wealth management industry research on human advisors.
2. Rankings informing consumers on robo-advice and other research.
3. The academic research on robo-advisors.

Industry overviews and rankings are considered to cover the information that potential customers will receive when they look for information online. It remains unclear which importance the different variables have. Furthermore, the literature treating objective features consists mostly of industry research. Thus, this and the following chapters can be seen as an exploratory endeavor introducing objective features into the robo-advisor adoption literature to identify significant relationships between features, customer attitudes, and robo-advisor adoption.

5.2.2 Derivation of Product Features

According to the Statista n.d. as well as Dorfleitner and Hornuf in Voß et al. 2021, robo-advisors in both the USA and Germany have achieved enormous inflows of funds in recent years. Nevertheless, the investment volumes in the American robo-advisors are significantly higher than in the German ones with $683B vs. 6.7B € in AuM in 2020. The investment volumes in robo-advisors in the USA are still significantly higher than in Germany when accounting for the higher population size of the USA, which is around 332.6M in the USA in 2020 (US Census Bureau 2017) and 83.2M in Germany (Statistisches Bundesamt n.d.). Although there are various suppliers in the field of robo-advisory in both the USA and Germany, the investment volume is concentrated on only a few providers (Vanguard, Scalable Capital, etc.).

To explain what drives the market penetration of different robo-advisors, it is important to consider all important factors. To include a diverse set of factors, three kinds of sources are considered:

1. Industry research on human advisors is examined to account for the expectations of clients of traditional human advisors, which possibly are also applied to robo-advisors.
2. Publicly available rankings and industry research on robo-advisors are included for factors that are considered important in the industry and by customers.
3. Academic research on robo-advisors is considered to include the academic perspective.

Industry research on success factors for human advisors is ample. Contributions from Vanguard and Spectrem Group 2014, CFA and Scorpio 2017, EY 2019, Reddel et al. 2020 from *Accenture*, and Qualtrics n.d. are considered. Epperson et al. 2015 from *A.T. Kearney* add to the scarce literature on clients' needs from robo-advisors.

Chowney and Fragnière 2014 concluded from their interviews with wealth managers and wealth management clients that service delivery primes over performance for client loyalty. Therefore, many variables related to service are included in the market overview to determine the most important service attributes of robo-advisors. Chan and Chan 2011 found that, apart from service and trust, a "feeling of cultural proximity" was important for Taiwanese nationals in mainland China to decide which wealth management service provider to choose. Thus, a variable accounting for the domestic or foreign origin of the robo-advisor is included in the overview.

According to Jung et al. 2018, some of their participants mentioned the wish to consult external comparison websites. To account for the most important criteria mentioned on these websites for the German and American market, the features mentioned on the ones that are most frequently consulted in terms of usage are included. Results from Google are considered to account for publicly available information because it is by far the most frequented search engine worldwide with a market share of 93.04% of hits in Germany and 88% of hits in the USA on desktop, mobile, tablet and console devices in 2020 according to the web traffic analysis website StatCounter.

The observable variables of the top 3 independent robo-advisor rankings on Google using the search term "robo-advisor ranking" both in English and German are included in the study. Using the website https://startpage.com/ to avoid an influence of my personal search history, I received the search results of a typical Google user in both Germany and the USA on March 23, 2021. The three top ranked American robo-advisor rankings on Google were Nerdwallet (ranking authored by Benson 2021), Investopedia (ranking authored by Silver and Chavarria 2021), and Money under 30 (ranking authored by Weliver 2021). The three top ranked German rankings on Google were Finanztip (ranking authored by Buhrs 2021), Brokervergleich.de and finanzen.net (ranking authored by Mencin 2021). I repeated this approach on January 17, 2022. The three top ranked robo-advisor rankings were Nerdwallet (ranking authored by Benson 2022), Forbes (ranking authored by Tepper 2022), and Investopedia (ranking authored by Sette et al. 2022) in the USA as well as finanzen.net (ranking authored by Mencin 2022), geldanlage-digital.de (ranking authored by Beutel 2022), and biallo.de in Germany. The change of the top ranked websites gives an indication of the high market dynamic in the field of robo-advisor rankings.

The academic literature considered in Section 5.1 provides evidence for the investigation of different product features (see Appendix A5.2.2 in the Electronic Supplementary Material), but also some product features not mentioned so far. The feature of a human name for a robo-advisor was adopted from Hodge et al. 2021. Jung et al. 2018 added the provision of explanatory videos to the list. One variable is collected measuring the length of time that the robo-advisor is on the market. Similar variables from different sources are matched with each other and merged to one. The complete list of variables and their respective sources can be found in the Appendix A5.2.2.

5.3 Results

In this section, I summarize the data collection process of the robo-advisor features derived in Section 5.2 in Germany and the USA. I compare the data from the German and American robo-advisor markets and present a personal take on the differences of these markets.

5.3.1 Data Collection

Data were collected between March 16–30, 2022.[8] The data collection was conducted by analyzing the websites of the robo-advisors. The data of 40 German and 34 American robo-advisors were collected. The 40 German robo-advisors included in the study constituted the whole German robo-advisor supplier market known to the author as of March 2022. The market overview represents the information as understood by Philipp Wierzchowski and the author to the best of our knowledge. The motive behind this process was to collect the data available to investors with a limited time budget. Thus, some fields in the data overview in the appendix remain empty if we were not able to collect all required data after due scrutiny of a robo-advisor's website. See *Table A5.2* in Appendix A5.3.1 in the Electronic Supplementary Material for a full overview of the data. The attribute numbers in *Table A5.2* are explained in the attribute legend (*Table A5.1*) in Appendix A5.2.2.

5.3.2 Findings

The German data summarized in *Table 5.1* encompass all robo-advisors in Germany in March, 2022, constituting a *survey of the entire statistical population.* Thus, all moments of the German data are deterministic and not probabilistic. On the other hand, the American data are a *sample* drawn from the entire American statistical population of robo-advisors. Thus, the share offering a specific feature, i.e., the sum of the robo-advisors in the sample offering a specific feature divided by the number of robo-advisors in the sample, of the American robo-advisor *sample* can be used as an *estimator* of the share of robo-advisors providing

[8] The author thanks Philipp Wierzchowski, doctoral student at the Professorship for Empirical Research in Economics at the University of Bremen, for his diligent support during the collection of the data.

this feature in the *American statistical population.* Therefore, the *estimators of the shares* derived from the American sample can be tested against the *deterministic shares* found in the data from Germany using a one-sample two-tailed t-test. The feature investment strategy is examined employing a chi-squared test where the null hypothesis postulates identical distributions in Germany and in the USA. As the number of data points collected in the American sample equals around 30 for each feature, the shares are assumed to be approximately normally distributed according to the central limit theorem. A t-test was impossible for features which lacked variation in the American sample, i.e., for features with a standard deviation of zero.

Years on the market

Years on the market is calculated as 2022 minus the year of foundation of the robo-advisor. German robo-advisors are significantly younger with an average age of 4.4 years as compared to 7.2 years of their American counterparts.

What is the minimum amount (€/$) that must be invested?

Most robo-advisors set a minimum investment amount. In Germany the average minimum investment amount is 12,494 € (median 750 €). However, the average in the USA is $34,655 (median $1,000). The difference is not statistically significant assuming currency parity. While $1 was equal to 0.903 € on March 31, 2022, $1 was equal to 1.025 € on November 3, 2022.

Robo-advice costs p.a. as % of AuM

For a majority of robo-advisors, fees as a percentage of the assets under management (AuM) are the main source of revenue. Robo-advisors often charge different fees for different offers, e.g., for providing personal advice. To establish comparability, the least expensive offer of each robo-advisor was considered. German robo-advisors have an average fee of 0.767% (median 0.75%). However, American robo-advisors only charge 0.31% (median 0.275%). Thus, American robo-advisors are significantly cheaper.

Third-party costs p.a. as % of AuM

Most robo-advisors use exchange-traded funds (ETFs) to allocate the investor's assets. These funds charge varying fees on the assets invested in them. The product fees of the cheapest configuration available with a robo-advisor were considered, i.e., mostly standard products as opposed to actively managed or ESG funds. As the fees for the products depend on the asset allocation, a standard case of 50% stocks and 50% bonds or the version approximating this allocation the most was

Table 5.1 Summary of the market overview of German and American robo-advisors

Attributes	Mean Germany (N = 40) (SD)	Mean USA (n = 34) (SD)	p-value of two-tailed one-sample (US sample) t-test
Years on the market	4.425 (1.842)	7.194 (3.664)	0.000***
What is the minimum amount (€/$) that must be invested?	12,493.800 *But median: 750.000* (34,911.816)	34,655.355 *But median: 1,000.000* (103,062.801)	0.241
Robo-advice costs p.a. as % of AuM	0.767 (0.364)	0.310 (0.272)	0.000***
Third-party costs p.a. as % of AuM	0.283 (0.259)	0.146 (0.159)	0.005**
	% of robo-advisors with feature Germany (SD)	**% of robo-advisors with feature USA (SD)**	**p-value of two-tailed one-sample (US sample) t-test**
Is the robo-advisor offered by an established institute?	 60.0 (0.490)	 55.9 (0.504)	0.637
Is this the robo-advisor's domestic market?	 85.0 (0.357)	 100.0 (0.000)	N/A

(continued)

Table 5.1 (continued)

Attributes	Mean Germany (N = 40) (SD)	Mean USA (n = 34) (SD)	p-value of two-tailed one-sample (US sample) t-test
Are the investment horizon and wealth objectives included in the investment recommendation?	 89.5 (0.307)	 100.0 (0.000)	N/A
Are risk attitudes factored into investment decisions?	 89.5 (0.307)	 100.0 (0.000)	N/A
Are the client's total assets included in the advice?	 78.4 (0.412)	 76.9 (0.430)	0.864
Is tax optimization offered?	 7.9 (0.270)	 46.9 (0.507)	0.000***
Is personal advice offered?	 62.5 (0.484)	 60.6 (0.496)	0.828

(continued)

Table 5.1 (continued)

Attributes	Mean Germany (N = 40) (SD)	Mean USA (n = 34) (SD)	p-value of two-tailed one-sample (US sample) t-test
Can the advice of the robo-advisor be used without opening an account?	 71.8 (0.450)	 47.1 (0.507)	0.008**
Is it possible to use a hotline?	 95.0 (0.218)	 79.4 (0.410)	0.034*
Does the robo-advisor have a mobile app?	 70.0 (0.458)	 79.4 (0.410)	0.190
Are investments made in other asset classes than stocks and bonds?	 63.2 (0.482)	 48.3 (0.509)	0.126
Does the robo-advisor also invest in individual stocks?	 23.7 (0.425)	 26.7 (0.450)	0.719

(continued)

Table 5.1 (continued)

Attributes	Mean Germany (N = 40) (SD)	Mean USA (n = 34) (SD)	p-value of two-tailed one-sample (US sample) t-test
Are ESG products offered?	 66.7 (0.471)	 43.3 (0.504)	0.017*
Are child deposit accounts offered?	 45.0 (0.497)	 50.0 (0.508)	0.582
Are donation projects advertised?	 15.0 (0.357)	 12.9 (0.341)	0.734
Does the robo-advisor provide information on its returns achieved in previous years?	 74.4 (0.437)	 33.3 (0.479)	0.000***

(continued)

Table 5.1 (continued)

Attributes	Mean Germany (N = 40) (SD)			Mean USA (n = 34) (SD)			p-value of two-tailed one-sample (US sample) t-test
Are explanatory videos offered?	85.0 (0.357)			79.4 (0.410)			0.433
Does the robo-advisor have a human name?	7.5 (0.263)			0.0 (0.000)			N/A
Which investment strategy is used?	**% of RA using strategy 1**		**% of RA using strategy 2**		**% of RA using strategy 3**		**p-value of chi-squared test**
1 = Passive **2 = Active timing** **3 = Active selection of investments**	**Germany**	**USA**	**Germany**	**USA**	**Germany**	**USA**	
	26.3	64.7	34.2	2.9	39.5	32.4	0.001**

Note: * $p < 0.05$. ** $p < 0.01$. *** $p < 0.001$.

included, e.g., 60% stocks and 40% bonds. Whereas the German robo-advisors employ products charging on average 0.283% of AuM (median 0.21%), American robo-advisors on average used products charging 0.146% (median 0.12%), which is significantly less.

Is the robo-advisor offered by an established institute?

It was investigated whether the institution offering the robo-advisor was an established institute or a start-up. Institutions are defined as start-ups if they were founded since 2008 and crucially rely on technology for their services. With 60% of robo-advisors being offered by established institutes in Germany and 56% in the USA, there was no significant difference between the German and the American sample.

Is this the robo-advisor's domestic market?

Robo-advisors were counted as being domestic if the institute which offers the robo-advisors has its main presence in this market. 85% of robo-advisors in Germany were domestic, compared to all investigated institutes in the USA.

Are the investment horizon and wealth objectives included in the investment recommendation?

This condition was fulfilled if the investment horizon was discussed in the robo-advisor's questionnaire. Whereas all American robo-advisors incorporated this question, 90% of the German advisors did.

Are risk attitudes factored into investment decisions?

Risk attitudes were considered as factored into the investment decisions by the robo-advisor if a question relating to the investor's risk attitudes was featured in the questionnaire. While all American robo-advisors incorporated this question, 90% of the German advisors did.

Are the client's total assets included in the advice?

The total amount of assets of an investor was considered by the robo-advisor if a question relating to total assets, i.e., also those that are not to be invested with the robo-advisor, was featured in the questionnaire. 78% of the German and 77% of the American robo-advisors included such a question. Thus, there was no significant difference.

Is tax optimization offered?

Tax optimization is defined as any strategy executed by a robo-advisor in order to lower the investor's tax burden. While only 8% of German robo-advisors offered such a service, 47% of American robo-advisors did (constituting a significant difference). This result can be seen in the light of differences between the American and German legislation as most of the tax optimization strategies were not possible in Germany such, e.g., tax loss harvesting. According to this strategy, assets that show a net loss are sold and substituted with a very similar asset to use the incurred loss to lower the taxes on the profits on other assets.

Is personal advice offered?
This question was answered with yes if it was possible to avail the advice of a human being. This does not mean that this service is offered in the standard package or without further fees, i.e., often personal assistance results in additional costs. The percentages of robo-advisors offering personal advice is similar with 63% in Germany and 61% in the USA.

Can the advice of the robo-advisor be used without opening an account?
This question was answered positively when it was possible to fill in a questionnaire and receive investment advice from the robo-advisors without providing more personal information than an e-mail address. 72% of German robo-advisors provided information without opening an account. However, this was only true for 47% of their American counterparts. This difference is statistically significant.

Is it possible to use a hotline?
A hotline was defined as a phone number which could be reached to discuss topics relating to the robo-advisor service. Whereas 95% of German robo-advisors offered this service, only 79% of the American ones did, which is a significant difference.

Does the robo-advisor have a mobile app?
This attribute was considered as offered by the robo-advisor if a mobile application could be found on the robo-advisors website or in the major app stores. While 70% of German robo-advisors offer a mobile application, 79% of American robo-advisors do so. This difference is not significant.

Are investments made in other asset classes other than stocks and bonds?
This question relates to the availability of portfolios which contain other assets than stocks and bonds, although in most cases stocks and bonds are the foundation of the portfolios offered. The options with other assets than stocks and bonds are not necessarily the standard portfolios with the lowest prices. Whereas 63% of German robo-advisors offer portfolios that contain other assets than stocks and bonds,

only 48% of their American counterparts do so. This difference is not statistically significant.

Does the robo-advisor also invest in individual stocks?
Investments in individual assets refer to investments apart from exchange-traded funds (ETFs) or mutual funds, i.e., individual stocks and bonds. With 24% of Germany and 27% of American robo-advisors investing in individual stocks, there is no significant difference.

Are ESG products offered?
This attribute was considered as provided by the robo-advisor when it was possible to include ESG products in the portfolio. Often these ESG portfolios had a higher price than the standard portfolio, while some robo-advisors focus exclusively on ESG portfolios. 67% of German robo-advisors provide that option, but only 43% of the American ones do so. This difference meets a significant level.

Are child deposit accounts offered?
This question was marked positively if investors can open accounts for their children. This option was offered by 45% of the German and 50% of the American robo-advisors. This does not constitute a significant difference.

Are donation projects advertised?
This question was answered positively if the robo-advisor mentioned charitable causes to which the robo-advisor contributes. 15% of the German and 13% of the American robo-advisors mentioned charitable contributions, which does not constitute a significant difference.

Does the robo-advisor provide information on its returns achieved in previous years?
This question was noted as positive if it was possible to derive exact information on past returns. Charts providing rough estimations or requiring intense calculation by the investor to infer the exact returns were considered as not providing information on past returns. While 74% of German robo-advisors reported their past returns, only 33% of their American counterparts did so. Thus, the provision of information on past returns was handled in a significantly different manner.

Are explanatory videos offered?
Explanatory videos are videos on the website of the robo-advisor or links to social media platforms (e.g., YouTube) that explain the function and usage of robo-advisors in a simple manner. While 85% of German robo-advisors offer explanatory videos, 79% of American robo-advisors provide this offer. This does not constitute a significant difference.

Does the robo-advisor have a human name?
This question was answered positively if the robo-advisor itself has a human name. None of the American robo-advisors have a human name, whereas 8% of German robo-advisors have one[9].

Which investment strategy is used?
I have assigned the differentiated investment strategies to three basic ones: strategy 1 in which the robo-advisor invests passively in order to match the markets, strategy 2 in which the robo-advisor conducts active market timing, and strategy 3 in which the robo-advisor actively chooses investment assets, e.g., individual stocks. In Germany, strategy 1 was adopted by 26%, strategy 2 by 34%, and strategy 3 by 39% of the robo-advisors. In the USA, strategy 1 was pursued by 65%, strategy 2 by 3%, and strategy 3 by 32% of the robo-advisors. Statistically, this constitutes a significant difference.

5.3.3 Personal Take

When considering the impressions made during the collection of the data two points seem worth mentioning that are not evident from the data alone:

1. The share of American robo-advisors that offer ESG products is significantly lower than in Germany. Moreover, the importance that the various providers put on them were quite distinct from each other. While the ESG products were often presented as an optional add-on by the American robo-advisors, they were an essential part of the product story for some German robo-advisors, sometimes being the only investment option.

[9] The robo-advisors are named OSKAR (offered by the fintech OSKAR), CARL (offered by Bankhaus Spängler), and ROBIN (offered by Deutsche Bank).

2. The American robo-advisors seemed on average less transparent than their German counterparts, as can be seen from the data on information on past returns, which is more readily available for German robo-advisors. This lesser degree of transparency can also be illustrated in a quantitative manner: Whereas precise product costs were not available for 18% of German robo-advisors, this applied to 56% of American robo-advisors. I do not conclude though, that American firms try to hide the costs from the investors to make a profit. The recommendation of the American robo-advisors often consisted of 20 to 30 ETFs without providing a single number for product costs. Thus, in these cases precise costs were available for each ETF (with very reasonable costs), but not in an aggregated form. This is astonishing as both transparency and costs seem to be lower in the USA. One possible explanation might be a lower focus on low product costs by American customers. This interpretation will be supported in Chapter 6.

5.4 Discussion

Section 5.4 summarizes the theoretical contributions of Chapter 5 including limitations and opportunities for future research. Managerial implications of the results of this chapter are deducted from a comparison with the customer preferences elicited in the next chapter, thus, they are discussed in Chapter 6.

5.4.1 Theoretical Contributions

The literature review provides an overview of past research on features and robo-advisors. Thereby, it summarizes topics that have received attention from the research community, such as human versus robot financial advisory, humanization, and the impact of trust. Furthermore, it allows to identify topics that are not yet treated in detail by the relevant literature. Importantly, a research gap was identified concerning the impact of objective features on the acceptance of robo-advice, although such a connection is at the heart of technology acceptance models such as TAM. Chapter 7 will contribute to closing this gap. Lastly, the literature review has provided a list of features relevant for a market overview accounting for sources from research, the wealth management industry, and rankings informing consumers.

The theoretical contribution of investigating the objective attributes of robo-advisors consists in comparing the robo-advisor industry in Germany and the

USA by attributes deemed important by the academic, financial advisory literature as well as major websites giving advice on the selection of robo advisors. Although there are some academic comparisons between robo-advisors (Jung et al. 2018; Fisch et al. 2019; Metzler et al. 2022), to my knowledge this is the most extensive one so far considering both the number of objective attributes and robo-advisors included. The high number of robo-advisors allows to compare the offers of robo-advisors quantitatively for the first time. I could show that German and American robo-advisors are characterized by significant differences in their average years on the market, robo-advice as well as third party costs, the offer of tax optimization, the accessibility of the advice of the robo-advisor without opening an account, information on past returns, and investment strategies used. This finding directly contrasts with the claim made in the literature that prices and minimum investments of robo-advisors only exhibit a "limited variation" (Rühr 2020).

5.4.2 Management Implications

The market comparison between German and American robo-advisors presented in this chapter offers by its very nature descriptive rather than normative insights. For normative insights, the descriptive evidence of the market overview has to be contrasted with some measure of desirability. As the importance that potential customers put on certain features provides such a measure, I refer to Section 6.4.2 for detailed management implications.

Nevertheless, this market overview offers industry practitioners an overview of the product features of the most important robo-advisors in major markets.

5.4.3 Limitations

Data for the comparison between German and American robo-advisor suppliers were collected to the best of knowledge and belief with the perspective of a common consumer, i.e., data were not checked individually with the suppliers of robo-advisory services. Therefore, human errors cannot be ruled out completely.

5.4.4 Future Research

As the competitive comparison was conducted with sources of information accessible to consumers, attributes were omitted that can only be collected within the organization of the robo-advisor supplier, e.g., the specifics of the robo-advisors' algorithm. Nevertheless, features hidden from customers might have a rather long-term and indirect effect on demand, e.g., through information on past returns evident to consumers. Thus, the effects of features hidden from customers are a potential field for future research.

Another potentially fruitful area for future research would be longitudinal studies on the effects of attributes on robo-advisor success, e.g., the impact of attributes on the assets under management (AuM) of robo-advisors over time.

Germany and especially the USA are major markets for robo-advisory services. Nevertheless, market overviews of other markets would be helpful to compare the different markets. This could even be extended to the attributes that were collected. As the attributes compared in this chapter are mostly derived from sources published in or for the American and German market, attributes that are deemed important in other markets might have been overlooked.

Analyzing Preferences of German and American Consumers using Choice-Based Conjoint Analysis (CBC)

6

Chapter 6 introduces conjoint analyses (CA) with a focus on choice-based conjoint analyses (CBC) to measure customer preferences regarding the features of robo-advisors in Germany and the USA empirically. The details of the data collection process are provided, while analysis techniques applicable to data derived from conjoint analyses are explained and executed yielding insights on customer preferences. The theoretical and practical implications of the empirical findings are discussed with a focus on the comparison between the market overview conducted in Chapter 5 and the customer preferences derived in this chapter.

6.1 Introduction to Conjoint Analyses (CA)

Chapter 5 has provided insights into the current state of the robo-advisor market in Germany and the USA as well as an overview of the current literature on the attributes of robo-advisors. But the market overview in Chapter 5 could not assess the relationship between the current state of the robo-advisor industry and the demand of (potential) customers. Investigating the match between demand for robo-advisor features and their supply may explain why the USA has higher robo-advisor adoption rates than Germany.

Conjoint analyses (CA) are an established method to elicit the preferences of consumers regarding different attributes (Green and Rao 1971). The market overview in Chapter 5 has shown that the pricing of robo-advisory services in

Supplementary Information The online version contains supplementary material available at https://doi.org/10.1007/978-3-658-44679-6_6.

M. Horn, *Technology Acceptance, Path Dependence, and the Demand for Robo-Advisory Services*, Forschung zur Digitalisierung der Wirtschaft | Advanced Studies in Business Digitization, https://doi.org/10.1007/978-3-658-44679-6_6

Germany and the USA is significantly different. Thus, the inclusion of price attributes is required. Hence, a choice-based conjoint analysis (CBC) is chosen for this study as it is the most established and recommended conjoint method to analyze pricing (Orme 2013). Choice-based conjoint analyses (CBC) require the estimation of part-worth utilities. In this section, CA, CBC, and part-worth utility estimation are introduced briefly. The study investigating robo-advisors' attributes using CBC is rolled out in the remainder of this chapter.

6.1.1 The Development of Conjoint Analyses

Conjoint analyses have been studied since the 1970 s (Green and Rao 1971; Srinivasan and Shocker 1973; Johnson 1974) to quantify the trade-off between attributes that buyers of multi-attributed products and services face. Using CA, preferences regarding the levels of the attributes of a product can be transferred to utility values, or part-worth utilities. Summing up the part-worth utilities equates to the utility of a product attribute to a consumer or how much it influences a customer's decision to choose a specific product. Thus, more or less preferred levels of attributes compensate each other and, therefore, constitute a trade-off.

I follow Naous and Legner 2021 providing an overview of CA from the perspective of information systems (IS). Conjoint analysis has been established by Green and Rao 1971 for marketing research based on the conjoint measurement proposed by Luce and Tukey 1964. According to Green and Rao 1971, conjoint analysis measures "the joint effects of a set of independent variables on the ordering of a dependent variable". In conjoint analysis consumer preferences are investigated by estimating how respondents *con*sider *joint*ly (conjoint) different product attributes with specific attributes levels. As utility measures a person's preferences regarding a set of alternatives, conjoint analyses derive a utility function from consumer assessments of product attributes and levels (Green and Srinivasan 1978). The preference structure influencing the person's product choice can be derived from this utility function. Hence, the preference structure incorporates information on the importance of attributes and their levels for a person's overall preference (Hair et al. 2010).

Common conjoint analyses comprise three phases (Naous and Legner 2021):

1. Product profiles are built with different attributes and attribute levels.
2. Consumers evaluate the profiles in a survey.
3. Different analysis techniques are used on the data that can be structured by the insights that they add. The first three clusters of analysis techniques can

be traced back to Green and Rao 1971, while the fourth one was proposed by Johnson 1974:

- **Relative importance:** The relative importance of product attributes and levels is derived from participants' choices in the survey, which allows a ranking of the attributes included in the study. It should be noted that the relative importance is always dependent on the attributes and attribute levels included in the study.
- **Cost-benefit analyses:** The willingness to pay (WTP) of consumers for specific attributes and attribute levels is quantified.
- **Clustering of customers:** The estimated utility functions of customers are used to cluster them into groups sharing similar preferences.
- **Market simulation:** Market shares of current or new products are derived on the basis of consumer preferences.

According to Green and Srinivasan 1978, six steps are necessary to plan a conjoint analysis (CA). Each step offers alternative approaches to choose from:

1. **Selection of the preference model:** The preference model forms the basis of the estimation of the preference function from respondents' utilities regarding attributes. Hence, the partial benefit values of the attributes are determined based on the selection of the preference model. Major models include the vector, the ideal-point, and the port-worth models:
   - **The vector model:** The set of t attributes that have been selected for the study are designated with p = 1, 2, …, t. Furthermore, y_{jp} describes the level of the pth attribute for stimulus j (i.e., product profiles), while w_p denotes the weight that an individual puts on an attribute. Note that the preference w_p will differ among individuals. The vector model has also been referred to as Composite Criterion Model (Srinivasan and Shocker 1973; Parker and Srinivasan 1976). According to the vector model, the preference s_j towards the stimulus j is given by:

$$s_j = \sum_{p=1}^{t} w_p y_{jp} \tag{6.1}$$

   - **The ideal-point model:** The ideal-point model is based on the idea that there is an ideal point x_p for every individual. The model measures the squared and weighted (w_p) distance of the stimulus y_{jp} from this ideal point. Thus, smaller distances indicate more preferred stimuli, i.e., higher s_j. This squared distance of the stimulus j from the ideal point is denoted as d_j^2 and defined as:

$$d_j^2 = \sum_{p=1}^{t} w_p \left(y_{jp} - x_p\right)^2 \tag{6.2}$$

- **The part-worth function:** The part-worth function assumes that there is a function f_p that denotes the part-worth of various levels of y_{jp} for the pth attribute. As the measurement can only be conducted for the levels included in the study, the part-worths of intermediate levels are measured using linear interpolation. Thus, to avoid extrapolation, it is recommendable to include the full range of possible levels for each attribute. According to the part-worth model, the preference s_j regarding the stimulus j is denoted as:

$$s_j = \sum_{p=1}^{t} f_p\left(y_{jp}\right) \tag{6.3}$$

The part-worth function was widely accepted as early as 1978 (Green and Srinivasan 1978) due to its interpretability and flexibility. It can be shown that the vector model is a special case of the ideal-point model (Carroll 1972 in Shepard et al. 1972). Similarly, both the vector and the ideal-point model can be demonstrated to be special cases of the part-worth model (Green and Srinivasan 1978) giving the part-worth model the highest degree of flexibility.

2. **Data collection method:** Traditional approaches include the full-profile and pairwise evaluation. In the traditional full-profile evaluation, consumers rank different product profiles (called stimuli) having a specific set of attributes and attribute levels. Thus, complete products were ranked. In the pairwise approach proposed by Johnson 1974, respondents provide evaluations of pairs of attributes allowing to determine trade-offs among product features. Although a higher number of attributes can be investigated using the pair-wise approach, the full-profile method is the most frequently used among the traditional CA approaches.
3. **Stimulus set construction:** Different methods can be used to reduce the number of stimuli and facilitate evaluation. One main method is the fractional factorial orthogonal design, which assumes no interaction effects of the selected attributes. Another frequently used method is balanced overlap, which allows co-occurrences of the same attribute levels but forbids an inclusion of the same concepts within one choice task. The balanced overlap design permits a more precise estimation of interaction effects.

4. **Stimulus presentation:** Stimuli can be presented with a variety of forms depending on the subject of the study: verbal description, graphical representation, prototypes, or even actual products.
5. **Measurement scale:** In the traditional approaches, rankings can be used for full-profile and pairwise data collection. Furthermore, ratings on a numbered scale can be used on full-profile studies to rate stimuli by their perceived benefit. Furthermore, choice-based methods, as described below, use a choice of one stimulus among several stimuli as a measurement.
6. **Estimation method:** The estimation model is based on the dependent variable type determined by the measurement scale. Methods include ordinary least squares (OLS) for interval-scaled variables, MONANOVA for ordinal-scaled variables, and LOGIT or PROBIT for choice-based data. The particular estimation methods used in this study will be explained below in more detail.

Adaptive conjoint analysis (ACA) uses self-explicated tasks combined with an evaluation of partial profile stimuli (Green 1984; Johnson 1987). ACA allows researchers to deal with a higher number of attributes, as respondents exclude unacceptable attribute levels already in the self-explicated task reducing the necessary evaluations of the partial profile stimuli (Johnson 1987). While the computer-based ACA was developed by the software vendor Sawtooth Software (Johnson 1987), it was validated by research (Huber and Hansen 1987; Green et al. 1991).

Choice-based conjoint analysis replaces measurements using rankings and ratings with direct decisions. This method tries to simulate a competitive marketplace (Johnson et al. 2003; Naous and Legner 2021) by providing hypothetical product choices. While participants have to evaluate a large number of scenarios, it successfully incorporates the complexity of competitive scenarios (Green et al. 2001).

An adaptive choice-based conjoint analysis (ACBC) contains self-explicated tasks, which are included to short-list the most relevant levels and attributes. The relevant levels and attributes are then studied using a CBC. This combination of approaches allows to estimate part-worth utilities from studies with fewer than 100 participants (Johnson et al. 2003; Naous and Legner 2021).

Conjoint methods have seen further developments over time to tackle existing application issues (Green and Srinivasan 1978; Green and Srinivasan 1990; Rao 2008; Netzer et al. 2008). Orme 2013 discusses the advantages and disadvantages of the different methods based on the criteria: number of attributes, interview method and time, sample size, and inclusion of pricing. Adaptive methods are recommended for a large number of attributes or for a small sample size, while choice-based methods are favored for studies that involve pricing.

6.1.2 A primer on Choice-based Conjoint Analyses

Choice-based conjoint analyses (CBC) have been introduced for the estimation of consumer preferences and the utility of the entire product (Louviere and Woodworth 1983; Louviere 1988) and developed into the most frequently applied conjoint method. CBC constitutes a repeated-design choice experiment using a decompositional analysis method in which potential consumers hypothetically choose their preferred product out of different alternatives. This reduces mental effort increasing accuracy of preference estimation compared to the ranking or rating systems of traditional conjoint analyses methods (Green and Srinivasan 1990). The product alternatives, or stimuli, are characterized by different attributes with predefined attribute levels. During a CBC, several choice sets, i.e., a collection of differing product alternatives presented to the participants at the same time, are used to derive data for coefficient estimation relying on the decisions of the participants. In many CBC studies, potential consumers are not forced to decide for one offer, but also have an option to vote against all offers with a none-option (Brazell et al. 2006). Thus, participants in CBC studies do not evaluate each attribute separately, but they choose their preferred alternative as in real-life situations (Cohen 1997). As pointed out by Naous and Legner 2021 conjoint analyses have been used in the information systems domain in one-time applications rather than providing a cumulative research pattern. Nevertheless, conjoint analyses have been applied to different technologies in the realm of IS: VoIP technology (Zubey et al. 2002), mobile couponing (Mueller-Lankenau and Wehmeyer 2005), mobile service bundles (Haaker et al. 2006), wireless grid applications (Van de Wijngaert and Bouwman 2009), WebOS (Lilienthal et al. 2010), transactional e-government services (Venkatesh et. al 2012), e-payment service (See-To and Ho 2016), personal cloud storage (Naous and Legner 2019), and data sharing (Schomakers et al. 2020). Thus, attributes' importance to consumers is investigated by a CBC to compare and rank their influence on consumer preferences.

6.1.3 Introduction to Part-worth Utility Estimation

Many analysis methods of conjoint data involve the estimation of part-worth utilities. Therefore, I will describe the general principle in more detail in this section and will discuss specifics of the analysis methods in the next sections. I follow Orme and Chrzan 2021 in their depiction of the random utility model (RUM) and the multinomial logistic regression (MNL), also referred to as multinomial logit, which provide a basis for estimating part-worth utilities.

The RUM treats every of J respondents as a rational decision-maker choosing the option providing the highest utility in a choice set with M alternatives, e.g., a choice-based conjoint study. In the model, the total utility of each alternative is given by the following formula:

$$U_{jm} = V_{jm} + \varepsilon_{jm} = \sum_{k=1}^{n} b_j^k x_m^k + \varepsilon_{jm} \tag{6.4}$$

- U_{jm} is respondent j's true utility from the mth alternative.
- V_{jm} corresponds to respondent j's representative utility from the mth alternative that can be estimated statistically.
- ε_{jm} represents a right-skewed Gumbel distributed random variable which is independent and identically distributed.
- b_j^k designates respondent j's $1 \times L^k-1$ (when using effects-coding) vector of part-worth utilities towards attribute k, where L^k is the number of levels of attribute k.
- x_m^k denotes the L^k-1 (when using effects-coding) $\times$ 1 design vector of independent variables describing attribute k in alternative m, where L^k is the number of levels of attribute k.

In the RUM, choices of people can be conceptualized as being influenced by unobservable utility vectors. These part-worth utility vectors cannot be measured directly, but they can be estimated by analyzing the choice behavior of respondents.

The multinomial logit (MNL) was developed by McFadden 1974 allowing to compute part-worth utilities. The goal of MNL is to find a set of part-worth utility vectors that maximizes the fit to the respondents' choices in the questionnaire. The computation of the logit model is based on an estimation of the choice of a specific alternative from a choice set under the assumption that RUM holds:

$$P_i = \frac{e^{U_i}}{\sum_1^k e^{U_i} + \ldots + e^{U_k}} \quad (6.5)$$

- P_i is defined as the probability for the choice of alternative i
- U_i is defined as the utility of alternative i

This closed-form expression allows an estimation of choice probabilities while avoiding an integration across the RUM equation over an infinite number of choices and drawings of ε. The MNL algorithm is repeated until it fails to improve the quality criterion, which is the log-likelihood by less than a cut-off value, typically 0.00001. The log-likelihood measures the predictive accuracy of the model. This measure relies on the likelihood that a respondent would choose the concept that he/she actually did in the questionnaire given the estimated parameters of the model. The likelihood of each choice task would have to be multiplied to derive the probability of a perfect prediction of all choice tasks using the estimates of the model. An addition instead of a multiplication of the terms can be applied when the natural logarithms of the likelihoods are used. The usage of natural logarithms reduces data volume, which was scarce when the method was developed in the 1970 s, because this method decreases the number of decimals that a computer retains while performing this task.

6.2 Empirical Methodology

Chapter 5 provides evidence on the robo-advisor features of the German and American markets. As only a limited number of these features can be included in a choice-based conjoint analysis (CBC), Section 6.2 explains which criteria are used to determine the attributes of the study and how the questionnaire employed to collect survey data is designed.

6.2.1 Decision on Attributes Included in the Study

The number of attributes that can be studied using a choice-based conjoint analysis is limited. While Green and Srinivasan 1978 suggested a maximum of six attributes, a recent study by Peitz et al. 2020 suggests that full-profile CBC is a viable option for up to 10 attributes, while partial-profile adaptive CBC (ACBC) is recommendable for studies involving more than 15 attributes. In order to choose as many attributes as possible without risking the loss of attention of participants, I included eight attributes with up to four attribute levels. Therefore, not all attributes of robo-advisors gathered in Germany and the USA in the market overview in Chapter 5 could be included in the study. Although objective criteria can serve as a decision aid, it is important to stress that the selection of attributes of a CBC always contains an arbitrary element. I chose the attributes to be included in the CBC analysis from the attributes examined in the market overview in Chapter 5 based on the following criteria:

1. Data from the market overview in Chapter 5 suggests a notable difference between robo-advisors in Germany and the USA regarding this attribute:
   - Decision for: Robo-advice costs, third-party costs, tax optimization, investment strategy, ESG products, and information on past returns.
2. It relates to the findings of Chapter 4:
   - Decision for: The minimum investment amount can be seen as the counterpart to household wealth, which was included as a facilitating condition in the PDA-UTAUT model applied to robo-advisors. It is important to investigate the impact of affordability on customer preferences as a lower minimum amount enables more people to invest.
3. This attribute does **not** constitute a "hygiene" factor which is easy to implement by robo-advisor suppliers and offered by a vast majority of robo-advisors:
   - Decision against: Inclusion of horizon and wealth objectives in the investment recommendation, factoring in of risk attitudes, and possible usage of the advice of the robo-advisor before opening an account.
4. To restrict the number of attributes to the target level of eight, I decided against an attribute that cannot be influenced by robo-advisors after their foundation and, thus, might have a minor practical importance for their management:
   - Decision against: Years on the market.

6.2.2 Questionnaire Design

This study uses choice-based conjoint analysis (CBC) to understand potential customers' preferences and the value they place on key attributes, focusing on robo-advisory service pricing in Germany and the USA. CBC is a recommended method to conduct pricing research (Orme 2013; Orme and Chrzan 2021). The influence of the attributes with the highest importance to customers in the CBC are studied for their effects on customers' attitudes and adoption intention.

The questionnaire was developed and conducted with the software Lighthouse Studio 9 from Sawtooth Software. This design was pretested with selective students from the University of Bremen, who were requested to note down feedback and understanding issues. The original English questionnaire for the American sample was designed based on the students' feedback. The questionnaire consisted of three sections. In the first section the participants were introduced to the concept of robo-advice, the attributes to be investigated and their definitions. The robo-advisor and attribute descriptions can be found in the Appendix A6.2.2 in the Electronic Supplementary Material. In the second section, participants were presented with 12 random choice tasks containing four concepts, i.e., stimuli, with all eight attributes (full-profile CBC). Each concept described one robo-advisor model with a specific selection of attribute levels. After making their choice, participants were asked whether they would pay for this service in their current life situation, thus, providing the none-option. See *Figure 6.1* for an example of the random choice tasks.

In the third section of the questionnaire, participants were asked for their demographic data and whether they currently invest with a robo-advisor and on the stock market. Furthermore, the two attention checks employed in Chapter 4 were included in this study.

I adhered to the recommendations of Orme and Chrzan 2021 to include at least 300 respondents in total for CBC studies. The balanced overlap method was employed to design the questionnaire due to the method's efficiency and ability to estimate interaction terms.

The attribute levels of the robo-advice costs and third-party costs were developed based on the competitive overview of German and American robo-advisors to capture the entire price curve, which ranged from 0–1.95% in the case of robo-advice costs and from 0–1.19% for third-party costs (see Appendix A5.3.1 in the Electronic Supplementary Material). The levels of the minimum amount to be invested were derived with the same intention, but the highest level of minimum investment was capped at $100,000 (instead of the highest minimum investment of $500,000 found in the market overview required by Elm Wealth) to be still relevant for the participant group of this online survey.

Please select the most attractive offer for you.
The explanation of the terms is repeated below the table.

Robo-advice costs p.a.	2.0%	2.0%	1.0%	0%
Third-party costs p.a.	0%	0.5%	0.25%	0.5%
Is personal advice offered?	No	Yes	No	Yes
Is tax optimization offered?	Yes	No	Yes	Yes
Are ESG products (see definition) offered?	No	Yes	Yes	No
Which investment strategy is used?	Active selection of investment	Passive	Passive	Passive
What is the minimum amount of money that must be invested?	10000$	100000$	1000$	0$
Does the robo-advisor provide information on its returns achieved in previous years?	No	Yes	Yes	No
	Select	Select	Select	Select

Considering your current life situation, would you pay for the offer you selected above as the most attractive?

Yes | No

Figure 6.1 Exemplary choice task

6.3 Results

The empirical methodology designed in Section 6.2 is implemented in Section 6.3. In the following, the data collection and cleansing process is summarized, an empirical strategy for the data analysis is developed and applied to the data deriving major findings on customer preferences regarding the features of robo-advisors. The data analysis techniques employed include counts-analysis, Hierarchical-Bayes analysis, latent class analysis, and willingness to pay analysis.

6.3.1 Data Collection and Cleansing

Data for the American sample were collected between May 16–17, 2022 on Amazon MTurk with in total 479 participants of which 17 were not considered for the further study as they did not answer the attention checks correctly or took less than 100 seconds to complete the survey. Based on the recommendations by Orme 2019, I calculated a root likelihood (RLH) value using 500 random respondents on the questionnaire design. The RLH value allows to judge the consistency of answers, i.e., whether participants paid attention. Based on the recommendation, I chose the 95th percentile of the random respondents' RLH value as a cutoff for the study participants, i.e., only 5% of random answers could reach such a value. Removing all participants who exhibited a worse RLH value left, 288 participants in the American sample, whose answers are analyzed in the following.

Data for the German sample were collected between July 13–16, 2022 on Clickworker with in total 400 participants of which 32 participants were excluded as they failed to answer the attention checks correctly or took less than 100 seconds to complete the survey. Using the RLH methodology on the German sample removed further 38 participants. Key demographic data of the samples are summarized in *Table 6.1*.

Table 6.1 Sample description—choice-based conjoint study (CBC)

Sample	Sample size	Mean age	% of women	% of investors on the stock market	% of investors using a robo-advisor
Germany	330	42.3	36.4	51.2	2.7
USA	288	36.6	41.3	80.2	53.8

6.3.2 Empirical Strategy

I analyzed the cleansed data using four distinct analysis methods. I outline the principle and the aim of the analyses below, while the details and results of these analysis methods will be discussed in the following sections. The four analyses conducted with the CBC data were:

- **Counts-analysis:** I aim at eliciting the impact that different attribute levels have on the overall market share of robo-advisors with specific attribute levels, e.g., I compare the number of robo-advisor designs chosen which offer personal advice versus the number of robo-advisor designs chosen which do not offer personal advice. In principle, this analysis is conducted by comparing the number of times designs with different attribute levels of one attribute were chosen among all participants. The numbers are compared using chi-squared tests to establish significant differences among choices of robo-advisors with different attribute levels.
- **Hierarchical-Bayes-analysis:** The purpose of the Hierarchical-Bayes-analysis (HB) is to quantify the impact that attributes have on the decision for a robo-advisor and to find out which attribute levels are preferred by average customers. The idea behind a Hierarchical-Bayes-analysis is to estimate the customers' preferences on an individual basis and aggregate those estimates. This method allows a ranking of the contribution of each attribute to the decision for specific robo-advisor designs.
- **Latent class analysis:** I employ the latent class analysis to identify customer segments with distinct preferences. Furthermore, the aim is to investigate

whether differences between German and American participants as well as between investors and non-investors emerge from the samples, which would establish the impact of path dependence for the preferences regarding features. In principle, the latent class algorithm assigns individuals to different customer segments according to their preferences. The number of customer segments emerging from a data set is unknown a priori and is determined based on statistical criteria. The algorithm is used on a pooled sample of German and American participants as well as on the German and the American samples separately. I use a t-test to analyze whether the German and American participants have a differing probability of affiliation to the segments emerging from the pooled German and American sample and whether investors and non-investors have a differing probability of affiliation to the segments emerging from the separate German and American samples.

- **Willingness to pay analysis:** I use the willingness to pay analysis (WTP) to quantify the increase in robo-advisor costs in percentage of AuM p.a. that participants are willing to take to get a certain attribute, e.g., how much increase in robo-advisor costs p.a. participants endure to avail personal advice. This information offers decision support for suppliers of robo-advisory services by allowing them to quantify what they could charge for the addition of a certain service without losing market share. The basic idea of the willingness to pay analysis is to investigate the price increase that equalizes the market shares of a design with a more preferred attribute level compared a less preferred attribute level. To provide an example, the price of a robo-advisor with personal advice is increased up to a point that it equals the market share of this robo-advisor without personal advice in a different market.

6.3.3 Findings

Section 6.3.3 renders the empirical findings based on the data collected in Germany and the USA according to the analysis technique with which they are derived: counts-analysis, Hierarchical-Bayes analysis, latent class analysis, and willingness to pay analysis.

6.3.3.1 Counts-analysis

The counts-analysis allows to analyze CBC data on an aggregate level, by comparing how often the designs incorporating a specific attribute with a specific level are selected by the participants. Thus, it does not involve a multinomial logit regression (MNL). A chi-squared test was used to find out whether the null hypothesis of an identical distribution of customer choices among the different levels of each attribute can be rejected. Joint or interaction effects are reported if they reached the $p < 0.05$ level of significance in the specific sample. See *Table 6.2* for an overview of the German and American counts-analysis.

Table 6.2 Counts-analysis—German and American samples

Total respondents Germany: 330
Total respondents USA: 288
Levels of analysis: Main effects, two-way

Attributes	Attribute levels	Proportion of wins	
		Germany	USA
Robo-advice costs p.a.	0%	0.355	0.275
	0.5%	0.292	0.258
	1.0%	0.216	0.242
	2.0%	0.137	0.225
	Within Att. Chi-Square	424.907	18.799
	D.F.	3.000	3.000
	Significance	p = 0.000***	p = 0.000***
Third-party costs p.a.	0%	0.305	0.245
	0.25%	0.265	0.260
	0.5%	0.260	0.258
	1.5%	0.169	0.236
	Within Att. Chi-Square	156.839	5.519
	D.F.	3.000	3.000
	Significance	p = 0.000***	p = 0.138
Is personal advice offered?	Yes	0.281	0.284
	No	0.219	0.216
	Within Att. Chi-Square	62.125	65.560
	D.F.	1.000	1.000
	Significance	p = 0.000***	p = 0.000***

(continued)

Table 6.2 (continued)

Total respondents Germany: 330
Total respondents USA: 288
Levels of analysis: Main effects, two-way

Is tax optimization offered?	Yes	0.280	0.275
	No	0.220	0.225
	Within Att. Chi-Square	56.497	35.649
	D.F.	1.000	1.000
	Significance	p = 0.000***	p = 0.000***
Are ESG products (see definition) offered?	Yes	0.284	0.265
	No	0.216	0.235
	Within Att. Chi-Square	73.228	12.639
	D.F.	1.000	1.000
	Significance	p = 0.000***	p = 0.000***
Which investment strategy is used?	Passive	0.242	0.228
	Active timing	0.249	0.254
	Active selection of investments	0.259	0.268
	Within Att. Chi-Square	3.087	15.677
	D.F.	2.000	2.000
	Significance	p = 0.214	p = 0.000***
What is the minimum amount of money that must be invested?	0 € / $0	0.377	0.259
	1.000 € / $1.000	0.329	0.305
	10.000 € / $10.000	0.208	0.246
	100.000 € / $100.000	0.086	0.190
	Within Att. Chi-Square	807.089	93.501
	D.F.	3.000	3.000
	Significance	p = 0.000***	p = 0.000***
Does the robo-advisor provide information on its returns achieved in previous years?	Yes	0.307	0.279
	No	0.193	0.221

(continued)

Table 6.2 (continued)

Total respondents Germany: 330
Total respondents USA: 288
Levels of analysis: Main effects, two-way

	Within Att. Chi-Square		208.657	45.490
	D.F.		1.000	1.000
	Significance		p = 0.000***	p = 0.000***
Level of analysis: joint effects				
Robo-advice costs p.a. x Are ESG products (see definition) offered?	0%	Yes	0.382	US: No joint effects
	0%	No	0.329	
	0.5%	Yes	0.331	
	0.5%	No	0.252	
	1.0%	Yes	0.257	
	1.0%	No	0.175	
	2.0%	Yes	0.165	
	2.0%	No	0.109	
	Interaction Chi-Square		10.536	
	D.F.		3.000	
	Significance		p = 0.001**	
Robo-advice costs p.a. x What is the minimum amount of money that must be invested?	0%	0 €	0.523	US: No joint effects
	0%	1.000 €	0.455	
	0%	10.000 €	0.299	
	0%	100.000 €	0.141	
	0.5%	0 €	0.431	
	0.5%	1.000 €	0.392	
	0.5%	10.000 €	0.237	

(continued)

Table 6.2 (continued)

Total respondents Germany: 330
Total respondents USA: 288
Levels of analysis: Main effects, two-way

	0.5%	100.000 €	0.112	
	1.0%	0 €	0.322	
	1.0%	1.000 €	0.286	
	1.0%	10.000 €	0.194	
	1.0%	100.000 €	0.058	
	2.0%	0 €	0.229	
	2.0%	1.000 €	0.184	
	2.0%	10.000 €	0.103	
	2.0%	100.000 €	0.033	
	Interaction Chi-Square		18.004	
	D.F.		9.000	
	Significance		p = 0.035*	
Robo-advice costs p.a. x Does the robo-advisor provide information on its returns achieved in previous years?	0%	Yes	0.415	US: No joint effects
	0%	No	0.295	
	0.5%	Yes	0.366	
	0.5%	No	0.218	
	1.0%	Yes	0.268	
	1.0%	No	0.164	
	2.0%	Yes	0.180	
	2.0%	No	0.093	
	Interaction Chi-Square		10.898	
	D.F.		3.000	
	Significance		p = 0.012*	

Note: * $p < 0.05$. ** $p < 0.01$. *** $p < 0.001$.

In the German sample, all main effects apart from the investment strategy were significant at the $p < 0.01$ level. The direction of the effect becomes evident by comparing the percentages with which the robo-advisor designs with specific price and service levels were selected. Robo-advisor designs with lower levels of robo-advice and third-party costs as well as more services, e.g., the offer of personal advice, were chosen more frequently by the participants than more expensive robo-advisor designs with less services. Furthermore, there were a few joint effects that showed a significant influence. A joint effect was detected at the $p < 0.05$ level such that the influence of the offer of ESG products was larger for robo-advisors with higher robo-advice costs. Moreover, the effects of minimum investment and information on past returns were larger for robo-advisors with higher robo-advice costs. The effect of the information on past returns was stronger if no personal advice or no ESG products were offered.

The results in Germany give support for the effects on the population level of all attributes apart from the investment strategy. Additionally, high robo-advisor fees lead to the expectation of more favorable attributes, i.e., the more expensive a robo-advisor is, the more important the service quality becomes to participants.

In the American sample, all main effects apart from third-party costs are significant at the $p < 0.01$ level in the expected direction, i.e., less expensive robo-advisor designs with more services were more frequently selected. Active investment strategies are preferred to passive ones. No significant joint effects are detected in the American sample. The lacking significance of third-party costs is counterintuitive, as investors should have a clear financial motive to pay less for the services that they use.

6.3.3.2 Hierarchical-bayes-analysis

By conducting a Hierarchical-Bayes-analysis (HB), I derive the average part-worth utilities that the German and American participants ascribe to the different attribute levels of the robo-advisors included in this study. I follow Orme and Chrzan 2021 in their explanation of the HB. The Hierarchical-Bayes method was first applied by Allenby et al. 1995 for the estimation of part-worth utilities and quickly developed into a popular estimation method for utilities, as it allows to derive utilities on the respondent-level. It is only applicable in cases in which multiple choice tasks are available for each respondent. The hierarchy of the Hierarchical-Bayes-analysis consists of the following two levels:

- At the superordinate level, the part-worths of individuals are summarized by a multivariate normal distribution with a vector of means and a matrix of covariances.
- At the subordinate level, a multinomial logit model predicts the probabilities of choosing specific alternatives given an individuals' part-worths.

This can be formalized as:

$$\beta_i \sim Normal(\alpha, D) \tag{6.6}$$

with the following definitions:

- β_i denotes individual i's vector of part-worths.
- α describes the vector of means of the distribution of part-worths.
- D corresponds to a matrix of the variances and covariances of the part-worths' distribution across individuals.

A three-step iterative process is used to derive the parameters β, α, and D. As a default, the vectors β and α are set to zero and D to the identity matrix. The following three steps are conducted for each iteration:

1. Generate a new estimation of α based on the current estimates of β and D. α is normally distributed with the average of β as a mean and D as a covariance matrix divided by the count of respondents. That distribution is used to draw a new estimate of α employing a Cholesky decomposition. I refer to Orme and Chrzan 2021 for further details.
2. Draw a new estimate of D from an inverse Wishart distribution based on the current estimates of β and α.
3. Generate new estimates of β based on the current estimates of α and D. β are drawn using a Metropolis Hastings algorithm. I refer to Orme and Chrzan 2021 for further details.

The HB in this study was conducted based on the recommendations by Orme and Chrzan 2021. A Monte Carlo Markov Chain algorithm was used to estimate the part-worth utilities on the individual level. As recommended, 10,000 iterations were taken before using the results and an additional 10,000 draws were used for each respondent. Prior variance was set to 0.3 based on the recommendation from Orme and Williams 2016 for CBC studies with 7–9 attributes and three covariates were used: Investment on the stock market, investment with a robo-advisor, and household wealth. These covariates were chosen based on the recommendation of Orme and Howell 2009 to include covariates that relate to behavior of respondents. The importance of the three covariates for the adoption of robo-advisors was demonstrated in Chapter 3 and Chapter 4.

As the results of a HB are conjoint utilities or part-worths, they are interval data scaled to an arbitrary constant within each attribute. In this case, the conjoint utilities are scaled so that they sum up to zero, i.e., they are referred to as zero-centered. A negative utility value of a level does not indicate that respondents would not have chosen this attribute level, but that the level with the positive utility is preferred to the level with the negative value.

To find out which attribute is important to the participants, the range of an attribute's utility values is considered. This range equates to the attribute's contribution to the total utility of the robo-advisor. The percentage of the range of one attribute x compared to the ranges of the other attributes provides a value for the average relative importance of this attribute x, i.e., the relative importance values of all attributes sum up to 100%. The relative importance of an attribute depends on its attribute levels in the study, i.e., the wider the ranges in the values of the attribute levels, the higher the estimated relative importance value of the attribute. For a summary of the HB results, see *Table 6.3* for Germany and *Table 6.4* for the USA.

The average importance values show that the minimum investment as well as robo-advice costs and third-party costs are the most important attributes in both samples. Furthermore, the ranking of importance values of the remaining attributes is very similar in Germany and the USA. The only notable difference is the position of ESG products in the list, which seem to be relatively more important to German participants. It is noticeable that the attributes which did not reach a significant level in the counts-analysis (investment strategy in Germany and third-party costs in the USA) were important to participants: The investment strategy is the fourth most important attribute in Germany, while third-party costs are the third most important attribute in the USA. *Figure 6.2* and *Figure 6.3* visualize the relative importance of the respective attributes.

Interestingly, participants preferred the active investment strategies as compared to the passive one in both samples. While the German participants preferred the active timing, the American ones preferred the active selection of investments. Apart from the preferences of participants in financial decision making, a further potential reason for this finding might include more positive associations of the word "active" in comparison to the word "passive".

Noticeably, the none-option, i.e., the decision against the robo-advisors on offer available for each of the sets of robo-advisors presented to the participants, receives a positive utility value of 214.5 in Germany, while the corresponding value for the USA is negative with a utility of -297.5. This suggests that in Germany, only a combination of very preferable attribute levels of a robo-advisor as judged by German participants led them to choose the robo-advisor over the rejection of all offers on display. The negative utility of the none-option in the USA suggests that a lot of combinations of levels in a robo-advisor would have been preferred by American participants over the none-option. This suggests a

Table 6.3 HB analysis Germany

Attributes	Average importance	Standard deviation	Attribute levels	Average utilities (zero-centered)	Standard deviation
Robo-advice costs p.a.	19.773	10.374	0%	59.981	50.775
			0.5%	33.211	24.211
			1.0%	−11.051	22.283
			2.0%	−82.141	54.386
Third-party costs p.a.	13.215	7.762	0%	33.793	34.012
			0.25%	13.098	19.715
			0.5%	9.828	15.143
			1.5%	−56.718	46.025
Is personal advice offered?	5.684	5.070	Yes	19.338	23.550
			No	−19.338	23.550
Is tax optimization offered?	5.000	4.354	Yes	18.180	19.313
			No	−18.180	19.313
Are ESG products (see definition) offered?	6.546	6.726	Yes	21.214	30.984
			No	−21.214	30.984
Which investment strategy is used?	8.126	6.422	Passive	−6.934	47.176
			Active timing	3.676	25.241
			Active selection of investments	3.258	31.542
What is the minimum amount of money that must be invested?	31.837	14.310	0 €	84.199	79.865
			1,000 €	66.414	45.579
			10,000 €	−9.946	58.925
			100,000 €	−140.666	70.634
Does the robo-advisor provide information on its returns achieved in previous years?	9.819	8.801	Yes	35.155	39.330
			No	−35.155	39.330
None[1]				214.534	220.332

Note: 1 = None corresponds to the respondents' option to decide against all robo-advisor designs included in a choice task.

Table 6.4 HB analysis USA

Attributes	Average importance	Standard deviation	Attribute levels	Average utilities (zero-centered)	Standard deviation
Robo-advice costs p.a.	15.596	8.320	0%	19.409	58.597
			0.5%	7.029	38.449
			1.0%	−4.698	41.884
			2.0%	−21.739	65.762
Third-party costs p.a.	11.478	5.736	0%	−7.505	42.825
			0.25%	11.053	28.719
			0.5%	4.900	34.590
			1.5%	−8.448	47.630
Is personal advice offered?	8.875	6.607	Yes	22.798	37.966
			No	−22.798	37.966
Is tax optimization offered?	6.741	5.505	Yes	14.877	31.501
			No	−14.877	31.501
Are ESG products (see definition) offered?	5.454	4.060	Yes	8.890	25.731
			No	−8.890	25.731
Which investment strategy is used?	9.521	6.368	Passive	−18.877	41.602
			Active timing	6.762	29.602
			Active selection of investments	12.115	37.369
What is the minimum amount of money that must be invested?	33.415	15.358	$0	−4.110	131.749
			$1,000	48.106	89.157
			$10,000	13.826	80.590
			$100,000	−57.822	124.088
Does the robo-advisor provide information on its returns achieved in previous years?	8.921	7.527	Yes	21.464	41.498
			No	−21.464	41.498
None[1]				−297.534	383.633

Note: 1 = None corresponds to the respondents' option to decide against all robo-advisor designs included in a choice task.

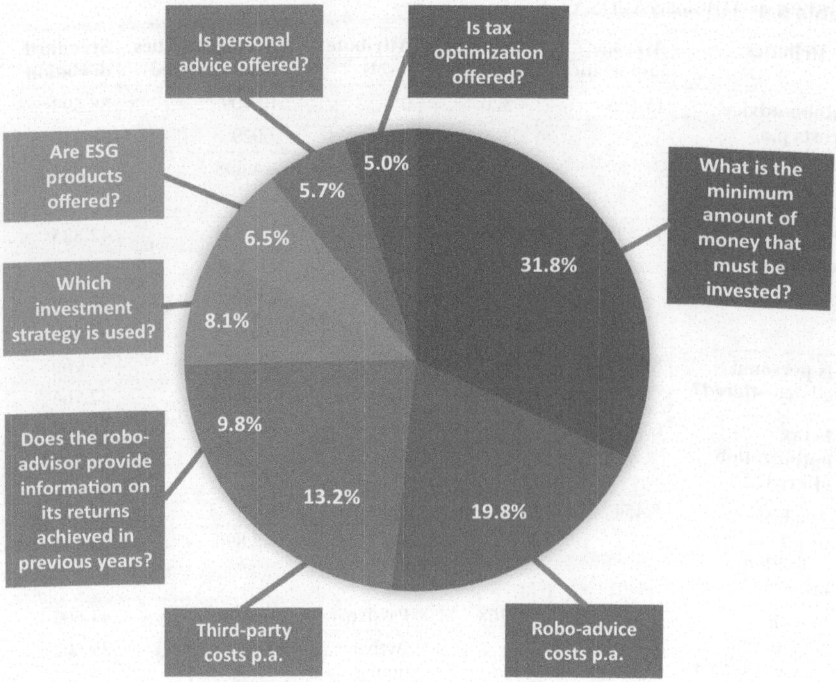

Figure 6.2 Average importance values Germany

more favorable climate towards robo-advisors in the USA as compared to Germany, at least of the participants included in this study towards robo-advisors with the features that were included. This result is consistent with the fact that only 2.7% of the German participants in this study, but 53.8% of American participants in this study used robo-advisors for investing. This finding also supports the significance of path dependence in the adoption of robo-advice. The American sample, which comprised 80.2% investors, judged the none-option less favorably compared to the German sample, where investors constituted 51.2%.

6.3.3.3 Latent Class Analysis

I conduct a latent class analysis to assign respondents to different groups according to their preferences regarding robo-advisors. The latent class analysis is applied to the German, the American, and a pooled sample. The detected solutions help to develop market segmentation strategies. I follow the depiction of

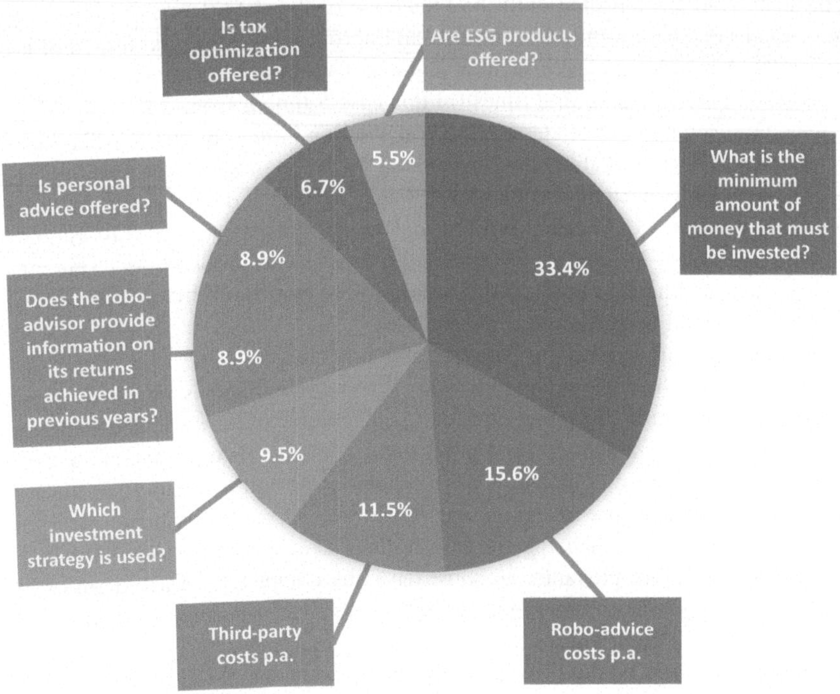

Figure 6.3 Average importance values USA

and suggestions regarding latent class multinomial logit (MNL) by Orme and Chrzan 2021.

The latent class algorithm has 4 distinct steps:

1. A number of classes is set with initially equal sizes and random small initial part-worths for each class.
2. The respondents' data is fit to the part-worths of each class. Thus, the probability of each respondent to belong to each class is computed using the logit equation. This probability is multiplied by the size of the class from the first step as a prior.
3. With the respondents' probabilities of belonging to the respective classes, a weighted logit solution is estimated for each class.
4. Given the part-worths, the likelihood of the data is estimated.

The steps 2.-4. are repeated until the likelihood of the data does not increase by more than a certain cut-off criterion, e.g., an improvement in log-likelihood of less than 0.01. As finding a local instead of a global maximum is a potential pitfall, the calculation is repeated several times (in this case 5 times) from different starting points. For each number of classes, the best solution judged by the log-likelihood is selected. The log-likelihood is calculated by estimating the probability that each respondent selected the alternative that he or she did in the questionnaire given the estimates of segment utilities and group sizes derived in this solution. The log-likelihood is equal to the summed logs of these probabilities. Thus, the optimal log-likelihood is zero, as this would imply that the individual choices of participants could be predicted perfectly.

It would be of value to researchers and practitioners alike to compare the utility values of the different groups. This direct comparison is impeded by the inverse influence of the response error on the magnitude of utilities. Thus, the raw utilities of each respondent group depend on the response error of this group. This issue cannot be solved completely, as the scale factor and the utility are always estimated together. I use the proposed remedy by Orme and Chrzan 2021 of zero-centering and normalizing the raw utilities to a constant range. Although this remedy does not guarantee to solve the issue completely, it avoids most of the associated problem. Therefore, the zero-centered and normalized part-worth utilities of the different groups are compared.

In the following, I would like to show that key demographic variables predict the group membership within a latent class analysis. Thus, the latent class multinomial logit is employed to find out whether different customer classes emerge from a combined German and American sample as well as from the separate German and American samples.

The latent class analysis builds customer segments based on individual preferences and calculates probabilities for every individual to belong to a certain segment. I chose solutions between 1 and 5 groups to assure interpretability (Orme and Chrzan 2021).

To determine the optimal number of segments, various information criteria have been proposed in the literature: the Akaike Information Criterion (AIC; Akaike 1973; Akaike 1998), the "Consistent Akaike Information Criterion" (CAIC; Bozdogan 1987; Ramaswamy et al. 1993), and the Bayesian Information Criterion (BIC; Schwarz 1978). The information criteria are based on the log-likelihood and are defined as:

$$AIC = -2 * Log\text{-}likelihood + 2 * (nk + k - 1) \tag{6.7}$$

$$CAIC = -2 * Log - likelihood + (nk + k - 1) * (ln\ N + 1) \tag{6.8}$$

$$BIC = -2 * Log - likelihood + (nk + k - 1) * ln\ N \tag{6.9}$$

with:

- k denotes the number of groups.
- n indicates the number of independent parameters estimated per group.
- N describes the number of choice tasks in the data set.

Among the information criteria, the BIC is the most widely used and trusted (Masyn 2013 edited by Little 2013; Nylund-Gibson and Choi 2018) and has been established empirically as the best performing one (Nylund et al. 2007). The BIC value can be used in two distinct ways (Nylund et al. 2007; Orme and Chrzan 2021):

1. The model with the lowest BIC might be chosen.
2. The model for which the addition of another segment leads to a diminished change in BIC (ΔBIC) can be selected.

As the purpose of this latent class analysis consists in interpretability rather than the improvement of predictive validity, the second usage of the BIC value is adopted (Orme and Chrzan 2021).

6.3.3.3.1 Segmentation of the Pooled German and American Sample

See *Table 6.5*, *Table 6.6*, and *Table 6.7* for the segmentation results of the pooled German and American sample. As *Table 6.5* depicts, the transition from a solution with one group to a two-group solution is associated with a considerably higher change in BIC than any other transition, so that the two-group solution is selected.

As shown in *Table 6.6*, the preferences of the two groups are different, while the ranks at the top of the list remain the same, with the minimum amount of investment and robo-advice costs constituting rank 1 and 2 of the importance scores in both groups. In general, group 2 showed higher preferences for cheaper robo-advisor options (both robo-advice and third-party costs) and a low minimum investment, while having a high utility for the none-option. Group 1 on the other hand showed higher preferences for the service attributes (tax optimization, personal advice, investment strategy, ESG products, and information on past returns) and a low preference for the none-option. Interestingly, group 1 shows only a very low preference for high levels of third-party costs, but no clear trend for middle levels of third-party costs. Both groups show the highest preference for an active selection of investments and the lowest for passive investments.

Table 6.7 provides an overview of the affiliation of the German and American sample to group 1 and group 2: While 62.4% of the German participants belong to group 2, 84.7% of American participants belong to group 1. Thus, most Americans belong to the group which is relatively more likely to use a robo-advisor and have developed preferences for robo-advisory services and is less sensitive to costs as well as the size of the initial investment. Furthermore, group 2 to which most Germans belong to is less likely to use a robo-advisor, has a high preference for cheap options with low initial investment, and less preferences for service attributes. A t-test rejects the null hypothesis that the probabilities of German participants to belong to group 1 and group 2 equal the probabilities of American participants to be part of group 1 and group 2.

Table 6.5 Quality criteria latent class analysis of the pooled sample (Germany and USA)

Summary of best replications for latent class analysis German and American data					
No. of groups	**Log-likelihood**	**AIC**	**CAIC**	**BIC**	**Δ BIC**
1	−13995.53	28023.06	28154.06	28138.06	/
2	−12217.16	24500.31	24770.51	24737.51	**−3400.55**
3	−11688.24	23476.49	23885.88	23835.88	−901.63
4	−11438.50	23010.99	23559.57	23492.57	−343.31
5	−11241.48	22650.95	23338.73	23254.73	−237.84

Table 6.6 Latent class analysis estimation results of the pooled sample (Germany and USA)

Solution for two groups (Best replication: 3)				**Group 1**	**Group 2**
			Segment sizes	59.8%	40.2%
Attributes	**Attribute importance**		**Rescaled utilities (Zero-centered differences)**		
	Group 1	**Group 2**	**Attribute levels**	**Group 1**	**Group 2**
Robo-advice costs p.a.	17.450	22.280	0%	58.132	85.437
			0.5%	39.817	38.263
			1.0%	−16.472	−30.927
			2.0%	−81.477	−92.773
Third-party costs p.a.	8.080	13.980	0%	15.956	42.616
			0.25%	18.731	12.411
			0.5%	11.185	14.170
			1.5%	−45.872	−69.196
Is personal advice offered?	9.290	6.610	Yes	37.166	26.433
			No	−37.166	−26.433
Is tax optimization offered?	8.720	5.750	Yes	34.861	23.005
			No	−34.861	−23.005
Are ESG products (see definition) offered?	7.610	5.840	Yes	30.439	23.352
			No	−30.439	−23.352
Which investment strategy is used?	6.450	2.620	Passive	−25.290	−12.031
			Active timing	−1.015	3.076
			Active selection of investments	26.305	8.955
What is the minimum amount of money that must be invested?	28.460	31.720	0 € / $0	48.783	106.406
			1,000 € / $1,000	89.876	55.777
			10,000 € / $10,000	−0.860	−14.811
			100,000 € / $100,000	−137.799	−147.372

(continued)

Table 6.6 (continued)

Solution for two groups (Best replication: 3)				Group 1	Group 2
			Segment sizes	59.8%	40.2%
Attributes	Attribute importance		Rescaled utilities (Zero-centered differences)		
	Group 1	Group 2	Attribute levels	Group 1	Group 2
Does the robo-advisor provide information on its returns achieved in previous years?	13.950	11.200	Yes	55.792	44.817
			No	−55.792	−44.817
None[1]				−450.129	385.584

Note: 1 = None corresponds to the respondents' option to decide against all robo-advisor designs included in a choice task.

Table 6.7 Group affiliation of the pooled sample (Germany and USA)

	Germany	USA
Group 1	37.6%	84.7%
Group 2	62.4%	15.3%
t-test[1] of group affiliation German vs. US respondents	p-value = 0.000***	

Note: 1 = two-tailed unequal variances t-test, * $p < 0.05$, ** $p < 0.01$, *** $p < 0.001$.

6.3.3.3.2 Segmentation of the German Sample

Table 6.8, Table 6.9, and *Table 6.10* provide the results of the latent class analysis in Germany. *Table 6.8* shows that the change in BIC considerably peaks during the transition from a solution with one group to two-group solution, again the solution with two groups is considered in the following.

As depicted in *Table 6.9*, both groups rank the minimum investment amount the highest, followed by the robo-advice costs and the third-party costs. Thus, participants of both groups show a straightforward preference for cheaper and more accessible robo-advisors. The differences between the groups are not very pronounced regarding the preferences towards services. Exceptions might include the difference of preferences regarding the information on past returns reaching higher values in group 2, while some services like personal advice and tax optimization show a higher importance for group 1. The none-option is more preferred by the group 1 as compared to group 2. Both groups prefer an active selection of assets, especially compared to the passive investment strategy.

Table 6.10 provides an overview of the group affiliation probabilities of German investors and non-investors: While 75.1% of German investors belong to group 2, only 57.1% of German non-investors belong to group 2. Thus, the null hypothesis that German investors and non-investors have the same probabilities to belong to the groups 1 and 2 can be rejected. Nevertheless, the majority of

Table 6.8 Quality criteria latent class analysis German data

Summary of best replications for latent class analysis German data					
No. of groups	**Log-likelihood**	**AIC**	**CAIC**	**BIC**	**Δ BIC**
1	−8284.49	16600.99	16726.32	16710.32	/
2	−7320.40	14706.80	14965.29	14932.29	**−1778.03**
3	−7075.19	14250.38	14642.03	14592.03	−340.26
4	−6886.10	13906.20	14431.01	14364.01	−228.02
5	−6739.35	13646.70	14304.67	14220.67	−143.34

Table 6.9 Latent class analysis estimation results Germany

Solution for two groups (Best replication: 3)				**Group 1**	**Group 2**
			Segment sizes	34.0%	66.0%
Attributes	**Attribute importance**		**Rescaled utilities (zero-centered differences)**		
	Group 1	**Group 2**	**Attribute levels**	**Group 1**	**Group 2**
Robo-advice costs p.a.	23.551	21.740	0%	82.296	81.470
			0.5%	40.456	39.760
			1.0%	−16.639	−28.770
			2.0%	−106.113	−92.450
Third-party costs p.a.	13.600	14.740	0%	46.095	44.850
			0.25%	9.491	15.800
			0.5%	7.081	12.420
			1.5%	−62.667	−73.070

(continued)

Table 6.9 (continued)

Solution for two groups (Best replication: 3)				**Group 1**	**Group 2**
			Segment sizes	34.0%	66.0%
Attributes	**Attribute importance**		**Rescaled utilities (zero-centered differences)**		
	Group 1	**Group 2**	**Attribute levels**	**Group 1**	**Group 2**
Is personal advice offered?	5.820	4.970	Yes	23.265	19.890
			No	−23.265	−19.890
Is tax optimization offered?	7.120	5.170	Yes	28.461	20.690
			No	−28.461	−20.690
Are ESG products (see definition) offered?	5.090	6.590	Yes	20.344	26.380
			No	−20.344	−26.380
Which investment strategy is used?	1.350	2.520	Passive	−5.468	−9.510
			Active timing	0.135	−1.130
			Active selection of investments	5.333	10.650
What is the minimum amount of money that must be invested?	36.010	31.190	0 €	113.931	101.030
			1,000 €	65.682	66.350
			10,000 €	−5.475	−18.860
			100,000 €	−174.137	−148.520
Does the robo-advisor provide information on its returns achieved in previous years?	7.480	13.060	Yes	29.910	52.260
			No	−29.910	−52.260
None[1]				653.734	98.510

Note: 1 = None corresponds to the respondents' option to decide against all robo-advisor designs included in a choice task.

investors and non-investors is part of the same group. Thus, this outcome reinforces the conclusion derived from the estimation results in *Table 6.9* that the differences in the German sample are limited.

Table 6.10 Group affiliation of German investors and non-investors

	Investors	Non-investors
Group 1	24.9%	42.9%
Group 2	75.1%	57.1%
t-test[1] of group affiliation investors vs. non-investors respondents	p-value = 0.000***	

Note: 1 = two-tailed unequal variances t-test, * $p < 0.05$, ** $p < 0.01$, *** $p < 0.001$.

6.3.3.3.3 Segmentation of the American sample

See the *Table 6.11*, *Table 6.12*, and *Table 6.13* for an overview of the segmentation results in the USA. The results depicted in *Table 6.11* demonstrate that the transition from a solution with one group to a solution with two groups brings a considerably higher change in BIC than any other transition, which is why the two-group solution is also used in the analysis below.

The results for attribute importance values provided in *Table 6.12* show remarkable differences between the customer groups compared to the segmentation of the German sample in Section 6.3.3.3.2. While the minimum investment is the most important attribute in both groups, robo-advice costs are on the second place in the group 1, but they constitute the least important attribute to members of group 2. Personal advice constitutes the second most important feature for members of group 2. Comparatively, members of group 1 focus on cheap solutions (robo-advice and third-party costs), while the services attributes (personal advice, tax optimization, ESG products, and investment strategy) are more valued by the members of group 2. Interestingly members of group 2, although attributing a high importance to the minimum investment and third-party costs, prefer offers in the middle of the range of attribute levels, thus neither the cheapest nor the most accessible. These preferences might account for the insignificant effect of third-party costs in the counts-analysis of the American sample. Compared to group 1, group 2 shows a very low utility for the none-option. Both groups show a preference for an active selection of investments and the lowest preference for the passive strategy.

Table 6.13 provides an overview of the group affiliations of investors and non-investors in the American sample: A majority of investors (75.8%) belongs to group 2, while most non-investors (59.6%) belong to group 1. Hence, the null hypothesis of an equal probability of American investors and non-investors to be part of the groups 1 and 2 can be rejected.

Table 6.11 Quality criteria latent class analysis American data

Summary of best replications for latent class analysis American data					
No. of groups	**Log-likelihood**	**AIC**	**CAIC**	**BIC**	**Δ BIC**
1	−6953.41	13938.82	14057.60	14041.60	/
2	−6281.39	12628.78	12873.76	12840.76	**−1200.84**
3	−6066.26	12232.52	12603.70	12553.70	−287.06
4	−5934.29	12002.58	12499.96	12432.96	−120.74
5	−5835.12	11838.24	12461.81	12377.81	−55.15

Table 6.12 Latent class analysis estimation results USA

Solution for two groups (Best replication: 2)				**Group 1**	**Group 2**
			Segment sizes	31.7%	68.3%
Attributes	**Attribute importance**		**Rescaled utilities (Zero-centered differences)**		
	Group 1	**Group 2**	**Attribute levels**	**Group 1**	**Group 2**
Robo-advice costs p.a.	19.263	2.284	0%	71.032	−4.741
			0.5%	34.232	8.025
			1.0%	−22.193	−10.245
			2.0%	−83.070	6.961
Third-party costs p.a.	9.607	10.151	0%	26.675	−37.404
			0.25%	1.636	43.806
			0.5%	21.870	6.104
			1.5%	−50.182	−12.506
Is personal advice offered?	10.074	14.677	Yes	40.296	58.707
			No	−40.296	−58.707
Is tax optimization offered?	6.884	11.354	Yes	27.537	45.417
			No	−27.537	−45.417
Are ESG products (see definition) offered?	4.711	5.653	Yes	18.844	22.614
			No	−18.844	−22.614

(continued)

Table 6.12 (continued)

Solution for two groups (Best replication: 2)				Group 1	Group 2
			Segment sizes	31.7%	68.3%
Attributes	**Attribute importance**		**Rescaled utilities (Zero-centered differences)**		
	Group 1	**Group 2**	**Attribute levels**	**Group 1**	**Group 2**
Which investment strategy is used?	5.249	8.696	Passive	−24.262	−37.635
			Active timing	6.530	5.704
			Active selection of investments	17.732	31.931
What is the minimum amount of money that must be invested?	32.948	35.713	$0	140.825	−151.131
			$1,000	34.781	134.572
			$10,000	−52.847	74.587
			$100,000	−122.759	−58.028
Does the robo-advisor provide information on its returns achieved in previous years?	11.263	11.472	Yes	45.053	45.887
			No	−45.053	−45.887
None[1]				223.037	−1801.350

Note: 1 = None corresponds to the respondents' option to decide against all robo-advisor designs included in a choice task.

Table 6.13 Group affiliation of American investors and non-investors

	Investors	**Non-investors**
Group 1	24.2%	59.6%
Group 2	75.8%	40.4%
t-test[1] **of group affiliation investors vs. non-investors respondents**	p-value = 0.000***	

Note: 1 = two-tailed unequal variances t-test, * $p < 0.05$, ** $p < 0.01$, *** $p < 0.001$.

The results of the analyses of the American sample and the comparison between Germany and the USA demonstrate: American participants and especially American investors are more likely to belong to customer segments paying more attention to services attributes and less attention to prices at the same time, indicating a certain willingness to pay for service-related options. The German groups, on the other hand, did not show many notable differences, meaning that costs and minimum investments are most important to the German participants, irrespective of their investment behavior.

6.3.3.4 Willingness to Pay Analysis

A willingness to pay (WTP) analysis seeks to quantify the monetary value of features or characteristics of a product, in this case a robo-advisor. The willingness to pay analysis was conducted according to the recommendations by Orme and Chrzan 2021 as well as Orme 2021. I calculated the willingness to pay of participants using market simulations accounting for competition. Two markets are considered for this approach, one in which the product is facing competition without the specific feature and one in which the product is facing competition with this feature. The price of the product in the second market is raised until the product has the same market share as in the first market. The price difference is an estimate of the willingness to pay.

As the WTP estimate would depend on the robo-advisors' attribute levels as well as the competition, a Sampling of Scenarios (SOS) approach is applied. In each scenario, random attribute levels and prices for the robo-advisor in question and its competition are drawn. In each scenario, a price is estimated to equalize the market shares in a market in which the robo-advisor does not have the feature against a market in which the robo-advisor has the feature. Accounting for competition with the same feature solves the "Gilligan's Island" problem present in situations in which no competition exists. As people stranded on an island without other possibilities of rescue, participants might be willing to pay inflated prices if no competition is available.

To provide stable results, the median WTP of the scenarios is chosen. This approach has the advantage that consumers who are on the cusp of choosing this robo-advisor have a more pronounced effect on the WTP. Approaches in which the WTP is measured by an average of the population depend more strongly on participants, who are very unlikely to opt for this robo-advisor independent of pricing. As the WTP are estimated by a change in just one attribute level, the WTP values cannot be added for several features.

As recommended by Orme 2021, the share of preferences was used to simulate the results. 30 competitors were included in each sample including the none-option. 1000 bootstrap samples were considered in the analysis. The preferences of customers were based on a Hierarchical-Bayes-analysis (HB) constraining higher prices to be less preferred to avoid nonsensical negative WTP estimates. As services of robo-advisors are usually remunerated with a price in proportion to the assets under management (AuM), the price is given as %. Reference levels are always the attribute levels which are least preferred by the participants in the respective group.

See *Table 6.14* and *Table 6.15* for the willingness to pay analysis results in Germany and the USA. The results for stock market investors and non-investors are reported as their different preferences regarding robo-advisors were substantiated in Chapter 4 and in Section 6.3.3.3.

The willingness to pay results provide companies with a first estimate of the value that specific features have for their customers. This estimate can be compared with the costs of introducing this feature. Average German participants have a WTP of around 0.5% of AuM p.a. for a robo-advisor which offers personal advice as compared to one that does not. Thus, providers of robo-advisory services can decide whether they are able to offer personal advice at that price. Subgroup analyses can provide an opportunity to tailor features specifically to subgroups of the population.

Nevertheless, the WTP should be treated with caution, especially as some reference levels might be strictly prohibitive for some of the participants. The minimum investment amount of $100,000 is so high that many participants would not be able to make such a payment, thus, the WTP values might be distorted.

The WTP for third-party costs p.a. might be especially interesting for suppliers of robo-advisors in the USA which offer both the robo-advisor as well as investment vehicles, i.e., the third-party products. The numbers suggest that increasing third-party costs to decrease direct robo-advice costs might make American customers more satisfied with the robo-advisor while increasing overall profits.

Table 6.14 Willingness to pay results Germany

Attributes	Attribute levels	Willingness to pay in % of AuM (SD)		
		Total	Stock investors	Non-investors
Third-party costs p.a.	1.5%	Reference level		
	0%	1.335 (0.071)	1.328 (0.083)	1.326 (0.098)
	0.25%	0.997 (0.067)	1.049 (0.081)	0.910 (0.079)
	0.5%	1.055 (0.071)	1.042 (0.089)	1.045 (0.083)
Is personal advice offered?	No	Reference level		
	Yes	0.508 (0.082)	0.369 (0.087)	0.722 (0.119)
Is tax optimization offered?	No	Reference level		
	Yes	0.516 (0.079)	0.398 (0.084)	0.688 (0.100)
Are ESG products (see definition) offered?	No	Reference level		
	Yes	0.625 (0.096)	0.547 (0.101)	0.770 (0.155)
Which investment strategy is used?	Active timing	Reference level		
	Passive	−0.017 (0.067)	0.062 (0.082)	−0.195 (0.098)
	Active selection of investments	0.023 (0.031)	0.051 (0.028)	−0.025 (0.072)
What is the minimum amount of money that must be invested?	100.000 €	Reference level		
	0 €	3.813 (1.125)	2.848 (1.405)	4.750 (1.548)
	1.000 €	2.531 (0.534)	2.359 (0.766)	2.598 (0.792)
	10.000 €	1.438 (0.168)	1.492 (0.277)	1.250 (0.278)
Does the robo-advisor provide information on its returns achieved in previous years?	No	Reference level		
	Yes	1.008 (0.135)	0.832 (0.130)	1.346 (0.232)

Table 6.15 Willingness to pay results USA

Attributes	Attribute levels	Willingness to pay in % of AuM (SD)		
		Total	Stock investors	Non-investors
Third-party costs p.a. **Is personal advice offered?**	1.5%	Reference level		
	0%	0.063 (0.148)	0.076 (0.174)	0.065 (0.178)
	0.25%	0.613 (0.149)	0.521 (0.181)	0.865 (0.173)
	0.5%	0.402 (0.148)	0.352 (0.174)	0.586 (0.227)
	No	Reference level		
	Yes	1.445 (0.257)	1.469 (0.345)	1.328 (0.479)
Is tax optimization offered?	No	Reference level		
	Yes	1.070 (0.170)	1.273 (0.210)	0.434 (0.210)
Are ESG products (see definition) offered?	No	Reference level		
	Yes	0.549 (0.152)	0.605 (0.183)	0.429 (0.168)
Which investment strategy is used?	Passive	Reference level		
	Active timing	0.707 (0.178)	0.820 (0.228)	0.395 (0.197)
	Active selection of investments	1.000 (0.198)	1.188 (0.261)	0.416 (0.272)
What is the minimum amount of money that must be invested?	$100.000	Reference level		
	$0	1.086 (0.397)	0.813 (0.424)	1.600 (0.741)
	$1.000	2.953 (2.366)	3.563 (3.247)	2.086 (1.787)
	$10.000	1.777 (0.762)	2.109 (1.550)	1.070 (0.540)
Does the robo-advisor provide information on its returns achieved in previous years?	No	Reference level		
	Yes	1.281 (0.196)	1.387 (0.276)	0.941 (0.229)

6.4 Discussion

In Section 6.4, I summarize the findings of Chapter 6 focusing on theoretical as well as management implications. The management implications focus on a comparison with the findings from Chapter 5 to derive mismatches between supply and demand in Germany and the USA. Limitations and opportunities for future research are outlined.

6.4.1 Theoretical Contributions

The choice-based conjoint analysis (CBC) demonstrated the significant impact of the eight objective attributes included in the study regarding consumer preferences: robo-advice costs p.a., third-party costs p.a., personal advice, tax optimization, ESG products, investment strategy, minimum investment amount, and information on past returns. While all attributes influence preferences on the individual level (Hierarchical-Bayes-analysis) and most on the aggregate level (counts-analysis), with the exceptions of investment strategy in Germany and third-party costs p.a. in the USA, important differences could be demonstrated between Germany and the USA.

Latent class analyses were used to cluster respondents according to their preferences deriving valuable insights for marketing purposes. The number of groups for each sample is not fixed a priori but determined by using statistical quality criteria. These statistical quality criteria indicated an optimum of a solution with two groups for each of the three samples: German and American participants combined, German participants, and American participants. By means of the latent class analyses, differences between the customer groups were determined:

- The latent class analysis of the pooled sample of German and American participants revealed that German participants were more likely to be part of a customer segment with a high level of price sensitivity and interested in a low minimum investment amount, while American participants were more likely to be part of a customer segment interested in services (tax optimization etc.).
- The latent class analysis revealed two customer segments within the group of American participants: One customer segment showed no clear interests in low robo-advice and third-party costs and preferred a small minimum investment of $1,000 over $0 and put a relatively high focus on services (tax optimization etc.), while the other customer segment showed preferences for low prices and a low minimum investment. While investors were significantly more likely

to be part of the former customer segment, non-investors had a significantly higher probability of belonging to the latter one.

- The latent class analysis found two customer segments within the German sample: The differences between the customer segments were more gradual than in the other samples. One group showed a higher importance towards the feature of minimum investment amount and the option not to select any of the robo-advisors offered, i.e., the none-option. This group had a significantly higher proportion of non-investors.

Interestingly, the finding of the influence of path dependent attitudes on the adoption of robo-advisors developed in the Chapters 2 and 3 and confirmed in Chapter 4 receives further evidence in this chapter, especially in the American sample. American investors and non-investors had significantly different probabilities to belong to specific customer groups showing different preferences towards the attributes of robo-advisors, but also towards adopting robo-advisors. While the effect of the non-price attributes was very high on the American investors, the effect on the American non-investors was lower.

Thus, this study provides a first step of the solution to overcome the hesitation of non-investors to use robo-advisors by eliciting which attributes and attribute levels are important to this group: offers with low robo-advice costs, low third-party costs, and a low minimum investment amount.

6.4.2 Management Implications

The data gathered for this investigation combined with the findings from Chapter 5 suggests one principal reason for the worse performance of robo-advisors in Germany as compared to the USA: pricing. There is a strong mismatch between customer preferences in Germany and the offers made by robo-advisors on the German market. While German participants, irrespective of whether they are investors or not, have preferences for inexpensive robo-advisors, German robo-advisors are almost twice as expensive when compared to the USA. Despite the lower costs of robo-advice in the USA, the American participants have a less pronounced interest in low costs. Furthermore, the customer segment that American investors are more likely to belong to shows no clear preference for lower costs. Thus, the assumption made in Chapter 5 that American consumers are less price-conscious (at least compared to German consumers) is supported as a possible explanation for the low transparency of third-party pricing in the USA.

Interaction effects could be detected in the German sample such that the effects of ESG products, minimum investment, and information on past returns are stronger if the robo-advisor is more expensive, thus, service expectations towards more expensive robo-advisors are higher in Germany. This further highlights that German robo-advisors might reconsider their pricing or adjust their service offer. Although price levels for robo-advisory services are significantly higher in Germany than in the USA, German robo-advisors do not consequently offer better services than American ones. Considering the three attributes with interaction effects with the price level (ESG products, minimum investment amount, and information on past returns), German robo-advisory services only stand out positively in the attribute of information on past returns compared to their American counterparts.

As already being successful, American suppliers of robo-advisory services might avoid changing their core strategies, but some opportunities for improvement remain. One opportunity might be the introduction of an active selection of investment, which is rarely offered when compared to Germany, although this corresponds to the preferences of American investors and non-investors alike.

Furthermore, American suppliers of robo-advisors might try to raise costs slightly as around two thirds of the American sample (mostly consisting of investors) showed no clear direction of preferences towards prices of robo-advice. Nevertheless, this pricing policy might deter non-investors, as they are more likely to belong to a customer segment with a higher degree of price sensitivity. Another aspect that might be improved by American robo-advisors is their transparency, especially in the form of information on past returns, which is only provided by the minority of robo-advisors analyzed in the US sample in contrast to the German sample.

The willingness to pay analysis offers suppliers of robo-advisory services the opportunity to receive a rough estimate of what potential customers (divided into investors and non-investors) might be willing to pay for a specific feature. Suppliers of robo-advisory services can use the willingness to pay analysis to compare their own costs for the introduction of a specific feature with the willingness to pay of their target group. Nevertheless, they should be aware that the willingness to pay estimates cannot be added for several features.

The data also suggest that in most groups and subgroups, with only minor exceptions in the German sample, the willingness to pay for lower third-party costs is less than the saving in third-party costs would suggest. This implies that suppliers could try to move costs from the robo-advice costs to third-party costs, especially in the USA. Suppliers might be advised to use their own products for their robo-advisor, as already done by Vanguard Digital Advisor, set relatively high prices for these products, and reduce the fee for the robo-advice. Alternatively, partnering up with a company offering ETFs and negotiating kickbacks might be a rewarding strategy.

As the overall robo-advisor market size is still low in Germany, which also has a low share of stock market investors (17.1% in 2021 according to Balonier et al. 2022 from *Deutsches Aktieninstitut*), suppliers of robo-advisory services could seize a sizable untapped market. According to the empirical results, there is a straightforward way to ease the access of non-investors to robo-advisors: Offer a robo-advisor with low robo-advice and third-party costs, as well as a low minimum investment amount. One caveat remains: The customer segments to which the German participants and the non-investors in both the German and U.S. samples were more likely to belong showed a relatively strong preference for the none-option. This finding suggests that these groups are relatively reluctant to adopt robo-advice.

6.4.3 Limitations

The number of attributes that can be investigated using a CBC is limited. Therefore, the focus of this chapter was on the attributes that showed a significant difference between the American and German robo-advisor suppliers in the market comparison in Chapter 5. Thus, other objective attributes that influence demand for robo-advisors might have been omitted in the CBC.

Importantly, the data of the CBC study are not representative of the American and German population. Especially, the group of investors were overrepresented. Nevertheless, I have treated the topic of investors and non-investors in detail demonstrating their differing preferences.

Due to the lack of representativeness of the sample, the results and management implications should be considered as explorative. Nevertheless, due to the scale of the robo-advisor market, a repetition of the study design provided in this chapter using a representative sample might prove commercially promising.

6.4.4 Future Research

As there is only a limited number of attributes that can be compared by participants in a choice-based conjoint analysis (CBC), I restricted the scope of my CBC model to eight attributes. Therefore, many attributes, e.g., the ones included in Chapter 5 but omitted in Chapter 6, might be investigated using a choice-based conjoint analysis (CBC).

7 Studying the Impact of Objective Product Features on the Independent UTAUT Constructs

Chapter 6 provides insights into the value that customers place on selected features, which priorities customer groups have, and how the preferences of customers translate into a willingness to pay for these attributes. This approach compares market offerings to customer preferences. However, it does not explain how attributes shape attitudes towards robo-advisors. Chapter 6 has shown *that* attributes influence purchase and spending decisions, but not *how* they do this—which is the main question of this chapter.

The empirical investigation of this chapter has an explorative character, i.e., the focus is on establishing the role of features for the acceptance of robo-advice rather than explaining cross-country or group-specific differences. Thus, I concentrate on American sample data because American participants were found to be significantly more likely to be part of a customer group with a keen interest in the features of robo-advisors as compared to Germans in the latent class analysis in Section 6.3.3.3. Furthermore, American participants in the empirical studies of the Chapters 4 and 6 were significantly more likely to invest with robo-advisors than Germans, e.g., 53.8% in the USA and 2.7% in Germany in Chapter 6. Hence, it is plausible that American participants have more differentiated expectations towards robo-advisors, as their familiarity with the technology is higher.

Supplementary Information The online version contains supplementary material available at https://doi.org/10.1007/978-3-658-44679-6_7.

M. Horn, *Technology Acceptance, Path Dependence, and the Demand for Robo-Advisory Services*, Forschung zur Digitalisierung der Wirtschaft | Advanced Studies in Business Digitization, https://doi.org/10.1007/978-3-658-44679-6_7

7.1 Empirical Concept

In this section, I will derive the empirical concept to investigate the impact of features on the adoption of robo-advice. While Section 7.1.1 derives a UTAUT model with exogenous path dependence accounting for features that might be generalized to other technologies than robo-advice, Section 7.1.2 adapts the model to robo-advice. Details of the survey are discussed in 7.1.3.

7.1.1 Accounting for Features in Models of Technology Acceptance

Chapter 2 outlines how technology acceptance models help explore technology usage and usage intentions. The most frequently used models of technology acceptance are the unified theory of acceptance and use of technology (UTAUT) by Venkatesh (Venkatesh et al. 2003) and its precursor, the technology acceptance model (TAM) by Davis (Davis 1985; Davis et al. 1989). Chapter 5 explains that TAM was created to study how product features influence its constructs. Therefore, I choose a model of technology acceptance to investigate the influence of features. As the UTAUT model was introduced thoroughly in Chapter 2, Chapter 3, and Chapter 4 to verify the influence of individual path dependence on the intention to use and usage of robo-advisors, it is the model of choice in this chapter.[1]

As the aim of this chapter is to identify the effect of attributes on the attitudes towards robo-advisors, attributes are introduced through descriptions of robo-advisory services including these additional attributes. These attributes do not constitute robo-advisor technology in general, but adjustments within the same technological concept. As the addition of these attributes to the general robo-advisor technology creates specific and hypothetical offers, the adoption behavior of robo-advisor technology cannot be measured directly as the specific offers are not available on the market. Thus, the adoption behavior is not part of this investigation.

As the adoption behavior cannot be modeled in this study, other options for the dependent variable have to be considered: Both *the intention to use robo-advisor technology (IURA)* and *the intention to invest using a robo-advisor (IIRA)* are intention constructs that are influenced by the attitudes towards a technology and, thus,

---

[1] Nevertheless, I do not claim that the UTAUT model is a better fit than TAM for this endeavor, but I deem both models as equally suited.

by the attributes a specific offer is equipped with. Nevertheless, *the intention to use robo-advisor technology (IURA)* is the most directly affected one by the attitudes towards a technology, as it has no other direct independent factors than the exogenous drivers, e.g., performance expectancy, effort expectancy, and interpersonal influence. In contrast to *IURA*, *the intention to invest using a robo-advisor (IIRA)* is also influenced by *the intention to invest on the stock market (IINV)* (see Chapter 3). Nevertheless, there is no reason to assume that the attributes or the exogenous drivers of *the intention to use robo-advisor technology (IURA)* of one specific robo-advisor, as included in this study could influence the *intention to invest on the stock market (IINV)* or the investment on the stock market. Thus, *the intention to invest on the stock market (IINV)* and the investment on the stock market can be assumed as constant and unaffected in this chapter. Hence, *the intention to invest using a robo-advisor (IIRA)* contains no additional information regarding the adoption of one specific robo-advisor compared to *the intention to use robo-advisor technology (IURA)* in the scope of this study. Therefore, I choose *the intention to use robo-advisor technology (IURA)* as the dependent variable in this study.

Moreover, the extension for path dependence, which makes the investment on the stock market an endogenous construct, is not affected by the attributes nor the attitudes towards robo-advisor technology. Nevertheless, path dependence is accounted for because the investment on the stock market, i.e., the basic technology, has been shown to have a significant impact on the attitudes towards robo-advisor technology in Chapter 4. Hence, a traditional UTAUT model accounting for the effect of path dependence on the attitudes towards robo-advice, i.e., the new technology, is selected in this study. See *Figure 7.1* for a depiction of the generalized version of the model used in this chapter. Be aware of the changed position of the adoption of the basic product/technology compared to the depictions in Chapter 2, Chapter 3, and Chapter 4. The change of position reflects the role of the basic technology, as it does not influence the adoption behavior directly but shapes the attitudes towards robo-advice in this model.

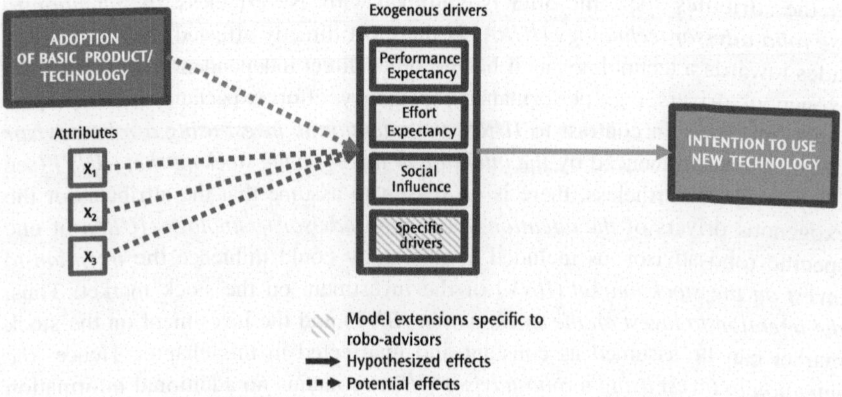

Figure 7.1 UTAUT model with exogenous path dependence accounting for features

7.1.2 Adapting the Model to Robo-advisor Technology

In the following paragraphs, I will explain how I adapted the independent drivers of *the intention to use robo-advisor technology (IURA)* to the case of specific robo-advisor offers equipped with the attributes analyzed in Chapter 6. To investigate the influence of attributes on the attitudes and adoption intentions of robo-advisors, attributes have to be considered that are important to potential users—as they seem most likely to influence the attitudes of customers—and relate to the technology itself. The first criterion would suggest that the attributes most important to potential customers, as found by the Hierarchical-Bayes-analysis (HB) based on the choice-based conjoint (CBC) data in Chapter 6, are included in the study. Nevertheless, the attributes with the highest average importance values to study participants (minimum investment, robo-advice costs, and third-party costs) do not directly relate to the robo-advisor technology or service itself, but to the pricing and marketing. Therefore, the attributes that are ranked on the places 4–6 in the HB in the USA are selected for the study:

- Investment strategy
- Personal advice
- Information on past returns (abbreviated as "past returns" in the model)

To not only assess how a particular product feature influences respondents to adopt a certain product, but also with which mechanism this specific feature influences the attitudes of respondents, a set of factors from the technology acceptance literature is included in the research model. Considering the factors included in the Chapter 3, the traditional UTAUT model factors performance expectancy, effort expectancy, and interpersonal influence should be included in the research model.[2] These factors express direct opinions on robo-advisors or an appraisal which attitudes other people might have towards robo-advisors (interpersonal influence).

The attributes investigated in this chapter (personal advice, information on past returns, and an active investment strategy) directly relate to the technology of robo-advice. To assure model parsimony, only those independent constructs are included in the model which can be influenced by the attributes. Four constructs from Chapter 4 which related to the intention to use robo-advice are **not** included in the model of this chapter:

- Personal innovativeness: Personal innovativeness relates to a person's attitudes towards technology in general, thus, it cannot be changed by the inclusion of an attribute of a robo-advisor.
- Perceived privacy risk: The attributes included in the study do not relate to questions of privacy issues, therefore, no effect of the attributes could be expected.
- Financial literacy: Financial literacy is a measure of competence, which cannot be influenced by the inclusion or exclusion of attributes.
- External influence: External influence relates to the media depiction of a technology. As this study deals with the adoption intention of a hypothetical specification of robo-advice, it is outrightly impossible that the attributes influence external influence.

Apart from the constructs already considered in Chapter 3 and Chapter 4, possible new constructs might emerge from the literature review in Chapter 5. Specifically, the role of trust for the acceptance of robo-advice with interacting effects with human or humanized advice has been established empirically in selected papers reviewed in Chapter 5:

[2] As in the Chapter 3, no direct effect of effort expectancy on performance expectancy is modeled because its initial inclusion was due to the technologies investigated by Davis 1985, which were part of the job of the participants, thus, consuming a non-trivial amount of their time. This condition is not met by robo-advisors.

- Morana et al. 2020 found social cues (names, avatars, etc.) to have a positive impact on social presence increasing trusting beliefs, which in turn positively influenced the likeliness to follow advice.
- Zhang et al. 2021 found that trust and the intention to hire towards high-expertise human advisors was higher than for robo-advisors. This difference could not be found between low-expertise human advisors and robo-advisors.

Thus, I conclude that humanization of robo-advice or human advice might influence trusting beliefs and the intention to use, while the direction of the effect is not clear. As this study includes personal advice by human advisors as an add-on to robo-advice, the effect on trust and the intention to use the technology are worth studying.

The definition and questionnaire items for trusting beliefs are adapted from Komiak and Benbasat 2006, who define trusting beliefs—based on the works of Gefen et al. 2003, Komiak and Benbasat 2004, and McKnight et al. 2002—as: "Trusting beliefs are the trustor's cognitive beliefs resulting from the trustor's attributional processes. In other words, the trustee's actions are observed, and the causes are attributed to the trustee's internal trust-related characteristics (e.g., competence and integrity)."

As already argued in Section 3.3, individual path dependence is also reflected in an influence of the adoption of the basic technology on the attitudes towards the new technology. It was explained that the specific influences are not considered as hypotheses, as their direction is not evident a priori and dependent on the specific experiences of the participants.

As an influence of path dependence, the influence of the investment on the stock market on performance and effort expectancy was investigated. A potential effect of stock market investment on performance expectancy is plausible, as investors might have a better grasp of the value that a robo-advisor can add. Effort expectancy might be influenced as investors might have used other services from suppliers of robo-advisory services, as many suppliers of robo-advisory services are also online brokers facilitating stock market investment. While a positive effect of the investment on the stock market on effort expectancy could be shown in the German and the American samples in Chapter 4, no effect was found on performance expectancy.

As the acquaintance with companies supplying robo-advisory services might give investors a better assessment of these services, it might also shape their trust perceptions regarding these companies. As with performance and effort expectancy, the effect might be positive, negative, or neutral depending on the experiences of the participants. Thus, the influence of stock market investment on trust in competence and trust in integrity (the trust perception constructs included in this study) are investigated.

As the direction of the influence of the product features and the investment on the stock market on the drivers of *the intention to use robo-advisor technology (IURA)* is not specified a priori, I will test all potential moderating effects of control variables. The effects that reach statistical significance will remain in the model. As the direction of the influence of the product features and investment on the stock market is not specified, no assumptions are made regarding the direction of the moderating effects. Consider *Figure 7.2* for an overview of the research model to combine product features, individual path dependence, and the UTAUT model.

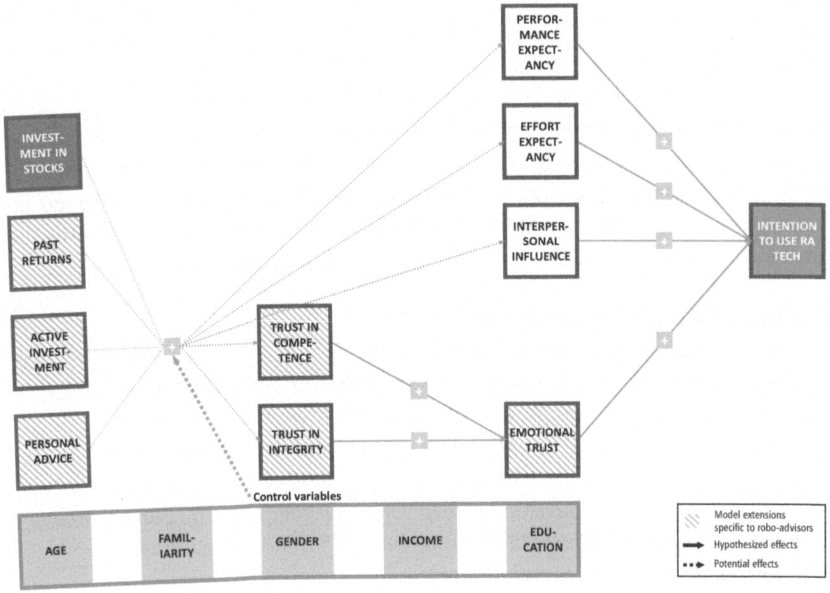

Figure 7.2 UTAUT model with exogenous path dependence accounting for features applied to robo-advisors

7.1.3 Study Design

The survey instrument began with a short description of a fictitious robo-advisor, Robo 1:

"Please read the following text carefully as it is vital to respond to the questionnaire! The text describes the service that the robo-advisor "Robo 1" offers:

You can use the service of Robo 1 if you want to invest money on the stock market. Robo 1 is an automated, digital service that distributes the invested money to various financial investments without requiring human intervention (robo-advisor). Like other robo-advisors, Robo 1 is offered for relatively low fees. Before using Robo 1, you would state your personal investment preferences in a questionnaire. Robo 1 takes your answers into account when automatically investing the total amount. Further personal intervention in the investment decision and subsequent adjustments are not necessary. Investing money using robo-advisors is associated with the typical risks and opportunities as other investments on the stock market."

Although the description defined a specific robo-advisor, it was very general to describe a common robo-advisor without any extraordinary characteristics. This description was extended upon in the treatment groups with a description of the specific attributes added to the robo-advisor. The control group received no extension of the description. Apart from the description, the study design was the same for all groups. Consider the three additional texts employed:

- **Additional text for past returns:**
  "Robo 1 offers you personal advice:
  Unlike many of its competitors, Robo 1 offers you a personal human advisor. Therefore, every time you have a question about your personal finances or the investment with Robo 1, you have access to a human advisor with who you can get in touch with by phone, online or even personally to discuss your questions. Furthermore, a human advisor can help you reach your financial goals by making a targeted plan and adjust your investments with Robo 1 accordingly."
- **Additional text for personal advice:**
  "Robo 1 offers you personal advice: Unlike many of its competitors, Robo 1 offers you a personal human advisor. Therefore, every time you have a question about your personal finances or the investment with Robo 1, you have access to a human advisor with who you can get in touch with by phone, online or even personally to discuss your questions. Furthermore, a human advisor can help you reach your financial goals by making a targeted plan and adjust your investments with Robo 1 accordingly."

- **Additional text for active selection of investments:**
  "Robo 1 offers you an active selection of investments:
  Unlike many of its competitors which exclusively invest in exchange traded funds (ETFs) to achieve the performance of a certain benchmark stock market index (like the S&P 500), Robo 1 tries actively to achieve a better performance than the S&P 500. Based on detailed analyses, Robo 1's investment team (consisting of experienced financial professionals) chooses assets to add to the portfolio by considering investments in stocks, bonds, money market, gold, commodities, hedge funds, and real estate. To reduce risks and increase profits further, Robo 1's investment team invests in an anticyclical way by investing when markets or asset prices are down and selling when they are up."

In the remainder of the study, the respondents expressed their attitudes towards Robo 1 by answering the indicators of the UTAUT model as described above. In contrast to the study in Chapter 4, the indicators in this study asked respondents about their assessment of Robo 1 and not about robo-advisor technology in general. Furthermore, demographic questions were included as control variables in the questionnaire.

7.2 Results

7.2.1 Online Survey

As for the UTAUT study in Chapter 4, data for this sample were collected employing an online survey conducted on Amazon Mechanical Turk with a sample size of 935 American participants on May 30 and 31, 2022.

As in Chapter 4, the additional latent constructs, e.g., trust in competence, are measured using indicators shown in the Appendix A7.2.1 in the Electronic Supplementary Material. Furthermore, the constructs already used in Chapter 4 are derived from the same literature but adapted to the case of the robo-advisor service in question "Robo 1" (see Appendix A7.2.1). Psychometric indicators were measured using a 7-step Likert-scale ranging from "Strongly disagree" to "Strongly agree".

7.2.2 Survey Data Quality Control

As in Chapter 4, a two-stage process was used to ensure attention and seriousness of participants (Oppenheimer et al. 2009; Aust et al. 2013; Berinsky et al. 2014). The two-stage process consisted of an instructional manipulation check (IMC) controlling whether participants read the instructions diligently and a seriousness check assuring that the participants are confident enough of their answers to use them for academic research. Excluding all participants who failed in at least one of the tests, all participants who took less than 100 seconds to answer the survey, all who provided impossible age values, and all participants who only gave one answer on the Likert-scale across all indicators without any variation reduced the overall sample size from 935 to 750. See *Table 7.1* for an overview of sample sizes in the different groups and key demographic data.

Table 7.1 Overview of key demographic data

Sample	Sample size	Mean age	% of women	% of investors on the stock market	% of investors using a robo-advisor
Control	204	36.6	34.8	79.4	52.0
Information on past returns	178	35.6	34.3	85.4	66.3
Personal advice	191	37.1	44.5	77.5	47.1
Active selection of investments	177	37.3	37.9	79.7	61.6
Entire sample	750	36.7	37.9	80.4	56.4

7.2.3 Findings

As in Chapter 4, data were analyzed using partial least squares regressions (PLS regressions) with the software SmartPLS 3 (Ringle et al. 2015). This is, to the author's knowledge, the first study investigating the impact of information on past returns, personal advice, and active selection of investment on the adoption of robo-advice. Thus, the study is explorative in the sense that the effects of the attributes on the constructs in the UTAUT model are not hypothesized in advance but estimated during the analysis. This makes the PLS-SEM method a useful tool, as it is more likely to detect effects that are indeed present in the population as significant, i.e., reject the null hypothesis (H_0), as compared for example to factor-based SEM (Sarstedt et al. 2021). Thus, PLS-SEM has a greater statistical power. As in Chapter 4, the analysis of the data follows the recommendations of Benitez et al. 2020 and Sarstedt et al. 2021. See the Appendix A7.2.3 in the Electronic Supplementary Material for an overview of the indicator loadings and crossloadings.

The data were analyzed in three steps:

1. The measurement model was evaluated using statistical quality criteria.
2. The impact of attributes and investment on the stock market on the constructs of the UTAUT model was investigated. All relationships that showed significance at the $p < 0.1$ level remained in the final model.
3. The moderating effects of the control variables on the significant effects of the attributes on the constructs in the UTAUT model that were established in step 2 were checked sequentially. All moderating effects that were significant at the $p < 0.05$ level remained in the final model. Furthermore, the direct effects of the control variables with significant moderating effects on the constructs of the UTAUT model must be modeled explicitly to include the moderating effects in SmartPLS 3.

Consistent with Chapter 4, effect sizes are measured using Cohen's f^2. Values above 0.02 indicate a small, above 0.15 a medium and above 0.35 a large effect size (Cohen 1988; Benitez et al. 2020; Sarstedt et al. 2021). Values under 0.02 are considered as negligible.

7.2.3.1 Measurement Model Adaptation and Evaluation

The model was measured using the PLS algorithm and the PLS bootstrapping with 5000 subsamples (Benitez et al. 2020; Sarstedt et al. 2021). Although all constructs in the model are reflective, the traditional PLS as opposed to the consistent PLS algorithm was used as the measurement using the consistent PLS algorithm led to impossible results of path coefficients of >3 and <−3 for trust in competence and trust in integrity without reaching statistical significance. The author cites lacking discriminant validity between these concepts as a possible reason for these estimates as described below. According to Sarstedt et al. 2016, the biases of using a common factor model with the PLS algorithm are of a reasonably limited magnitude. As all constructs are reflective, they were measured with correlation weights (Mode A in PLS-SEM), i.e., the standard default setting.[3]

The results of the measurement model are presented above and are analyzed subsequently. See *Table 7.2* for the measurement model results. As all constructs are reflective, rho_alpha, average variance extracted (AVE), factor loadings, and discriminant validity are the decisive measures for the measurement model (Benitez et al. 2020). In the overall sample, rho_alpha providing information on composite reliability is consistently above the 0.707 threshold indicating that more than 50% of the variance of the construct scores are accounted for by the latent variable (Benitez et al. 2020; Dijkstra and Henseler 2015; Nunnally and Bernstein 1994), except for trust in competence, which falls slightly below this benchmark. The AVE is used to assess convergent validity providing information on the share of variance in the indicators that is explained by the underlying latent variable (Benitez et al. 2020). The threshold of 0.5 indicates that half of the variance of the indicators is explained by their latent variable, thus, more than by all other latent variables of the model combined (Fornell and Larcker 1981). All AVE-measures are above 0.5. Furthermore, all factor loadings are highly significant and above 0.707.

Discriminant validity is measured by the heterotrait-monotrait ratio (HTMT), as proposed by Henseler et al. 2015 with a recommended conservative threshold of 0.85 (Henseler et al. 2015; Voorhees et al. 2016), a more lenient threshold of 0.9 (Henseler et al. 2015), and a very lenient threshold, referred to as $HTMT_{inference}$ by the authors, of an inclusion of the value 1 in the 90% normal bootstrap interval with bias correction (Henseler et al. 2015). The conservative HTMT is met by all constructs apart from the following exceptions: Performance expectancy and intention to use robo-advisor technology, trust in integrity and emotional trust, and trust in integrity and performance expectancy. The lenient threshold is surpassed by the following: Intention to use robo-advisor technology and emotional trust, interpersonal influence and intention to use robo-advisor

[3] See Sarstedt et al. 2021, p. 11.

Table 7.2 Measurement model results—UTAUT model with exogenous path dependence accounting for features applied to robo-advisors

Construct	Indicator	rho_a	AVE	Weight	Loading
Effort expectancy (EE)		0.775	0.592		
	EE_1			0.303***	0.765***
	EE_2			0.350***	0.767***
	EE_3			0.285***	0.756***
	EE_4			0.360***	0.788***
Emotional trust (ET)		0.841	0.758		
	ET_1			0.380***	0.869***
	ET_2			0.392***	0.873***
	ET_3			0.377***	0.870***
Intention to use robo-advisor technology (IURA)		0.856	0.774		
	IURA_1			0.366***	0.867***
	IURA_2			0.395***	0.884***
	IURA_3			0.375***	0.889***
Interpersonal influence (II)		0.853	0.771		
	II_1			0.381***	0.879***
	II_2			0.363***	0.856***
	II_3			0.395***	0.898***
Performance expectancy (PE)		0.776	0.691		
	PE_1			0.402***	0.815***
	PE_2			0.397***	0.840***
	PE_3			0.404***	0.838***
Trust in competence (TC)		0.697	0.766		
	TC_1			0.585***	0.882***
	TC_2			0.557***	0.869***
Trust in integrity (TI)		0.739	0.644		
	TI_1			0.345***	0.731***
	TI_2			0.445***	0.826***
	TI_2			0.450***	0.845***

Note: * $p < 0.05$. ** $p < 0.01$. *** $p < 0.001$.

technology, trust in competence and emotional trust, trust in competence and intention to use robo-advisor technology, and trust in competence and performance expectancy. The HTMT between trust in integrity and trust in competence does not meet the minimum threshold for discriminant validity. A deletion or reassignment of indicators, as suggested by Henseler et al. 2015 did not solve the issue. As the constructs trust in integrity and trust in competence are established (McKnight et al. 2002; Gefen et al. 2003; Komiak and bBenbasat 2004; Komiak and Benbasat 2006; Cheng et al. 2019; Morana et al. 2020; Zhang et al. 2021) and can be easily differentiated theoretically, they were left in the model. See Appendix A7.2.3.1 in the Electronic Supplementary Material for the complete list of HTMT values and the construct correlation matrix.

7.2.3.2 Model Evaluation and the Constructs' Impacts

As all data analyzed in this study are self-reported, common method bias is a potential pitfall. All VIF-values of the latent variables are well below the conservative threshold of 3.3 showing that collinearity was not an issue (Kock 2015; Kock and Lynn 2012).

I will describe the results of the PLS estimation starting from the exogenous variables (robo-advisors features and investment on the stock market) to the key endogenous construct intention to use robo-advisor technology. See *Table 7.3* and *Figure 7.3* for an overview of the estimation results.

In order to investigate the impact of the robo-advisor features, I tested the effect of personal advice, active selection of investment, and information on past returns on the independent constructs of the model. Active selection of investment is shown to have a significant positive effect on trust in competence with a negligible effect size. Personal advice has a significantly positive effect on trust in integrity with a negligible effect size. The attribute of information on past returns was not found to have any significant effect on the attitudes of participants, i.e., on the independent constructs of the UTAUT model.

To account for the impact of path dependence on the constructs of the UTAUT model, I tested the effect of investment on the stock market on performance expectancy, effort expectancy, trust in competence and trust in integrity. The data confirmed that investment on the stock market has a significant negative effect on all of these attitudes towards robo-advisor technology. The effect on trust in integrity reached a small effect size, while all other effect sizes were negligible.

Age and income have a positive moderating effect on the relationship between investment on the stock market and performance expectancy, although both effects are of negligible size. These moderating effects might be considered as

Table 7.3 Path coefficients results—UTAUT model with exogenous path dependence accounting for features applied to robo-advisors

	Path coefficient	Standard deviation	95%-Confidence interval	t-statistic	p-value	Cohen's f^2
Active selection of investment → Trust in competence	0.073	0.036	[0.004, 0.141]	2.021	0.043*	0.005
Age → Performance expectancy	−0.017	0.034	[−0.083, 0.049]	0.498	0.619	0.000
Age on investment → Performance expectancy	0.101	0.035	[0.033, 0.170]	2.885	0.004**	0.010
Effort expectancy → IURA	0.024	0.034	[−0.037, 0.094]	0.727	0.467	0.001
Emotional trust → IURA	0.449	0.050	[0.347, 0.543]	8.920	0.000***	0.306
Income → Performance expectancy	−0.023	0.039	[−0.099, 0.054]	0.583	0.560	0.001
Income on investment → Performance expectancy	0.102	0.034	[0.036, 0.171]	2.948	0.003**	0.013
Interpersonal influence → IURA	0.328	0.037	[0.256, 0.401]	8.915	0.000***	0.201
Investment → Effort expectancy	−0.094	0.038	[−0.168, −0.021]	2.494	0.013*	0.009
Investment → Performance expectancy	−0.120	0.037	[−0.191, −0.046]	3.217	0.001**	0.014

(continued)

Table 7.3 (continued)

	Path coefficient	Standard deviation	95%-Confidence interval	t-statistic	p-value	Cohen's f^2
Investment → Trust in competence	−0.127	0.041	[−0.208, −0.048]	3.107	0.002**	0.016
Investment → Trust in integrity	−0.163	0.040	[−0.241, −0.085]	4.068	0.000***	0.027
Performance expectancy → IURA	0.179	0.048	[0.091, 0.275]	3.762	0.000***	0.058
Personal advice → Trust in integrity	0.062	0.033	[−0.002, 0.126]	1.908	0.056+	0.004
Trust in competence → Emotional trust	0.472	0.049	[0.373, 0.565]	9.711	0.000***	0.251
Trust in integrity → Emotional trust	0.345	0.049	[0.249, 0.440]	7.083	0.000***	0.134

Note: + < 0.1. * $p < 0.05$. ** $p < 0.01$. *** $p < 0.001$.

Table 7.4 R^2 results—UTAUT model with exogenous path dependence accounting for features applied to robo-advisors

Endogenous variable	R^2	Adjusted R^2
Effort expectancy (EE)	0.009	0.007
Emotional trust (ET)	0.578	0.577
Intention to use robo-advisor technology (IURA)	0.760	0.758
Performance expectancy (PE)	0.042	0.035
Trust in competence (TC)	0.021	0.019
Trust in integrity (TI)	0.029	0.027

circumstantial, as they were not detected in the German and American samples analyzed in Chapter 4 raising doubts on the pervasiveness of the effect.

The effects of trust in competence and trust in integrity on emotional trust are highly significant. The effect size of trust in competence on emotional trust is medium, while the effect size of trust in integrity is small.

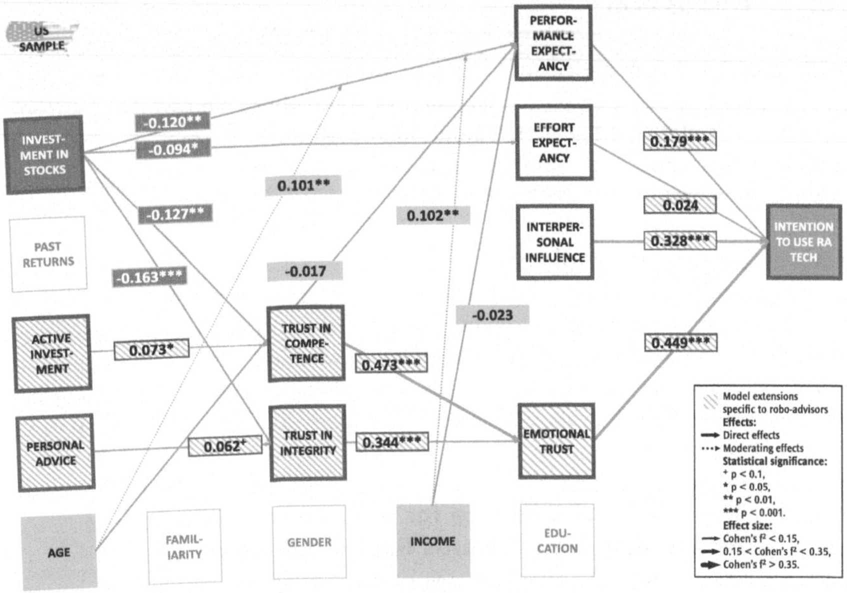

Figure 7.3 Summary of path coefficient results—UTAUT model with exogenous path dependence accounting for features applied to robo-advisors

All path coefficients of the attitudes towards robo-advisor technology had the expected direction. All except for effort expectancy were highly significant.[4] The effect size of emotional trust on the intention to use this robo-advisor technology is medium. Interestingly, performance expectancy has only a small effect size in contrast to the findings in Chapter 4 in the absence of the construct of emotional trust. Interpersonal influence has a medium effect size on the intention to use robo-advisor technology.

The adjusted R^2 values in *Table 7.4* suggest that the variations in the intention to use robo-advisor technology and emotional trust can be fairly well explained, while the respective values for the other constructs are relatively low.

[4] The lacking direct effect of effort expectancy could already be observed in Chapter 4 and was found in the literature for technologies that are relatively easy to use (Subramanian 1994) and for more experienced participants (Davis et al. 1989).

7.3 Discussion

In Section 7.3, I summarize the empirical findings of Chapter 7 with a focus on the impact of features on the adoption of robo-advice and further evidence for path dependence. Managerial implications are derived from the empirical findings, while limitations and future research opportunities are outlined.

7.3.1 Empirical Findings

The discussion of the empirical findings is divided into three topics: the impact of attributes on the attitudes towards robo-advice (Section 7.3.1.1), the impact of path dependence on the attitudes towards robo-advice (Section 7.3.1.2), and the impact of the attitudes on the intention to use robo-advisor technology (IURA) (Section 7.3.1.3).

7.3.1.1 The Empirical Evidence for the Impact of Attributes on the Attitudes Towards Robo-advice

The significant effects of active selection of investment and personal advice on the respective trust constructs show that technology acceptance models prove to be an acceptable tool to determine the mechanism by which an attribute influences actual usage. Thus, the study of attributes and their effects could enrich the robo-advisor acceptance research and add to the understanding of consumer choice. On the other hand, while the choice-based conjoint analysis (CBC) of Chapter 6 confirmed that American participants are interested in the investigated attributes, no attribute has a significant effect on the traditional constructs of the UTAUT model, i.e., performance expectancy, effort expectancy, and interpersonal influence. Furthermore, the effect sizes of active selection of investment and personal advice are negligible. Nevertheless, I hope that these results spark new interest in eliciting the connection between attributes and drivers of technology adoption as proposed by Davis 1985. Thus, this study directly answers the call for an investigation of the influence of antecedents (i.e., IT design and attributes) on the constructs of the technology acceptance models (Benbasat and Barki 2007).

The lacking influence of information on past returns, which was suggested to influence technology acceptance by Belanche et al. 2019 as well as Wu and Gao 2021 without empirical evidence, on any independent construct of the UTAUT model suggests that researchers should be very cautious in giving advice on how to influence the constructs of technology acceptance models by specific features without prior tests. Thus, even if a positive influence of the information on past returns is intuitive and found to be highly preferred by customers (see Chapter 6), this is no guarantee for a significant effect of this attribute on the constructs of technology acceptance models.

This study also provides further evidence for the important role of trust for the acceptance of robo-advisors and for the conclusion of Jung et al. 2018 that consumers rely on design to infer the trustworthiness of robo-advisors. Hence, my results are first empirical evidence for the influence of trust on robo-advisor adoption in technology acceptance models. Thus, they can be seen as a data-based justification for the large proportion of the literature on robo-advice covered in Chapter 5 which discusses the influence of trust (Tauchert and Mesbah 2019; Cheng et al. 2019; Morana et al. 2020; Zhang et al. 2021; Hodge et al. 2021).

The results from the American sample suggest that attributes mostly influence the trust of participants in the robo-advisor and their intention to use robo-advisor technology, i.e., changes in the attributes are likely to enhance trust rather than other attitudes and could enhance usage intention. Remarkably, neither performance expectancy nor effort expectancy were significantly impacted by the attributes, although active investment directly affects the service that a robo-advisor delivers.

7.3.1.2 The Empirical Evidence for Path Dependence

As the main purpose of this study was to investigate the effect of attributes on the attitudes towards a fictitious robo-advisor, robo-advisor adoption could not be included in the model. Hence, the direct impact of path dependence on robo-advisor adoption could not be observed. Nevertheless, the effect of path dependence in the form of stock market investment on the attitudes towards robo-advice could be estimated. It was demonstrated that stock market investment had a significantly negative effect on performance expectancy, effort expectancy, trust in competence, and trust in integrity. While the effect on trust in integrity was small, all other effect sizes were negligible.

Thus, the effects found in this sample are different from the effects detected in Chapter 4: Both the German and American sample in Chapter 4 showed no effect of investment on the stock market on performance expectancy, but a positive effect on effort expectancy. Hence, I consider the concrete effects of path dependence on the attitudes towards a technology to be highly context specific. However, this provides further evidence that path dependence has a significant effect on the attitudes towards robo-advice, corroborating the finding in Chapter 4.

7.3.1.3 The empirical Evidence for Drivers of the Intention to use Robo-advisor Technology (IURA)

The estimation results revealed the following major drivers of the intention to use robo-advisor technology (IURA):

- Emotional trust has a significantly positive influence on IURA with a medium effect size.
- Interpersonal influence has a significantly positive influence on IURA with a medium effect size.
- Performance expectancy has a significantly positive influence on IURA with a small effect size.

The effect size of performance expectancy is noticeably lower than in the estimation conducted in Chapter 4 in which the German sample showed a large and the American a medium effect size of performance expectancy on IURA. This might be attributed to the addition of emotional trust and trust in integrity to the model, which directly or indirectly influence IURA and have a relatively high correlation with performance expectancy. The respective correlations are both above 0.65.

Nevertheless, there is no doubt in the significance of the effect of performance expectancy on the intention to use robo-advisor technology (IURA). This effect was confirmed as the equivalent construct in the TAM model influenced the intention to use a robo-advisor with a sample of 96 participants from an unknown source in Germany (Seiler and Fanenbruck 2021) and with 404 American participants sourced through an online survey (Flavián et al. 2022). Furthermore, Figà-Talamanca et al. 2022 found that perceived usefulness has a significant positive effect on the attitude towards use among 214 members of the University of Perugia in Italy.

Corroborating the findings of Chapter 4, perceived ease of use was not found to have a significant positive effect on IURA. Nevertheless, Flavián et al. 2022 found a positive effect of the equivalent construct in the TAM model, perceived ease of use, on the intention to use a robo-advisor, while Figà-Talamanca et al. 2022 found no significant effect of perceived ease of use for people from the generation Y and older. Furthermore, Seiler and Fanenbruck 2021 found no effect of perceived ease of usage intentions.

In the model estimation of this chapter, emotional trust proves to have a high significant impact on the intention to use robo-advisor technology (IURA). This corresponds to the findings of Lourenço et al. 2020 obtained from a representative sample of 1,649 Dutch respondents sourced through a professional panel data firm demonstrating the effect that perceived trust has on the self-assessed likelihood to follow the advice of robo-advisor for pension advice. Nevertheless, Oehler et al. 2022 could not find an influence of trust on the willingness to use a robo-advisor at a German medium-sized university with 231 undergraduate business students. However, the lacking effect of trust in the study of Oehler et al. 2022 might be due to their trust measurement. They did not measure trust in the robo-advisor, but trust in different persons, groups, and institutions, e.g., police, neighbors, and the press.

7.3.2 Management Implications

The results of the study in this chapter touch directly on applied issues of the robo-advisor industry. It has been shown that personal advice and the active selection of investment are able to increase the trust perception of American participants. This is vital as emotional trust is a construct with a very high effect size on the intention to use robo-advisor technology. On the other hand, the role of these attributes on trust should not be overestimated due to the limited effect size of both attributes.

Most importantly, this study shows that advice on how to influence the independent constructs of technology acceptance models should be treated with a high degree of caution if no empirical evidence is presented to back the advice even when coming from the academic literature. The advice to include information of past returns in the model by Belanche et al. 2019 and Wu and Gao 2021 can be taken as an example. Even if the advice should be beneficial in the eyes of consumers, as in the case of information on past returns as shown in Chapter 6, it might not have the specific effect on technology acceptance as posited. Thus, this advice might be cautiously interpreted as a hypothesis and not as a result by practitioners.

7.3.3 Limitations

As this study was conducted using a convenience sample, it is not representative of the US population, especially stock market investors and investors with robo-advisors were considerably overrepresented in the sample. But as mentioned in Chapter 4, the usage of convenience samples is standard for research using the technology acceptance models UTAUT and TAM.

As in all self-reported studies the common method bias is a potential pitfall, but no strong indications of a common method bias were detected in my study.

7.3.4 Future Research

As this study merely draws on a convenience sample from the US population, further research with representative data from different countries is suggested to confirm the results of this study.

Future research might provide participants with a more realistic representation of the features than the verbal description chosen in this study, e.g., images or videos.

The effect of other attributes on the adoption of robo-advice could be investigated in future studies. The list of attributes in the market overview of the German and American robo-advisor market (see Chapter 5) can be employed as a starting point for the selection of attributes.

Summary

8

My dissertation aims at enhancing our understanding of technology acceptance in general and of the adoption of robo-advisory services in particular. I refine technology acceptance models by adding the theory of path dependence at the individual level. This leads to the introduction of the path dependence augmented unified theory of acceptance and use of technology model, or PDA-UTAUT model. The adoption of a new technology depends on the use of an established basic technology or product in this model. Moreover, the use of the basic technology or product can shape the attitudes towards the new technology. Investment on the stock market constitutes the necessary basic technology for the adoption of robo-advisory services. The PDA-UTAUT model gains explanatory power when endogenizing investment on the stock market by distinguishing between the intention to invest on the stock market from the intention to invest with a robo-advisor. The PDA-UTAUT model is empirically evaluated and confirmed with partial least squares structural equation modeling (PLS-SEM). The PDA-UTAUT model can be applied to a variety of new technologies which depend on the adoption of a basic product or technology.

I explore why American robo-advisors have attracted more assets under management (AuM) than their German counterparts. This involves comparing a comprehensive market overview of German and American robo-advisors with a choice-based conjoint analysis (CBC). This comparison helps detect supply and demand mismatches and identify the most relevant features of robo-advisors through a systematic process.

Using a systematic process, I identify key robo-advisor features. These features help address a critical question overlooked in current empirical research on technology acceptance: How do specific features influence the acceptance of new

M. Horn, *Technology Acceptance, Path Dependence, and the Demand for Robo-Advisory Services*, Forschung zur Digitalisierung der Wirtschaft | Advanced Studies in Business Digitization, https://doi.org/10.1007/978-3-658-44679-6_8

technology? I fill this research gap by integrating these (potential) supply side effects and path dependence in one research model to investigate the demand for robo-advisory services. The model is tested using PLS-SEM.

In this final chapter, I provide a summary of my theoretical results on path dependent technology acceptance in general (Section 8.1). The research models and approaches to investigate the impact of path dependence caused by stock market investment and product features on robo-advisor acceptance are derived in Section 8.2. Major empirical insights from applying the models to robo-advisor acceptance are set out in Section 8.3 from an information systems (IS) perspective. The deduction of managerial implications for both suppliers of robo-advisory services and governmental institutions is straightforward (Section 8.4). Finally, I address the limitations of this thesis and I point out worthwhile opportunities for future research in Section 8.5.

8.1 Introducing the PDA-UTAUT Model to Account for Path Dependence in Technology Acceptance Research

To address the first research question "*How does the individual investment behavior influence the demand for robo-advisory services?*", I introduce a general model described in this section. The model's application to robo-advice and empirical investigation are detailed in the next sections.

8.1.1 Insights on Individual Path Dependence and Technology Acceptance

By introducing individual path dependence into UTAUT models, I unite two influential strands of research: path dependence as established by Arthur (Arthur 1989; Arthur 1996) and models of technology acceptance (Davis 1985; Venkatesh et al. 2003).

Individual path dependence can have various reasons: Examples include customer groove-in derived from training or experience with a basic version of a product or technology which enables a user to become acquainted with a new version of a product or technology, e.g., a new generation of Airbus aircrafts (Arthur 1996). Network effects might compel users to use a specific basic software product, e.g., Microsystems' Java language (Arthur 1996), to be able to run the new software, i.e., the new technology, written by their network. Similarly, robo-advice *compels* users to invest on the stock market because providing advice on stock market investment is the main function of robo-advisors. Thus, stock market investment constitutes a basic product for the new technology of robo-advice.

The adoption of stock market investment is non-trivial due to learning costs, e.g., finding a broker and defining an investment strategy. Although, robo-advice might lower these learning costs, e.g., by defining an investment strategy for a new investor, I argue that the learning costs incurred by a stock market investor to adopt a robo-advisor are strictly lower than for non-investors, e.g., because the stock market investor already knows a broker that also offers robo-advisors.

Two conditions assure that accounting for path dependence is beneficial to explain the adoption of the new technology: Firstly, the basic technology serves a purpose which provides an independent advantage to the customer or user, which makes sure that the adoption of the basic product or technology is an independent decision from the adoption of the new technology. Secondly, the basic technology is not adopted by a vast majority of the population, which makes sure that the adoption is not yet ubiquitous and, thus, trivial, e.g., electricity in developed countries. Stock market investment meets both conditions because it evidently serves an independent purpose and major parts of the population in Germany (82.9% in 2021 according to Balonier et al. 2022 from *Deutsches Aktieninstitut*) and the USA (42% in 2022 according to Saad and Jones 2022 from *Gallup*) do not invest in stocks. Thus, I conclude that robo-advisor technology is ideal to study the impact of individual path dependence on technology acceptance.

8.1.2 Integrating Individual Path Dependence into UTAUT Models

The traditional UTAUT model established by Venkatesh et al. 2003 posits that performance expectancy[1], effort expectancy[2], and social influence[3] affect the

---

[1] Performance expectancy is defined as "the degree to which an individual believes that using the system will help him or her to attain gains in job performance" by Venkatesh et al. 2003.

[2] Effort expectancy represents "the degree of ease associated with the use of the system" according to Venkatesh et al. 2003.

[3] Social influence is characterized as "the degree to which an individual perceives that important others believe he or she should use the new system" by Venkatesh et al. 2003.

intention to use a new technology. These effects can be moderated by demographic and other factors. Facilitating conditions[4] and the intention to use a new technology explain the adoption of the new technology. Further constructs have been added to the UTAUT model when investigating the demand for specific technologies.

I derive a general path dependence augmented UTAUT model (PDA-UTAUT model) by introducing the acceptance of a basic product or technology, e.g., stock market investment, as the cause of path dependence into the UTAUT model. The basic technology enables the usage of the advanced or new technology, e.g., robo-advisor investment, and can shape the attitudes that respondents have towards that technology.

As the adoption of stock market investment, i.e., the basic product, is a necessary condition for the adoption of robo-advisory services, i.e., the new technology, the causes for the adoption of the basic product are of vital importance for understanding the adoption of the new technology. Thus, the adoption of the basic product is treated as an endogenous construct.

Incorporating the adoption of the basic product or technology allows us to explore three distinct intentions within the traditional UTAUT model:

- *The intention to use the basic product/technology* only relates to the basic product/technology without any interaction with attitudes towards the new technology.
- *The intention to use the new technology* exclusively concerns the new technology without a direct effect of the basic technology and possibly without the knowledge that the adoption of the basic technology is necessary.
- *The intention to use the basic product/technology with the new technology* relates to the combination of both the new and basic technology, i.e., the intention to use the new product is formed with the awareness that the basic product has to be used.

It remains an empirical question whether differentiating *the intention to use the new technology* from *the intention to use the basic product/technology with the new technology is worthwhile,* depending on the technology and population in focus.

The applicability of the PDA-UTAUT model is not confined to robo-advisors. Technologies (with their respective basic products or technologies) that might

[4] Facilitating conditions are the "degree to which an individual believes that an organizational and technical infrastructure exists to support use of the system" as defined by Venkatesh et al. 2003.

be studied using the PDA-UTAUT model include mobile payment without bank or credit cards (smartphones with NFC-technology), digital identity cards (smartphones with NFC-technology), video games (game consoles of a specific type and generation), etc. One new technology can also depend on more than one basic product or technology, e.g., a software that requires a certain operating system (Windows 11) and the programming language Java.

Moreover, I propose a reduced version of the PDA-UTAUT model applicable to those technologies in which the basic product or technology is not necessary to adopt the new technology: the UTAUT model with exogenous path dependence. This model might be applied to those technologies for which the path dependence is caused by customer groove-in, e.g., derived from experience with a different product of the same product family. The operating systems of Microsoft and Apple provide such a groove-in, as different products with the same operating system (either from Microsoft or Apple) share important properties of the user interface. Nevertheless, stock market investment is necessary for the adoption of robo-advice and, thus, I proceed by modifying the PDA-UTAUT model, which endogenizes the basic product, to the specific case of robo-advisory services.

8.2 Deriving Research Models and Hypotheses

8.2.1 Adapting the PDA-UTAUT Model to Robo-advisor Technology

I adapt the PDA-UTAUT model to robo-advisory by drawing on the IS literature (Venkatesh et al. 2003; Belanche et al. 2019; Agarwal and Prasad 1998; Featherman and Pavlou 2003; Remund 2010). I argue that the following constructs of the conventional UTAUT should affect *the intention to use robo-advisor technology (IURA)* positively: performance expectancy, effort expectancy, interpersonal[5] as

[5] Interpersonal influence represents the normative influence of social norms, specifically word-of-mouth influence by friends, colleagues, superiors, and other prior adopters in the social environment.

well as external influence[6], and personal innovativeness[7], while perceived privacy risk[8] and financial literacy[9] are hypothesized to have a negative impact on IURA.

Moreover, drawing from the literature on stock market participation (Van Rooij et al. 2011; Keller and Siegrist 2006; Pennings and Smidts 2000), I substantiate the following effects on *the intention to invest on the stock market (IINV)*: Financial literacy and financial risk attitude[10] are assumed to raise IINV, while the ethical stance towards the stock market[11] might have a negative effect on IINV.

Note that the PDA-UTAUT model can account for independent factors' diverging direction of effects on the basic and advanced technology, e.g., financial literacy in the case of robo-advice. Diverging effects are operationalized by influencing both *the intention to adopt the basic technology* and *the intention to use the new technology*.

Based on the properties of stock market investment and robo-advisor technology, I conclude that adoption of *investment on the stock market (INV)* has a feedback effect on selected attitudes towards robo-advice, i.e., the drivers of IURA: performance and effort expectancy, external influence, and perceived privacy risk.

---

[6] External influence, which describes nonpersonal information, is considered by decision makers to make a "rational" decision, specifically media reports, expert opinions, and other nonpersonal information and corresponds to the information influence.

[7] Personal innovativeness is conceptualized by Agarwal and Prasad 1998 to describe the willingness of an individual to try out any new information technologies.

[8] Perceived privacy risk is defined as "potential loss of control over personal information, such as when information about you is used without your knowledge or permission" by Featherman and Pavlou 2003.

[9] Financial literacy is characterized as "a measure of the degree to which one understands key financial concepts and possesses the ability and confidence to manage personal finances through appropriate, short-term decision-making and sound, long-range financial planning, while mindful of life events and changing economic conditions" by Remund 2010.

[10] Financial risk attitude does not follow one single definition (see Section 3.4.3). Nevertheless, a high financial risk attitude can be equated with a low loss-aversion for financial risks.

[11] Ethical stance towards the stock market is conceptualized by Keller and Siegrist 2006 as the view that profiting from the stock market is unethical or unfair.

8.2.2 An approach to Quantify the Influence of Features on the Demand for Robo-advisory Services

My second research question *"How do features influence the demand for robo-advisory services?"* addressed supply-side effects on technology acceptance. I develop a principled process to identify product features which influence the adoption of technology. In the initial process step, a longlist of product features considering the academic, industry, and consumer literature is derived. A market overview provides evidence on the offers of product features on the market. Different criteria can be chosen to shortlist product features for further analysis. In this thesis, I shortlisted criteria based on the differences between Germany and USA, relevance to the suppliers of robo-advisory services, or connection to previous findings of this thesis. A choice-based conjoint analysis (CBC) simulates the decisions of customers regarding product features and quantifies their relative importance for customer decision making. Technological features that are identified as important by the CBC are included in an adapted UTAUT model to test their impact on technology acceptance, adoption intention, and attitudes. A comparison of the CBC results with the market overview identifies potential mismatches between supply and demand.

The supply-side effects, i.e., the impact of features/attributes on the demand for robo-advisory services, on the intention to use the fictitious "Robo 1" are investigated using the UTAUT model with exogenous path dependence.[12] This model incorporates the approach of Davis 1985 to investigate the effect of attributes. Thus, it answers to the call of Benbasat and Barki 2007 for more research on the effect of features on technology acceptance while testing the effect of path dependence on the attitudes towards robo-advisors. In addition to the constructs of the initial UTAUT model by Venkatesh et al. 2003, I added the factors trust in integrity and competence, which are assumed to positively influence emotional trust[13], which in turn is hypothesized to have a positive effect on the intention to use robo-advisory services. Additionally, empirically derived product attributes are accounted for in the choice models: The product features

[12] This reduced form of the PDA-UTAUT model was chosen because supply-side effects can only influence IURA and not the drivers of the investment on the stock market. Furthermore, as "Robo 1" is fictitious, only the intention to adopt its services, but not adoption behavior could be modeled, which is one of the main influences of path dependence.

[13] I adopt the definition of Komiak and Benbasat 2006: "Trusting beliefs are the trustor's cognitive beliefs resulting from the trustor's attributional processes. In other words, the trustee's actions are observed, and the causes are attributed to the trustee's internal trust-related characteristics (e.g., competence and integrity)."

in this study are active selection of investment, personal advice, and information on past returns. Thus, as the exact product attributes are specific to each investigation and depend on the technology (market) in focus as well as the target population, they are unspecified a priori. Hence, their expected effects on the attitudes towards robo-advisors also remain unspecified in this section. I account for individual path dependence by estimating the feedback effects of stock market investment on performance and effort expectancy as well as on trust in integrity and trust in competence.

8.3 Empirical Findings

8.3.1 Empirical Evidence on the Influence of Path Dependence on the Demand for Robo-advisory Services

The PDA-UTAUT model was developed in this thesis to account for individual path dependence (Arthur 1989; Arthur 1996) in models of technology acceptance (Davis 1985; Venkatesh et al. 2003) by introducing the adoption of a basic technology, e.g., stock market investment, as an explanatory factor for the adoption of an advanced technology, e.g., robo-advisors. This theory was tested on robo-advisors in the Chapters 4 and 7 finding evidence for path dependence:

- The adoption of the investment on the stock market has a significantly positive impact on the adoption of robo-advice both in Germany and the USA (see Chapter 4).
- The adoption of the investment on the stock market has significant effects on the attitudes towards robo-advice both in Germany and the USA. Effects could be found both in models including and not including product features (see Chapter 4 and 7), although the direction of the effects depends on the concrete sample and model involved.
- *The intention to invest on the stock market* has a significant impact on *the intention to invest using robo-advisors* both in Germany and the USA. This effect is relatively stronger for non-investors than investors and, due to their higher share of non-investors, for Germans than for Americans (see Chapter 4). Thus, the importance of the investment decision is expected to decrease when the market matures.

- Accounting for path dependence increases the goodness-of-fit of the model even when accounting for the degrees of freedom. The goodness-of-fit of *the PDA-UTAUT model* is considerably higher than the goodness-of-fit of *the UTAUT model with exogenous path dependence*. The goodness-of-fit of *the UTAUT model with exogenous path dependence* is again markedly higher than the goodness-of-fit of *the traditional UTAUT model* (see Chapter 4).

The results of Chapter 4 provide significant insights into the use of adapted PDA-UTAUT models. These models are instrumental in disentangling the opposing effects of various independent factors on the adoption of both basic and advanced technologies. Specifically, the study found that financial literacy in both Germany and the USA, income in the USA, and gender in Germany influence *the intention to use robo-advisor technology (IURA)* and *the intention to invest (IINV)* in divergent ways. These diverging effects, which can only be modeled by accounting for individual path dependence, can explain the unsolved puzzle in the literature why financial literacy was found to have an overall negative effect on the intention to adopt robo-advisors (Fan and Chatterjee 2020; Todd and Seay 2020), although it was also found to increase stock market participation (Van Rooij et al. 2011; Lusardi and Mitchell 2011). Furthermore, the absence of a significant effect of gender in recent studies on the adoption of robo-advice (Belanche et al. 2019; Fan and Chatterjee 2020; Todd and Seay 2020; Wu and Gao 2021) can (at least in Germany) be explained by a positive effect of female gender on IURA and a negative effect on IINV potentially counteracting each other.

Testing the adapted PDA-UTAUT model with German and American survey data and the adapted UTAUT model with exogenous path dependence accounting for supply-side effects (Chapters 4 and 7) with an American sample has resulted in findings on the major drivers of the intention to use robo-advisor technology and the intention to invest. In summary, nearly all hypothesized effects proved to be statistically significant in the samples analyzed, corroborating the adjustments of the models to robo-advice in this thesis. However, many of these impacts showed only small or even negligible effect sizes.

8.3.2 Empirical Evidence on the Influence of features on the Demand for Robo-advisory Services

I have collected and compared the objective attributes of robo-advisors in Germany and the USA by attributes deemed important by the academic and financial advisory literature as well as major websites giving advice on the selection of robo-advisors (see Chapter 5). Although there are some academic comparisons between robo-advisors (Jung et al. 2018; Fisch et al. 2019; Metzler et al. 2022), to the best of my knowledge, this market overview is the most extensive and strictly principled one so far, considering both the number of objective attributes and robo-advisors included, e.g., the data of all German robo-advisors known to the author were collected. I found that American robo-advisors show notable differences compared to German robo-advisors in the following features: their average years on the market, robo-advice as well as third party costs, the offer of tax optimization, the accessibility of the advice of the robo-advisor without opening an account, information on returns achieved in the past, and investment strategies used.

A choice-based conjoint analysis (CBC) was used to determine the impact on the decision for robo-advisors of the following features: robo-advice costs p.a., third-party costs p.a., personal advice, tax optimization, ESG products, investment strategy, minimum investment amount, and information on past returns. A CBC simulates a customer's choice behavior between different product alternatives (designs) using different sets of designs. The CBC data can be analyzed using different analysis techniques: The counts-analysis relies on the number with which each robo-advisor design representing specific features is chosen to determine significant effects of the features. It confirmed the significant influence of almost all attributes on the choice of customers. A Hierarchical-Bayes-analysis (HB) builds aggregates of individual consumers' preferences and, thus, allows to derive preferred attribute levels as well as the relative importance of attributes. The HB found minimum amount of investment, robo-advice costs p.a., and third-party costs p.a. to be the most important attributes both in Germany and the USA. A latent class analysis revealed customer segments within the German, the American, and a pooled sample. Customer segments can mainly be differentiated by their focus on price and non-price features. A willingness to pay analysis (WTP) quantified the increase in robo-advisor costs that participants are willing to accept to avail a certain feature of a robo-advisor.

This thesis closed an evident research gap concerning the influence of attributes on the adoption of robo-advisor technology using a principled process as described above in Section 8.2.2. The most promising attributes were tested in a UTAUT model with exogenous path dependence adapted to robo-advisors accounting for supply-side effects with the following results: Active selection of investment and personal advice were shown to positively influence the intention to use "Robo 1" through the trust constructs. This finding provides preliminary evidence that trust might be a major path for the effect of features on the acceptance of technologies in fields which are adjacent to robo-advice, e.g., banking. Hence, researchers investigating the role of features on the adoption of technologies might consider including trust constructs in their models.

On the other hand, I found no evidence for a significant effect of information on past returns. This finding contrasts with unverified proposals that information on past returns would increase the number of robo-advisor users (Belanche et al. 2019) and promote robo-advisors' competence (Wu and Gao 2021). Thus, this serves as a reminder to be cautious when hypothesizing relationships between features and attitudes without conducting empirical research.

8.4 Practical Implications Drawn from the Empirical Findings

8.4.1 Implications for Suppliers of Robo-advisory Services

This thesis has provided ample evidence that individual path dependence based on the investment on the stock market influences the adoption of robo-advice (Chapter 4) as well as the attitude towards robo-advice (Chapters 4 and 7) providing suppliers of robo-advisory services with a starting point for their customer segmentation. Path dependence affects the relative importance of the decision for the robo-advisor technology and for stock market investments: While the technology is relatively more important to investors, the stock market investment is relatively more important to non-investors. Thus, targeting non-investors might require communicating the benefits of stock market investments in addition to marketing the robo-advisor technology.[14] Furthermore, the latent class analysis conducted with the CBC data revealed that customer segments in the USA are correlated with path dependence: The customer segment with a lower price sensitivity prioritizing product features consisted mostly of investors, while the customer segment with a higher price sensitivity comprised mostly non-investors.

A comparison of the market overview of robo-advisor features and the results of the CBC (Chapters 5 and 6) reveals one mismatch between supply and demand in Germany: The German market combines relatively high prices for robo-advice—prices are approximately twice as high as in the USA—with price sensitive customers. Suppliers of robo-advisory services in Germany might react

[14] The share of investors and non-investors differs between countries. While 58% (as of 2022 according to Saad and Jones 2022 from Gallup) of the US population are investors, only 17.1% of Germans invest on the stock market (as of 2021 according to Deutsches Aktieninstitut 2022).

to this mismatch by lowering their prices to increase their market share as well as the overall market size.

The latent class analysis has provided evidence that the American market harbors a customer segment, mostly comprising investors, with a limited concern for low prices of robo-advisory services. Thus, depending on the customer segment that they are catering to, American suppliers of robo-advisory services might profit from increasing their prices in the range of 0–2% of robo-advice costs p.a. tested in the CBC study and currently charged by robo-advisors in Germany and the USA. As steep cost increases alone might not be popular, suppliers of robo-advisory services might combine them with the introduction of new features.

The other customer segment comprising the American market, mostly including non-investors, is more price conscious. Although this customer segment also prefers low third-party prices, the impact of robo-advice costs is larger, especially for third-party prices between 0–1%. This might provide some suppliers of robo-advisory services with the opportunity to shift direct robo-advice costs to third-party costs. This can be achieved by using their own products for investment purposes, as already done by Vanguard Digital Advisor, or negotiate kickbacks with partners offering ETFs.

The features active selection of investment and personal advice influenced the intention use robo-advisor technology through trust constructs. Thus, suppliers and designers of robo-advisory services might consider consumers' trust beliefs when evaluating existing or new features of their robo-advisors.

The willingness to pay analysis (WTP) can serve as a starting point for suppliers of robo-advisory services to compare their internal costs for the introduction of a feature to the implementable increase in price. Furthermore, suppliers of robo-advisory services might consider segment-specific offers if the WTP among different customer groups diverges. Nevertheless, suppliers of robo-advisory services are advised to conduct representative market studies targeted to their requirements. Both the theoretical and empirical findings of this thesis might serve as a valid starting point.

8.4.2 Implications for Governmental Institutions

Some major countries like the USA have a longstanding history of promoting stock market participation for retirement planning, e.g., through 401(k) accounts[15]. Other major countries like Germany show interest in promoting stock market participation to add funded elements to the traditional pay-as-you-go pension schemes to counteract demographic change and achieve returns on the global financial markets. Thus, the empirical findings of this thesis are relevant for governmental institutions for their promotion of stock market participation.

The acceptance of the advanced technology of robo-advisory is shaped by path dependence, i.e., the individual decision to invest on the stock market. Thus, robo-advisor technology will not necessarily solve a low stock market participation, as the low stock market participation itself influences the adoption of robo-advice negatively. Therefore, the expectations towards robo-advice to increase the number of stock market participants should not be excessive. Nevertheless, the positive impact might be more pronounced for women (in Germany) than for men as shown in Section 8.3.1.

Thus, governmental institutions might consider influencing the intention to invest on the stock market directly. This thesis has provided levers to do so: financial literacy, education, the ethical stance towards stocks, and the financial risk attitude. While the ethical stance towards stocks and the financial risk attitude are based on personal values and, therefore, might show idiosyncratic differences between cultures, the financial literacy and education are measures of competence. Thus, they can be targeted directly in/with (governmental) education programs to increase private investments on the stock market contributing to a diversified retirement planning.

8.5 Limitations and Future Research

In this thesis, I have developed sound theoretical models (the PDA-UTAUT model and its adaption to robo-advisors) and applied appropriate econometric instruments (PLS regressions, market overviews, and CBC analyses) to the analysis of consumer preferences and behavior regarding robo-advisors. Most empirical findings of the thesis rely on parameter estimates as well as on statistical significance. All survey data were collected from the online platforms Amazon MTurk and Clickworker and, therefore, do represent convenience samples. Hence, the arguments based on statistical significance are subject to the reservation that they rely on data suffering from over- and undercoverage (or outright omission) of population segments and a self-selection of participants. Correcting for these

[15] A 401(k) account is an employer-sponsored, defined-contribution, personal pension account.

biases, e.g., by applying propensity scores, would call for both, an awareness of all confounding variables with an influence on a subject's participation in a survey and observations of these variables from participants as well as from non-participants.[16] Since neither the awareness nor the observations are usually available for these variables, a feasible remedy of sample selection issues is generally lacking and the usage of convenience samples is customary in IS research (Davis 1989; Venkatesh et al. 2003; Venkatesh et al. 2012; Belanche et al. 2019; Erjavec and Manfreda 2022; Al-Adwan et al. 2022). Nevertheless, I tried to approximate a representative sample by conducting the studies with generous sample sizes and from the relatively diverse pool of online surveys.[17] Nonetheless, any overconfident inferential reasoning should be avoided, and I do emphasize the exploratory nature of my empirical findings.

A more accurate understanding of consumer behavior promises higher profits for robo-advisors and insights for governmental institutions to foster the accessibility of financial markets for private investors. Furthermore, the robo-advisor market is very dynamic and, especially in Germany, not mature yet. Thus, I hope that robo-advisor companies and/or governmental institutions, having the financial means to conduct representative and longitudinal studies, might have an intrinsic interest in conducting their own empirical research drawing from the theoretical and empirical methods presented in this thesis. These methods might be advanced by further reliable evidence.

I have argued that the individual path dependence is vital to understanding mobile payment, mobile identity cards, and other technologies. Thus, I am convinced that an application of the PDA-UTAUT model to these technologies will also expand the understanding of the adoption of these technologies.

---

[16] See Hirschauer et al. 2022, Section 4.4, for an in-depth discussion on the statistical issues of convenience sampling.

[17] Note that some empirical IS research is based exclusively on students' responses (Morana et al. 2020; Hodge et al. 2021).

References

Agarwal, R., Karahanna, E., 2000. Time Flies When You're Having Fun: Cognitive Absorption and Beliefs about Information Technology Usage. MIS Quarterly 24, 665. https://doi.org/10.2307/3250951

Agarwal, R., Prasad, J., 1998. A Conceptual and Operational Definition of Personal Innovativeness in the Domain of Information Technology. Information Systems Research 9, 204–215. https://doi.org/10.1287/isre.9.2.204

Agarwal, R., Prasad, J., 1997. The Role of Innovation Characteristics and Perceived Voluntariness in the Acceptance of Information Technologies. Decision Sciences 28, 557–582. https://doi.org/10.1111/j.1540-5915.1997.tb01322.x

Ajzen, I., 1991. The theory of planned behavior. Organizational Behavior and Human Decision Processes 50, 179–211. https://doi.org/10.1016/0749-5978(91)90020-T

Akaike, H., 1998. Factor Analysis and AIC, in: Parzen, E., Tanabe, K., Kitagawa, G. (Eds.), Selected Papers of Hirotugu Akaike, Springer Series in Statistics. Springer, New York, NY, pp. 371–386. https://doi.org/10.1007/978-1-4612-1694-0_29

Akaike, H., 1973. Information theory and an extension of the maximum likelihood principle, in: Petrov, B.N., Csaki, B.F. (Eds.), Second International Symposium on Information Theory. Academiai Kiado: Budapest.

Akerlof, G.A., 1970. The Market for "Lemons": Quality Uncertainty and the Market Mechanism. The Quarterly Journal of Economics 84, 488–500. https://doi.org/10.2307/1879431

Al-Adwan, A.S., Yaseen, H., Alsoud, A., Abousweilem, F., Al-Rahmi, W.M., 2022. Novel extension of the UTAUT model to understand continued usage intention of learning management systems: the role of learning tradition. Educ Inf Technol 27, 3567–3593. https://doi.org/10.1007/s10639-021-10758-y

Albrecht, S., Strüker, J., Reichert, S., Neumann, D., Schmid, J., Fridgen, G., 2018. Dynamics of Blockchain Implementation—A Case Study from the Energy Sector. Proceedings of the 51st Hawaii International Conference on System Sciences. URL https://scholarspace.manoa.hawaii.edu/server/api/core/bitstreams/abc4d788-862f-421c-8ac9-dc549e333585/content

Al-Jabri, I.M., Sohail, M.S., 2012. Mobile Banking Adoption: Application of Diffusion of Innovation Theory. Journal of Electronic Commerce Research Vol. 13, 379–391.

M. Horn, *Technology Acceptance, Path Dependence, and the Demand for Robo-Advisory Services*, Forschung zur Digitalisierung der Wirtschaft | Advanced Studies in Business Digitization, https://doi.org/10.1007/978-3-658-44679-6

Almenberg, J., Dreber, A., 2015. Gender, stock market participation and financial literacy. Economics Letters 137, 140–142. https://doi.org/10.1016/j.econlet.2015.10.009

Alt, R., Puschmann, T., 2012. The rise of customer-oriented banking—electronic markets are paving the way for change in the financial industry. Electronic Markets 22, 203–215. https://doi.org/10.1007/s12525-012-0106-2

Al-Tamimi, H.A.H., 2006. Factors influencing individual investor behavior: an empirical study of the UAE financial markets. Bus. Rev. 5, 225–233.

Amel-Zadeh, A., Serafeim, G., 2018. Why and How Investors Use ESG Information: Evidence from a Global Survey. Financial Analysts Journal 74, 87–103. https://doi.org/10.2469/faj.v74.n3.2

Amoroso, D.L., Magnier-Watanabe, R., 2012. Building a Research Model for Mobile Wallet Consumer Adoption: The Case of Mobile Suica in Japan. J. theor. appl. electron. commer. res. 7, 13–14. https://doi.org/10.4067/S0718-18762012000100008

Anduiza, E., Galais, C., 2017. Answering Without Reading: IMCs and Strong Satisficing in Online Surveys. International Journal of Public Opinion Research 29, 497–519. https://doi.org/10.1093/ijpor/edw007

Apel, S., Lengauer, C., Möller, B., Kästner, C., 2008. An Algebra for Features and Feature Composition, in: Meseguer, J., Roşu, G. (Eds.), Algebraic Methodology and Software Technology, Lecture Notes in Computer Science. Springer Berlin Heidelberg, Berlin, Heidelberg, pp. 36–50. https://doi.org/10.1007/978-3-540-79980-1_4

Arrow, K.J., 1971. Essays in the theory of risk-bearing, Markham economics series. Markham Pub. Co, Chicago.

Arthur, W.B., 1996. Increasing Returns and the New World of Business. Harvard Business Review 11.

Arthur, W.B., 1989. Competing Technologies, Increasing Returns, and Lock-In by Historical Events. The Economic Journal 99, 116. https://doi.org/10.2307/2234208

Aust, F., Diedenhofen, B., Ullrich, S., Musch, J., 2013. Seriousness checks are useful to improve data validity in online research. Behav Res 45, 527–535. https://doi.org/10.3758/s13428-012-0265-2

Aversi, R., 1999. Demand dynamics with socially evolving preferences. Industrial and Corporate Change 8, 353–408. https://doi.org/10.1093/icc/8.2.353

Bailey, A.A., Pentina, I., Mishra, A.S., Ben Mimoun, M.S., 2017. Mobile payments adoption by US consumers: an extended TAM. International Journal of Retail & Distribution Management 45, 626–640. https://doi.org/10.1108/IJRDM-08-2016-0144

Balonier, S., Di Dio, D., Fey, G., 2022. Deutschland und die Aktie. Deutsches Aktieninstitut. URL https://www.dai.de/fileadmin/user_upload/220119_Aktionaerszahlen_2021_Deutsches_Aktieninstitut.pdf

Barnes, W., Gartland, M., Stack, M., 2004. Old Habits Die Hard:Path Dependency and Behavioral Lock-in. Journal of Economic Issues 38, 371–377. https://doi.org/10.1080/00213624.2004.11506696

Beer, J.M., Prakash, A., Mitzner, T.L., Rogers, W.A., 2011. Understanding Robot Acceptance. Georgia Institute of Technology School of Psychology. URL https://smartech.gatech.edu/bitstream/handle/1853/39672/HFA-TR-1103-RobotAcceptance.pdf

Belanche, D., Casaló, L.V., Flavián, C., 2019. Artificial Intelligence in FinTech: understanding robo-advisors adoption among customers. IMDS 119, 1411–1430. https://doi.org/10.1108/IMDS-08-2018-0368

Ben-Akiva, M., McFadden, D., Gärling, T., Gopinath, D., Walker, J., Bolduc, D., Börsch-Supan, A., Delquié, P., Larichev, O., Morikawa, T., Polydoropoulou, A., Rao, V., 1999. Extended Framework for Modeling Choice Behavior. Marketing Letters 10, 187–203. https://doi.org/10.1023/A:1008046730291

Ben-Akiva, M., Mcfadden, D., Train, K., Walker, J., Bhat, C., Bierlaire, M., Bolduc, D., Boersch-Supan, A., Brownstone, D., Bunch, D.S., Daly, A., De Palma, A., Gopinath, D., Karlstrom, A., Munizaga, M.A., 2002. Hybrid Choice Models: Progress and Challenges. Marketing Letters 13, 163–175. https://doi.org/10.1023/A:1020254301302

Benbasat, I., Barki, H., 2007. Quo vadis TAM? Journal of the Association for Information Systems 8, 7.

Bengtsson et al., 1999. The Impact of Anthropomorphic Interfaces on Influence, Understanding, and Credibility. Hawaii International Conference on System Sciences 15.

Benitez, J., Henseler, J., Castillo, A., Schuberth, F., 2020. How to perform and report an impactful analysis using partial least squares: Guidelines for confirmatory and explanatory IS research. Information & Management 57, 103168. https://doi.org/10.1016/j.im.2019.05.003

Benson, A., 2022. 11 Best Robo-Advisors of February 2022—NerdWallet [WWW Document]. NerdWallet. URL https://www.nerdwallet.com/best/investing/robo-advisors (accessed 2.17.22).

Benson, A., 2021. 12 Best Robo-Advisors of March 2021 [WWW Document]. NerdWallet. URL https://www.nerdwallet.com/best/investing/robo-advisors (accessed 3.23.21).

Berinsky, A.J., Margolis, M.F., Sances, M.W., 2014. Separating the Shirkers from the Workers? Making Sure Respondents Pay Attention on Self-Administered Surveys: Separating the Shirkers from the Workers? American Journal of Political Science 58, 739–753. https://doi.org/10.1111/ajps.12081

Bertaut, C.C., 1998. Stockholding Behavior of U.S. Households: Evidence from the 1983–1989 Survey of Consumer Finances. The Review of Economics and Statistics 13.

Beutel, M., 2022. Robo Advisor Performance 47 Live-Depots (01/22) Ø 3,50%. URL https://geldanlage-digital.de/robo-advisor/performance/ (accessed 2.17.22).

Beuth Verlag, 2022a. DIN EN ISO 9241-110:2020-10, Ergonomie der Mensch-System-Interaktion_- Teil_110: Interaktionsprinzipien (ISO_9241-110:2020); Deutsche Fassung EN_ISO_9241-110:2020. Beuth Verlag GmbH. https://doi.org/10.31030/3147467

Beuth Verlag, 2022b. DIN EN ISO 9241-210:2020-03, Ergonomie der Mensch-System-Interaktion_- Teil_210: Menschzentrierte Gestaltung interaktiver Systeme (ISO_9241-210:2019); Deutsche Fassung EN_ISO_9241-210:2019. Beuth Verlag GmbH. https://doi.org/10.31030/3104744

Bhattacherjee, A., 2001. Understanding Information Systems Continuance: An Expectation-Confirmation Model. MIS Quarterly 25, 351. https://doi.org/10.2307/3250921

Bhattacherjee, A., 2000. Acceptance of e-commerce services: the case of electronic brokerages. IEEE Trans. Syst., Man, Cybern. A 30, 411–420. https://doi.org/10.1109/3468.852435

biallo.de, 2022. Robo-Advisor im Performance-Vergleich | 02/2022 [WWW Document]. URL https://www.biallo.de/robo-advisor/ratgeber/performance-vergleich/ (accessed 2.17.22).

Bigné-Alcañiz, E., Ruiz-Mafé, C., Aldás-Manzano, J., Sanz-Blas, S., 2008. Influence of online shopping information dependency and innovativeness on internet shopping adoption. Online Information Review 32, 648–667. https://doi.org/10.1108/14684520810914025

Bonaccio, S., Dalal, R.S., 2006. Advice taking and decision-making: An integrative literature review, and implications for the organizational sciences. Organizational Behavior and Human Decision Processes 101, 127–151. https://doi.org/10.1016/j.obhdp.2006.07.001

Bourgarit, D., Plateau, J., 2005. Quand l'aluminium valait de l'or : peut-on reconnaître un aluminium «chimique» d'un aluminium «électrolytique»? archeosciences 95–105. https://doi.org/10.4000/archeosciences.560

Bozdogan, H., 1987. Model selection and Akaike's Information Criterion (AIC): The general theory and its analytical extensions. Psychometrika 52, 345–370. https://doi.org/10.1007/BF02294361

Brancheau, J.C., Wetherbe, J.C., 1990. The Adoption of Spreadsheet Software: Testing Innovation Diffusion Theory in the Context of End-User Computing. Information Systems Research 1, 115–143. https://doi.org/10.1287/isre.1.2.115

Brazell, J.D., Diener, C.G., Karniouchina, E., Moore, W.L., Séverin, V., Uldry, P.-F., 2006. The no-choice option and dual response choice designs. Market Lett 17, 255–268. https://doi.org/10.1007/s11002-006-7943-8

Brinberg, D., Durand, J., 1983. Eating at Fast-Food Restaurants: An Analysis Using Two Behavioral Intention Models. J Appl Social Pyschol 13, 459–472. https://doi.org/10.1111/j.1559-1816.1983.tb02330.x

Brokervergleich, 2015. Robo-Advisor Vergleich 2021 | Über 1.200 Erfahrungen und Bewertungen | Wer ist der beste Robo-Advisor? | Was ist ein Robo-Advisor (Definition) [WWW Document]. URL https://www.brokervergleich.de/robo-advisor/ (accessed 3.23.21).

Buhrs, H., 2021. Robo-Advisor Test: Die besten digitalen Anlagehelfer im Vergleich—Finanztip [WWW Document]. URL https://www.finanztip.de/robo-advisor/ (accessed 3.23.21).

Carroll, D.J., 1972. , in: Shepard, R.N., Romney, A.K., Nerlove, S.B. (Eds.), Individual Differences and Multidimensional Scaling. Seminar Press, New York, pp. 105–155.

Cenfetelli, R.T., Bassellier, G., 2009. Interpretation of Formative Measurement in Information Systems Research. MIS Quarterly 33, 689–707. https://doi.org/10.2307/20650323

CFA, Scorpio, 2017. The value of premium wealth management. URL https://www.cfainstitute.org/-/media/documents/support/membership/value-of-premium-wealth-management.ashx (accessed 3.22.21).

Chan, C., Chan, A., 2011. Attitude toward wealth management services: Implications for international banks in China. Intl Jnl of Bank Marketing 29, 272–292. https://doi.org/10.1108/02652321111145925

Chen, K., Zhang, W., Haiyan Zhao, Hong Mei, 2005. An approach to constructing feature models based on requirements clustering, in: 13th IEEE International Conference on Requirements Engineering (RE'05). Presented at the 13th IEEE International Conference on Requirements Engineering (RE'05), IEEE, Paris, France, pp. 31–40. https://doi.org/10.1109/RE.2005.9

Cheng, X., Guo, F., Chen, J., Li, K., Zhang, Y., Gao, P., 2019. Exploring the Trust Influencing Mechanism of Robo-Advisor Service: A Mixed Method Approach. Sustainability 11, 4917. https://doi.org/10.3390/su11184917

Cheng, Y.-M., 2021. Will robo-advisors continue? Roles of task-technology fit, network externalities, gratifications and flow experience in facilitating continuance intention. K 50, 1751–1783. https://doi.org/10.1108/K-03-2020-0185

Cheng, Y.-M., 2019a. How does task-technology fit influence cloud-based e-learning continuance and impact? Education + Training 61, 480–499. https://doi.org/10.1108/ET-09-2018-0203

Cheng, Y.-M., 2019b. A hybrid model for exploring the antecedents of cloud ERP continuance: Roles of quality determinants and task-technology fit. International Journal of Web Information Systems 15, 215–235. https://doi.org/10.1108/IJWIS-07-2018-0056

Cheng, Y.-M., 2018. What drives cloud ERP continuance? An integrated view. JEIM 31, 724–750. https://doi.org/10.1108/JEIM-02-2018-0043

Cheng, Y.-M., 2014a. Extending the expectation-confirmation model with quality and flow to explore nurses' continued blended e-learning intention. Information Technology & People 27, 230–258. https://doi.org/10.1108/ITP-01-2013-0024

Cheng, Y.-M., 2014b. What Drives Nurses' Blended e-Learning Continuance Intention? Journal of Educational Technology & Society 17, 203–215.

Chiang, H.-S., 2013. Continuous usage of social networking sites: The effect of innovation and gratification attributes. Online Information Review 37, 851–871. https://doi.org/10.1108/OIR-08-2012-0133

Chowney, P.E., Fragnière, E., 2014. Regaining Loyalty in Wealth Management: An Empirical Behavioural Inquiry in the Geneva Private Banking Sector. IJSSH 4, 254–259. https://doi.org/10.7763/IJSSH.2014.V4.358

Christensen, C.M., 1997. The innovator's dilemma: when new technologies cause great firms to fail, The management of innovation and change series. Harvard Business School Press, Boston, Mass.

Classen, A., Heymans, P., Schobbens, P.-Y., 2008. What's in a Feature: A Requirements Engineering Perspective, in: Fiadeiro, J.L., Inverardi, P. (Eds.), Fundamental Approaches to Software Engineering, Lecture Notes in Computer Science. Springer Berlin Heidelberg, Berlin, Heidelberg, pp. 16–30. https://doi.org/10.1007/978-3-540-78743-3_2

Cohen, J., 1988. Statistical power analysis for the behavioral sciences, 2nd ed. ed. L. Erlbaum Associates, Hillsdale, N.J.

Cohen, S.H., 1997. Perfect Union: CBC Marries the Best of Conjoint and Discrete Choice Models. Marketing Research 12–17.

Cohen, W.M., Levinthal, D.A., 1990. Absorptive Capacity: A New Perspective on Learning and Innovation. Administrative Science Quarterly 35, 128–152. https://doi.org/10.2307/2393553

Collier, J.E., Kimes, S.E., 2013. Only If It Is Convenient: Understanding How Convenience Influences Self-Service Technology Evaluation. Journal of Service Research 16, 39–51. https://doi.org/10.1177/1094670512458454

Compeau, D.R., Higgins, C.A., 1995. Computer Self-Efficacy: Development of a Measure and Initial Test. MIS Quarterly 19, 189. https://doi.org/10.2307/249688

Cramer, H., Evers, V., Ramlal, S., van Someren, M., Rutledge, L., Stash, N., Aroyo, L., Wielinga, B., 2008. The effects of transparency on trust in and acceptance of a content-based art recommender. User Model User-Adap Inter 18, 455–496. https://doi.org/10.1007/s11257-008-9051-3

Csikszentmihalyi, M., 1975. Beyond boredom and anxiety. Jossey-Bass Publishers, San Francisco.

D'Acunto, F., Prabhala, N., Rossi, A.G., 2019. The Promises and Pitfalls of Robo-Advising. The Review of Financial Studies 32, 1983–2020. https://doi.org/10.1093/rfs/hhz014

D'Acunto, F., Rossi, A.G., 2021. New Frontiers of Robo-Advising: Consumption, Saving, Debt Management, and Taxes (SSRN Scholarly Paper No. ID 3778244). Social Science Research Network, Rochester, NY. https://doi.org/10.2139/ssrn.3778244

David, P.A., 2001. Path dependence, its critics and the quest for "historical economics," in: Garrouste, P., Ioannides, S., Economy, E.A. for E.P. (Eds.), Evolution and Path Dependence in Economic Ideas: Past and Present. Edward Elgar Publishing, pp. 15–40.

David, P.A., 1985. Clio and the Economics of QWERTY. The American Economic Review 75, 332–337.

Davidson, A.R., Jaccard, J.J., 1979. Variables that moderate the attitude—behavior relation: Results of a longitudinal survey. Journal of Personality and Social Psychology 37, 1364–1376. https://doi.org/10.1037/0022-3514.37.8.1364

Davis, F.D., 1989. Perceived Usefulness, Perceived Ease of Use, and User Acceptance of Information Technology. MIS Quarterly 13, 319. https://doi.org/10.2307/249008

Davis, F.D., 1985. A technology acceptance model for empirically testing new end-user information systems: Theory and results. Massachusetts Institute of Technology.

Davis, F.D., Bagozzi, R.P., Warshaw, P.R., 1992. Extrinsic and Intrinsic Motivation to Use Computers in the Workplace. Journal of Applied Social Psychology 22, 1111–1132. https://doi.org/10.1111/j.1559-1816.1992.tb00945.x

Davis, F.D., Bagozzi, R.P., Warshaw, P.R., 1989. User Acceptance of Computer Technology: A Comparison of Two Theoretical Models. Management Science 35, 982–1003. https://doi.org/10.1287/mnsc.35.8.982

Diab, D.L., Pui, S.-Y., Yankelevich, M., Highhouse, S., 2011. Lay Perceptions of Selection Decision Aids in US and Non-US Samples: Selection Decision Aids. International Journal of Selection and Assessment 19, 209–216. https://doi.org/10.1111/j.1468-2389.2011.00548.x

Dijkstra, T.K., Henseler, J., 2015. Consistent Partial Least Squares Path Modeling. MIS Quarterly 39, 297–316.

Dimmock, S.G., Kouwenberg, R., 2010. Loss-aversion and household portfolio choice. Journal of Empirical Finance 17, 441–459. https://doi.org/10.1016/j.jempfin.2009.11.005

Dubé, J.-P., Hitsch, G.J., Rossi, P.E., 2010. State dependence and alternative explanations for consumer inertia. The RAND Journal of Economics 41, 417–445. https://doi.org/10.1111/j.1756-2171.2010.00106.x

Engel, J.F., Blackwell, R.D., Kollat, D.T., 1978. Consumer behavior, 3d ed. ed, The Dryden Press series in marketing. Dryden Press, Hinsdale, Ill.

Engel, J.F., Blackwell, R.D., Miniard, P.W., 1990. Consumer behavior, 6th ed. ed. Dryden Press, Chicago.

Epperson, T., Hedges, B., Singh, U., Gabel, M., 2015. Hype vs. Reality: The Coming Waves of "Robo" Adoption. A.T. Kearney 32.

Erjavec, J., Manfreda, A., 2022. Online shopping adoption during COVID-19 and social isolation: Extending the UTAUT model with herd behavior. Journal of Retailing and Consumer Services 65, 102867. https://doi.org/10.1016/j.jretconser.2021.102867

EY, 2019. 2019 Global Wealth Management Research Report.

Faff, R., Mulino, D., Chai, D., 2008. On the Linkage between Financial Risk Tolerance and Risk Aversion. J Financial Res 31, 1–23. https://doi.org/10.1111/j.1475-6803.2008.00229.x

Faloon, M., Scherer, B., 2017. Individualization of Robo-Advice. The Journal of Wealth Management Summer 2017 20, 30–36. https://doi.org/10.3905/jwm.2017.20.1.030

Fan, L., Chatterjee, S., 2020. The Utilization of Robo-Advisors by Individual Investors: An Analysis Using Diffusion of Innovation and Information Search Frameworks. Journal of Financial Counseling and Planning 31, 130–145. https://doi.org/10.1891/JFCP-18-00078

Featherman, M.S., Pavlou, P.A., 2003. Predicting e-services adoption: a perceived risk facets perspective. International Journal of Human-Computer Studies 59, 451–474. https://doi.org/10.1016/S1071-5819(03)00111-3

Fey, G., Stämmler, M., 2023. Deutschland kann Aktie! Deutsches Aktieninstitut. URL https://www.dai.de/fileadmin/user_upload/230117_Deutsches_Aktieninstitut_Aktionaerszahlen_2022.pdf (accessed 3.12.23).

Figà-Talamanca, G., Tanzi, P.M., D'Urzo, E., 2022. Robo-advisor acceptance: Do gender and generation matter? PLoS ONE 17, e0269454. https://doi.org/10.1371/journal.pone.0269454

Fisch, J.E., Labouré, M., Turner, J.A., 2019. The Emergence of the Robo-Advisor, in: The Disruptive Impact of FinTech on Retirement Systems. Oxford University Press, pp. 13–37. https://doi.org/10.1093/oso/9780198845553.003.0002

Fishbein, M., Ajzen, I., 1975. Belief, attitude, intention and behaviour: An introduction to theory and research. Reading, MA: Addison-Wesley.

Fisher, B., 2020. Contactless Competition and Digital Limitations Stifle Proximity Mobile Payment Growth in the UK [WWW Document]. eMarketer. URL https://www.emarketer.com/content/contactless-competition-and-digital-limitations-stifle-proximity-mobile-payment-growth-in-the-uk?ecid=NL1014

Flavián, C., Pérez-Rueda, A., Belanche, D., Casaló, L.V., 2022. Intention to use analytical artificial intelligence (AI) in services—the effect of technology readiness and awareness. JOSM 33, 293–320. https://doi.org/10.1108/JOSM-10-2020-0378

Fornell, C., Larcker, D.F., 1981. Evaluating Structural Equation Models with Unobservable Variables and Measurement Error. Journal of Marketing Research 18, 39–50. https://doi.org/10.1177/002224378101800104

Gartner, 2022. Number of smartphones sold to end users worldwide from 2007 to 2021 (in million units) [WWW Document]. Statista. URL https://www.statista.com/statistics/263437/global-smartphone-sales-to-end-users-since-2007/ (accessed 1.3.23).

Gastineau, G.L., 2002. The exchange-traded funds manual, Frank J. Fabozzi series. J. Wiley, New York.

Gefen, Karahanna, Straub, 2003. Trust and TAM in Online Shopping: An Integrated Model. MIS Quarterly 27, 51. https://doi.org/10.2307/30036519

Goodhue, D.L., 1995. Understanding User Evaluations of Information Systems. Management Science 41, 1827–1844. https://doi.org/10.1287/mnsc.41.12.1827

Goodhue, D.L., Thompson, R.L., 1995. Task-Technology Fit and Individual Performance. MIS Quarterly 19, 213. https://doi.org/10.2307/249689

Green, P.E., 1984. Hybrid Models for Conjoint Analysis: An Expository Review. Journal of Marketing Research 21, 155–169. https://doi.org/10.1177/002224378402100204

Green, P.E., Krieger, A.M., Wind, Y., 2001. Thirty Years of Conjoint Analysis: Reflections and Prospects, in: Wind, Y., Green, P.E. (Eds.), Marketing Research and Modeling: Progress and Prospects: A Tribute to Paul E. Green, International Series in Quantitative Marketing. Springer US, Boston, MA, pp. 117–139. https://doi.org/10.1007/978-0-387-28692-1_6

Green, P.E., Rao, V.R., 1971. Conjoint Measurement- for Quantifying Judgmental Data. Journal of Marketing Research 8, 355–363. https://doi.org/10.1177/002224377100800312

Green, P.E., Schaffer, C.M., Patterson, K.M., 1991. A Validation Study of Sawtooth Software's Adaptive Conjoint Analysis (ACA), in: Metegrano, M. (Ed.), Sawtooth Software. Presented at the Proceedings of the Sawtooth Software Conference 1991, Sun Valley, Idaho.

Green, P.E., Srinivasan, V., 1990. Conjoint Analysis in Marketing: New Developments with Implications for Research and Practice. Journal of Marketing 54, 3–19. https://doi.org/10.1177/002224299005400402

Green, P.E., Srinivasan, V., 1978. Conjoint Analysis in Consumer Research: Issues and Outlook. Journal of Consumer Research 5, 103. https://doi.org/10.1086/208721

Guiso, L., Haliassos, M., Jappelli, T., 2003. Household stockholding in Europe: where do we stand and where do we go? Economic Policy 18, 123–170. https://doi.org/10.1111/1468-0327.00104

Guiso, L., Paiella, M., 2008. Risk Aversion, Wealth, and Background Risk. Journal of the European Economic Association 6, 1109–1150. https://doi.org/10.1162/JEEA.2008.6.6.1109

Haaker, T., de Vos, H., Bouwman, H., 2006. Mobile Service Bundles: The Example of Navigation Services. Elec. Markets 17, 20–28. https://doi.org/10.1080/10196780601136757

Hair, J.F., Black, W.C., Babin, B.J., Anderson, R.E., Tatham, R., 2010. Multivariate Data Analysis. Pearson Prentice Hall, New Jersey.

Hair, J.F., Hult, G.T.M., Ringle, C.M., Sarstedt, M., Thiele, K.O., 2017. Mirror, mirror on the wall: a comparative evaluation of composite-based structural equation modeling methods. J. of the Acad. Mark. Sci. 45, 616–632. https://doi.org/10.1007/s11747-017-0517-x

Henseler, J., Ringle, C.M., Sarstedt, M., 2015. A new criterion for assessing discriminant validity in variance-based structural equation modeling. J. of the Acad. Mark. Sci. 43, 115–135. https://doi.org/10.1007/s11747-014-0403-8

Herr, P.M., Kardes, F.R., Kim, J., 1991. Effects of Word-of-Mouth and Product-Attribute Information on Persuasion: An Accessibility-Diagnosticity Perspective. Journal of Consumer Research 17, 454. https://doi.org/10.1086/208570

Hirschauer, N., Grüner, S., Mußhoff, O., 2022. Fundamentals of Statistical Inference: What is the Meaning of Random Error?, SpringerBriefs in Applied Statistics and Econometrics. Springer International Publishing, Cham. https://doi.org/10.1007/978-3-030-99091-6

Hodge, F.D., Mendoza, K.I., Sinha, R.K., 2021. The Effect of Humanizing Robo-Advisors on Investor Judgments. Contemp Account Res 38, 770–792. https://doi.org/10.1111/1911-3846.12641

Hofstede, G.H., Hofstede, G.J., Minkov, M., 2010. Cultures and organizations: software of the mind: intercultural cooperation and its importance for survival, 3rd ed. ed. McGraw-Hill, New York.

Hu, R., Pu, P., 2009. Acceptance issues of personality-based recommender systems, in: Proceedings of the Third ACM Conference on Recommender Systems - RecSys '09. Presented at the the third ACM conference, ACM Press, New York, New York, USA, p. 221. https://doi.org/10.1145/1639714.1639753

Huber, J., Hansen, D., 1987. Testing the Impact of Dimensional Complexity and Affective Differences of Paired Concepts in Adaptive Conjoint Analysis, Advances in Consumer Research. Association for Consumer Research, Provo, Utah.

Jiang, G., Deng, W., 2011. An empirical analysis of factors influencing the adoption of Mobile Instant Messaging in China. IJMC 9, 563. https://doi.org/10.1504/IJMC.2011.042777

Johnson, R., Huber, J., Bacon, L., 2003. Adaptive Choice-Based Conjoint. Presented at the 2003 Sawtooth Software Conference Proceedings, Sequim, WA.

Johnson, R.M., 1987. Adaptive Conjoint Analysis, in: Proceedings of the Sawtooth Software Conference on Perceptual Mapping, Conjoint Analysis, and Computer Interviewing 1987. Sun Valley, Idaho.

Johnson, R.M., 1974. Trade-Off Analysis of Consumer Values. Journal of Marketing Research 11, 121–127. https://doi.org/10.1177/002224377401100201

Jung, D., Dorner, V., Weinhardt, C., Pusmaz, H., 2018. Designing a robo-advisor for risk-averse, low-budget consumers. Electronic Markets 28, 367–380. https://doi.org/10.1007/s12525-017-0279-9

Kahneman, D., Tversky, A., 1979. Prospect Theory: An Analysis of Decision under Risk Econometrica, 263–292.

Kang, K.C., Cohen, S.G., Hess, J.A., Novak, W.E., Peterson, A.S., 1990. Feature-Oriented Domain Analysis (FODA) Feasibility Study: Defense Technical Information Center, Fort Belvoir, VA. https://doi.org/10.21236/ADA235785

Karahanna, E., Straub, D.W., Chervany, N.L., 1999. Information Technology Adoption Across Time: A Cross-Sectional Comparison of Pre-Adoption and Post-Adoption Beliefs. MIS Quarterly 23, 183. https://doi.org/10.2307/249751

Keller, C., Siegrist, M., 2006. Investing in stocks: The influence of financial risk attitude and values-related money and stock market attitudes. Journal of Economic Psychology 27, 285–303. https://doi.org/10.1016/j.joep.2005.07.002

Kennedy, B., Funk, C., 2016. 28% of Americans are 'strong' early adopters of technology. Pew Research Center. URL https://www.pewresearch.org/fact-tank/2016/07/12/28-of-americans-are-strong-early-adopters-of-technology/ (accessed 1.3.23).

Kilic, M., Heinrich, P., Schwabe, G., 2015. Coercing into Completeness in Financial Advisory Service Encounters, in: Proceedings of the 18th ACM Conference on Computer Supported Cooperative Work & Social Computing. Presented at the CSCW '15: Computer Supported Cooperative Work and Social Computing, ACM, Vancouver BC Canada, pp. 1324–1335. https://doi.org/10.1145/2675133.2675289

Kock, N., 2015. Common Method Bias in PLS-SEM: A Full Collinearity Assessment Approach. International Journal of e-Collaboration 11, 1–10. https://doi.org/10.4018/ijec.2015100101

Kock, N., Lynn, G., 2012. Lateral Collinearity and Misleading Results in Variance-Based SEM: An Illustration and Recommendations. JAIS 13, 546–580. https://doi.org/10.17705/1jais.00302

Komiak, S.X., Benbasat, I., 2006. The Effects of Personalization and Familiarity on Trust and Adoption of Recommendation Agents. MIS Quarterly 30, 941. https://doi.org/10.2307/25148760

Komiak, S.X., Benbasat, I., 2004. Understanding Customer Trust in Agent-Mediated Electronic Commerce, Web-Mediated Electronic Commerce, and Traditional Commerce. Information Technology and Management 5, 181–207. https://doi.org/10.1023/B:ITEM.0000008081.55563.d4

Korner, V., Zimmermann, H.-D., 2000. Management of customer relationship in business media-the case of the financial industry, in: Proceedings of the 33rd Annual Hawaii International Conference on System Sciences. Presented at the HICSS33: Hawaii International Conference on System Sciences, IEEE Comput. Soc, Maui, HI, USA, p. 10. https://doi.org/10.1109/HICSS.2000.926866

Krosnick, J.A., 1991. Response strategies for coping with the cognitive demands of attitude measures in surveys. Appl. Cognit. Psychol. 5, 213–236. https://doi.org/10.1002/acp.2350050305

Lee, M.-C., 2009. Factors influencing the adoption of internet banking: An integration of TAM and TPB with perceived risk and perceived benefit. Electronic Commerce Research and Applications 8, 130–141. https://doi.org/10.1016/j.elerap.2008.11.006

Lee, M.K.O., Cheung, C.M.K., Chen, Z., 2005. Acceptance of Internet-based learning medium: the role of extrinsic and intrinsic motivation. Information & Management 42, 1095–1104. https://doi.org/10.1016/j.im.2003.10.007

Liebowitz, S.J., Margolis, S.E., 1995. Path Dependence, Lock-In, and History. The Journal of Law, Economics, and Organization 11, 205–226. https://doi.org/10.1093/oxfordjournals.jleo.a036867

Lilienthal, M., Messerschmidt, C.M., Skiera, B., 2010. The Utility of TAM-Perceptions: Integration of Technology Perceptions into Choice-Based Conjoint Analysis. ACIS 2010 Proceedings. URL https://aisel.aisnet.org/cgi/viewcontent.cgi?article=1002&context=acis2010

Lin, C.-P., Bhattacherjee, A., 2008. Elucidating Individual Intention to Use Interactive Information Technologies: The Role of Network Externalities. International Journal of Electronic Commerce 13, 85–108. https://doi.org/10.2753/JEC1086-4415130103

Lin, K.-Y., Lu, H.-P., 2011. Why people use social networking sites: An empirical study integrating network externalities and motivation theory. Computers in Human Behavior 27, 1152–1161. https://doi.org/10.1016/j.chb.2010.12.009

Lin, T.-C., Huang, S.-L., 2014. Understanding the Determinants of Consumers' Switching Intentions in a Standards War. International Journal of Electronic Commerce 19, 163–189. https://doi.org/10.2753/JEC1086-4415190105

Littler, D., Melanthiou, D., 2006. Consumer perceptions of risk and uncertainty and the implications for behaviour towards innovative retail services: The case of Internet Banking. Journal of Retailing and Consumer Services 13, 431–443. https://doi.org/10.1016/j.jretconser.2006.02.006

Lohmöller, J.-B., 1989. Predictive vs. Structural Modeling: PLS vs. ML, in: Lohmöller, J.-B. (Ed.), Latent Variable Path Modeling with Partial Least Squares. Physica-Verlag HD, Heidelberg, pp. 199–226. https://doi.org/10.1007/978-3-642-52512-4_5

Lourenço, C.J.S., Dellaert, B.G.C., Donkers, B., 2020. Whose Algorithm Says So: The Relationships between Type of Firm, Perceptions of Trust and Expertise, and the Acceptance of Financial Robo-Advice. Journal of Interactive Marketing 49, 107–124. https://doi.org/10.1016/j.intmar.2019.10.003

Louviere, J.J., 1988. Conjoint Analysis Modelling of Stated Preferences: A Review of Theory, Methods, Recent Developments and External Validity. Journal of Transport Economics and Policy 22, 93–119.

Louviere, J.J., Woodworth, G., 1983. Design and Analysis of Simulated Consumer Choice or Allocation Experiments: An Approach Based on Aggregate Data. Journal of Marketing Research 18.

Lu, Y., Yang, S., Chau, P.Y.K., Cao, Y., 2011. Dynamics between the trust transfer process and intention to use mobile payment services: A cross-environment perspective. Information & Management 48, 393–403. https://doi.org/10.1016/j.im.2011.09.006

Lusardi, A., Mitchell, O.S., 2014. The Economic Importance of Financial Literacy: Theory and Evidence. Journal of Economic Literature 52, 5–44. https://doi.org/10.1257/jel.52.1.5

Lusardi, A., Mitchell, O.S., 2011a. Financial Literacy and Planning: Implications for Retirement Wellbeing (No. w17078). National Bureau of Economic Research. https://doi.org/10.3386/w17078

Lusardi, A., Mitchell, O.S., 2011b. Financial Literacy around the World: An Overview (No. w17107). National Bureau of Economic Research. https://doi.org/10.3386/w17107

Lusardi, A., Mitchell, O.S., 2008. Planning and Financial Literacy: How Do Women Fare? American Economic Review 98, 413–417. https://doi.org/10.1257/aer.98.2.413

Lyytinen, K., Damsgaard, J., 2001. What's Wrong with the Diffusion of Innovation Theory?, in: Ardis, M.A., Marcolin, B.L. (Eds.), Diffusing Software Product and Process Innovations, IFIP Advances in Information and Communication Technology. Springer US, Boston, MA, pp. 173–190. https://doi.org/10.1007/978-0-387-35404-0_11

Ma, S., Zhang, S., Li, G., Wu, Y., 2019. Exploring information security education on social media use: Perspective of uses and gratifications theory. AJIM 71, 618–636. https://doi.org/10.1108/AJIM-09-2018-0213

MacCrimmon, K.R., Wehrung, D.A., 1990. Characteristics of Risk Taking Executives. Management Science 36, 422–435. https://doi.org/10.1287/mnsc.36.4.422

Markowitz, H., 1959. Portfolio Selection. The Journal of Finance.

Masyn, K.E., 2013. , in: Little, T.D. (Ed.), The Oxford Handbook of Quantitative Methods, Oxford Library of Psychology. Oxford University Press, New York.

Mayring, P.A.E., 2015. Qualitative Inhaltsanalyse—Grundlagen und Techniken. Beltz, Weinheim.

McFadden, D., 2001. Economic Choices. The American Economic Review 91, 28.

McFadden, D., 1974. Conditional logit analysis of qualitative choice behavior. Frontiers in econometrics, Frontiers in econometrics.—New York [u. a.] : Academic Press, ISBN 0-12-776150-0.—1974, p. 105–142.

McKnight, D.H., Choudhury, V., Kacmar, C., 2002. Developing and Validating Trust Measures for e-Commerce: An Integrative Typology. Information Systems Research 13, 334–359. https://doi.org/10.1287/isre.13.3.334.81

Mencin, J., 2022. Bester Robo-Advisor: Vergleich und Test [WWW Document]. Ratgeber | finanzen.net. URL http://www.finanzen.net/ratgeber/wertpapiere/robo-advisor (accessed 2.17.22).

Mencin, J., 2021. Bester Robo-Advisor: Vergleich und Test [WWW Document]. Ratgeber | finanzen.net. URL http://www.finanzen.net/ratgeber/wertpapiere/robo-advisor (accessed 3.23.21).

Metzler, D.R., Neuss, N., Torno, A., n.d. The Digitization of Investment Management—An Analysis of Robo-Advisor Business Models. Wirtschaftsinformatik 2022 Proceedings. 2. URL https://aisel.aisnet.org/cgi/viewcontent.cgi?article=1052&context=wi2022

Mishra, S.K., Kumar, M., 2011. How mutual fund investors' objective and subjective knowledge impacts their information search and processing behaviour. J Financ Serv Mark 16, 27–41. https://doi.org/10.1057/fsm.2011.1

Mocker, V., Chapman, O., 2017. Digital Pulse: How ready are Germans for the digital life? Nesta. URL https://www.nesta.org.uk/report/digital-pulse-how-ready-are-germans-for-the-digital-life/

Morana, S., Gnewuch, U., Jung, D., Granig, C., 2020. The Effect of Anthropomorphism on Investment Decision-Making with Robo-Advisor Chatbots. Conference paper of Twenty-Eighth European Conference on Information Systems (ECIS2020).

Morey, T., Forbath, T. "Theo", Schoop, A., 2015. Customer Data: Designing for Transparency and Trust. Harvard Business Review.

Morosan, C., DeFranco, A., 2016. It's about time: Revisiting UTAUT2 to examine consumers' intentions to use NFC mobile payments in hotels. International Journal of Hospitality Management 53, 17–29. https://doi.org/10.1016/j.ijhm.2015.11.003

Morris, M.G., Venkatesh, V., Ackerman, P.L., 2005. Gender and age differences in employee decisions about new technology: an extension to the theory of planned behavior. IEEE Transactions on Engineering Management 52, 69–84. https://doi.org/10.1109/TEM.2004.839967

Mouakket, S., 2019. Information self-disclosure on mobile instant messaging applications: Uses and gratifications perspective. JEIM 32, 98–117. https://doi.org/10.1108/JEIM-05-2018-0087

Möwes, T., Puschmann, T., Alt, R., 2011. Service-based Integration of IT-Innovations in Customer- Bank-Interaction. Wirtschaftsinformatik Proceedings 2011. URL https://aisel.aisnet.org/cgi/viewcontent.cgi?article=1016&context=wi2011

Mueller, D.C., 1997. First-mover advantages and path dependence. International Journal of Industrial Organization 15, 827–850. https://doi.org/10.1016/S0167-7187(97)00013-1

Mueller-Lankenau, C., Wehmeyer, K., 2005. Mobile Couponing—Measuring Consumers, Acceptance and Preferences with a Limit Conjoint Approach. BLED 2005 Proceedings. 35. URL https://aisel.aisnet.org/cgi/viewcontent.cgi?article=1085&context=bled2005

Naous, D., Legner, C., 2021. Leveraging Market Research Techniques in IS: A Review and Framework of Conjoint Analysis Studies in the IS Discipline. CAIS 49, 126–155. https://doi.org/10.17705/1CAIS.04906

Naous, D., Legner, C., 2019. Understanding Users' Preferences for Privacy and Security Features—A Conjoint Analysis of Cloud Storage Services, in: Abramowicz, W., Corchuelo, R. (Eds.), Business Information Systems Workshops, Lecture Notes in Business Information Processing. Springer International Publishing, Cham, pp. 352–365. https://doi.org/10.1007/978-3-030-36691-9_30

Nass, C., Moon, Y., 2000. Machines and Mindlessness: Social Responses to Computers. J Social Isssues 56, 81–103. https://doi.org/10.1111/0022-4537.00153

Nelson, R.R., Winter, S.G., 1982. An evolutionary theory of economic change, digitally reprinted. ed. The Belknap Press of Harvard Univ. Press, Cambridge, Mass.

Netzer, O., Toubia, O., Bradlow, E.T., Dahan, E., Evgeniou, T., Feinberg, F.M., Feit, E.M., Hui, S.K., Johnson, J., Liechty, J.C., Orlin, J.B., Rao, V.R., 2008. Beyond conjoint analysis: Advances in preference measurement. Mark Lett 19, 337–354. https://doi.org/10.1007/s11002-008-9046-1

Nistor, N., Lerche, T., Weinberger, A., Ceobanu, C., Heymann, O., 2014. Towards the integration of culture into the Unified Theory of Acceptance and Use of Technology: Culture and the UTAUT. Br J Educ Technol 45, 36–55. https://doi.org/10.1111/j.1467-8535.2012.01383.x

Nueesch, R., Puschmann, T., Alt, R., 2014. Realizing Value From Tablet-Supported Customer Advisory: BLED 2014 Proceedings. URL https://aisel.aisnet.org/cgi/viewcontent.cgi?article=1011&context=bled2014

Nunnally, J.C., Bernstein, I.H., 1994. Psychometric theory, 3rd ed. ed, McGraw-Hill series in psychology. McGraw-Hill, New York.

Nussbaumer, P., Matter, I., Reto à Porta, G., Schwabe, G., 2012a. Designing for Cost Transparency in Investment Advisory Service Encounters. Bus Inf Syst Eng 4, 347–361. https://doi.org/10.1007/s12599-012-0237-1

Nussbaumer, P., Matter, I., Schwabe, G., 2012b. "Enforced" vs. "Casual" Transparency—Findings from IT-Supported Financial Advisory Encounters. ACM Trans. Manage. Inf. Syst. 3, 1–19. https://doi.org/10.1145/2229156.2229161

Nylund, K.L., Asparouhov, T., Muthén, B.O., 2007. Deciding on the Number of Classes in Latent Class Analysis and Growth Mixture Modeling: A Monte Carlo Simulation Study. Structural Equation Modeling: A Multidisciplinary Journal 14, 535–569. https://doi.org/10.1080/10705510701575396

Nylund-Gibson, K., Choi, A.Y., 2018. Ten frequently asked questions about latent class analysis. Translational Issues in Psychological Science 4, 440–461. https://doi.org/10.1037/tps0000176

Oehler, A., Horn, M., Wendt, S., 2022. Investor Characteristics and their Impact on the Decision to use a Robo-advisor. J Financ Serv Res 62, 91–125. https://doi.org/10.1007/s10693-021-00367-8

Oppenheimer, D.M., Meyvis, T., Davidenko, N., 2009. Instructional manipulation checks: Detecting satisficing to increase statistical power. Journal of Experimental Social Psychology 45, 867–872. https://doi.org/10.1016/j.jesp.2009.03.009

Orme, B., 2021. Estimating Willingness to Pay (WTP) Given Competition in Conjoint Analysis. Sawtooth Software, Inc. URL https://sawtoothsoftware.com/resources/technical-papers/estimating-willingness-to-pay-in-conjoint-analysis

Orme, B., 2019. Consistency Cutoffs to Identify "Bad" Respondents in CBC, ACBC, and MaxDiff [WWW Document]. URL https://sawtoothsoftware.com/resources/technical-papers/consistency-cutoffs-to-identify-bad-respondents-in-cbc-acbc-and-maxdiff (accessed 8.5.22).

Orme, B., 2013. Which Conjoint Method Should I Use? [WWW Document]. URL https://sawtoothsoftware.com/resources/technical-papers/which-conjoint-method-should-i-use (accessed 10.16.22).

Orme, B., Howell, J., 2009. Application of Covariates within Sawtooth Software's CBC/HB Program: Theory and Practical Example [WWW Document]. URL https://sawtoothsoft

ware.com/resources/technical-papers/application-of-covariates-within-sawtooth-softwares-cbc-hb-program-theory-and-practical-example (accessed 8.5.22).

Orme, B., Williams, W., 2016. What Are the Optimal HB Priors Settings for CBC and MaxDiff Studies? [WWW Document]. URL https://sawtoothsoftware.com/resources/technical-papers/what-are-the-optimal-hb-priors-settings-for-cbc-and-maxdiff-studies (accessed 8.5.22).

Orme, B.K., Chrzan, K., 2021. Becoming an expert in conjoint analysis: choice modelling for pros. Sawtooth Software, Orem.

Osterwalder, A., Pigneur, Y., 2010. Business Model Generation: A Handbook for Visionaries, Game Changers, and Challengers. John Wiley & Sons.

Paolacci, G., 2010. Running experiments on Amazon Mechanical Turk. Judgment and Decision Making 5, 9.

Parker, B.R., Srinivasan, V., 1976. A Consumer Preference Approach to the Planning of Rural Primary Health-Care Facilities. Operations Research 24, 991–1025. https://doi.org/10.1287/opre.24.5.991

Pavlou, P., 2003. Consumer Acceptance of Electronic Commerce: Integrating Trust and Risk with the Technology Acceptance Model. International Journal of Electronic Commerce 7, 101–134. https://doi.org/10.1080/10864415.2003.11044275

Peer, E., Brandimarte, L., Samat, S., Acquisti, A., 2017. Beyond the Turk: Alternative platforms for crowdsourcing behavioral research. Journal of Experimental Social Psychology 70, 153–163. https://doi.org/10.1016/j.jesp.2017.01.006

Peitz, M., Serpetti, M., Yardley, D., 2020. A Researcher's Guide to Studying Large Attribute Sets in Choice-Based Conjoint, in: Sawtooth Software Conference Proceedings 2019. San Diego, California.

Pennings, J.M.E., Smidts, A., 2000. Assessing the Construct Validity of Risk Attitude. Management Science 46, 1337–1348. https://doi.org/10.1287/mnsc.46.10.1337.12275

Pratt, J.W., 1964. Risk Aversion in the Small and in the Large. Econometrica 32, 122. https://doi.org/10.2307/1913738

Qiu, L., Benbasat, I., 2009. Evaluating Anthropomorphic Product Recommendation Agents: A Social Relationship Perspective to Designing Information Systems. Journal of Management Information Systems 25, 145–182. https://doi.org/10.2753/MIS0742-1222250405

Qualtrics, n.d. Financial Advisor Client Experience Research Report [WWW Document]. URL https://www.qualtrics.com/customer-experience/financial-advisor-report/ (accessed 3.22.21).

Ramaswamy, V., Desarbo, W.S., Reibstein, D.J., Robinson, W.T., 1993. An Empirical Pooling Approach for Estimating Marketing Mix Elasticities with PIMS Data. Marketing Science 12, 103–124. https://doi.org/10.1287/mksc.12.1.103

Rao, V.R., 2008. Developments in Conjoint Analysis, in: Wierenga, B. (Ed.), Handbook of Marketing Decision Models, International Series in Operations Research & Management Science. Springer US, Boston, MA, pp. 23–53. https://doi.org/10.1007/978-0-387-78213-3_2

Ray, A., Dhir, A., Bala, P.K., Kaur, P., 2019. Why do people use food delivery apps (FDA)? A uses and gratification theory perspective. Journal of Retailing and Consumer Services 51, 221–230. https://doi.org/10.1016/j.jretconser.2019.05.025

Reavley, N., 2005. Securing online banking. Card Technology Today 17, 12–13. https://doi.org/10.1016/S0965-2590(05)70389-3

Reddel, S., Silver, R., Spellacy, M., 2020. Financial advice reimagined. Accenture.

Reher, M., Sun, C., 2016. Robo Advisers and Mutual Fund Stickiness. SSRN Journal. https://doi.org/10.2139/ssrn.2872134

Remund, D.L., 2010. Financial Literacy Explicated: The Case for a Clearer Definition in an Increasingly Complex Economy. Journal of Consumer Affairs 44, 276–295. https://doi.org/10.1111/j.1745-6606.2010.01169.x

Ringle, C.M., Wende, S., Becker, J.-M., 2015. SmartPLS 3.

Rogers, E.M., 1962. Diffusion of Innovations. NY: Free Press, New York.

Rossi, B., Russo, B., Succi, G., 2011. Path dependent stochastic models to detect planned and actual technology use: A case study of OpenOffice. Information and Software Technology 53, 1209–1226. https://doi.org/10.1016/j.infsof.2011.05.002

Ruf, C., Back, A., Bergmann, R., Schlegel, M., 2015. Elicitation of Requirements for the Design of Mobile Financial Advisory Services—Instantiation and Validation of the Requirement Data Model with a Multi-method Approach, in: 2015 48th Hawaii International Conference on System Sciences (HICSS). IEEE, HI, USA, pp. 1169–1178. https://doi.org/10.1109/HICSS.2015.142

Ruf, C., Back, A., Burkhardt, M., 2016. Mobile First auch in Beratungsprozessen des Private Banking? Entwicklung und Validierung einer iPad-Applikation. Informationssysteme in der Finanzwirtschaft 12.

Rühr, A., 2020. Robo-Advisor Configuration: An Investigation of User Preferences and the Performance-Control Dilemma. In Proceedings of the 28th European Conference on Information Systems (ECIS). URL https://aisel.aisnet.org/cgi/viewcontent.cgi?article=1093&context=ecis2020_rp

Rühr, A., Berger, B., Hess, T., 2019. Can I Control My Robo-Advisor? Trade-Offs in Automation and User Control in (Digital) Investment Management. Twenty-fifth Americas Conference on Information Systems. URL https://www.researchgate.net/publication/334625614_Can_I_Control_My_Robo-Advisor_Trade-Offs_in_Automation_and_User_Control_in_Digital_Investment_Management

Saad, L., Jones, J.M., 2022. What Percentage of Americans Owns Stock? [WWW Document]. Gallup.com. URL https://news.gallup.com/poll/266807/percentage-americans-owns-stock.aspx (accessed 8.30.22).

Sarstedt, M., Hair, J.F., Ringle, C.M., Thiele, K.O., Gudergan, S.P., 2016. Estimation issues with PLS and CBSEM: Where the bias lies! Journal of Business Research 69, 3998–4010. https://doi.org/10.1016/j.jbusres.2016.06.007

Sarstedt, M., Ringle, C.M., Hair, J.F., 2021. Partial Least Squares Structural Equation Modeling, in: Homburg, C., Klarmann, M., Vomberg, A.E. (Eds.), Handbook of Market Research. Springer International Publishing, Cham, pp. 1–47. https://doi.org/10.1007/978-3-319-05542-8_15-2

Schomakers, E.-M., Lidynia, C., Ziefle, M., 2020. All of me? Users' preferences for privacy-preserving data markets and the importance of anonymity. Electron Markets 30, 649–665. https://doi.org/10.1007/s12525-020-00404-9

Schwarz, G., 1978. Estimating the Dimension of a Model. The Annals of Statistics 6, 461–464.

Scott, M., Watson, L., 2020. European Asset Allocation Survey 2020. Mercer.

See-To, E.W.K., Ho, K.K.W., 2016. A study on the impact of design attributes on E-payment service utility. Information & Management 53, 668–681. https://doi.org/10.1016/j.im.2016.02.004

Seiler, V., Fanenbruck, K.M., 2021. Acceptance of digital investment solutions: The case of robo advisory in Germany. Research in International Business and Finance 58, 101490. https://doi.org/10.1016/j.ribaf.2021.101490

Sette, M.L., Chavarria, A., Klammer, M.M., 2022. Best Robo-Advisors [WWW Document]. Investopedia. URL https://www.investopedia.com/best-robo-advisors-4693125 (accessed 2.17.22).

Sheppard, B.H., Hartwick, J., Warshaw, P.R., 1988. The Theory of Reasoned Action: A Meta-Analysis of Past Research with Recommendations for Modifications and Future Research. J CONSUM RES 15, 325. https://doi.org/10.1086/209170

Shorrocks, A., Davies, J., Lluberas, R., 2020. Global wealth report 2020. Crédit Suisse Research Institute. URL https://www.credit-suisse.com/about-us/en/reports-research/global-wealth-report.html

Siau, K., Shen, Z., 2003. Building customer trust in mobile commerce. Commun. ACM 46, 91–94. https://doi.org/10.1145/641205.641211

Silver, C., Chavarria, A., 2021. Investopedia's Robo-Advisor Ranking Methodology [WWW Document]. Investopedia. URL https://www.investopedia.com/robo-advisor-ranking-methodology-4693455 (accessed 3.23.21).

Srinivasan, V., Shocker, A.D., 1973. Estimating the weights for multiple attributes in a composite criterion using pairwise judgments. Psychometrika 38, 473–493. https://doi.org/10.1007/BF02291490

Srite, Karahanna, 2006. The Role of Espoused National Cultural Values in Technology Acceptance. MIS Quarterly 30, 679. https://doi.org/10.2307/25148745

StatCounter, 2021a. Search Engine Market Share Germany [WWW Document]. URL https://gs.statcounter.com/search-engine-market-share/all/germany/ (accessed 3.9.21).

StatCounter, 2021b. Search Engine Market Share United States Of America [WWW Document]. URL https://gs.statcounter.com/search-engine-market-share/all/united-states-of-america/ (accessed 3.9.21).

Statista, n.d. Robo-Advisors—United States | Statista Market Forecast [WWW Document]. URL https://www.statista.com/outlook/dmo/fintech/digital-investment/robo-advisors/united-states (accessed 1.3.23).

Statistisches Bundesamt, n.d. Bevölkerung nach Nationalität und Geschlecht (Quartalszahlen) [WWW Document]. Statistisches Bundesamt. URL https://www.destatis.de/DE/Themen/Gesellschaft-Umwelt/Bevoelkerung/Bevoelkerungsstand/Tabellen/liste-zensus-geschlecht-staatsangehoerigkeit.html (accessed 12.27.22).

Subramanian, G.H., 1994. A Replication of Perceived Usefulness and Perceived Ease of Use Measurement. Decision Sciences 25, 863–874. https://doi.org/10.1111/j.1540-5915.1994.tb01873.x

Tan, M., Teo, T., National University of Singapore, 2000. Factors Influencing the Adoption of Internet Banking. JAIS 1, 1–44. https://doi.org/10.17705/1jais.00005

Tang, T., Ho, A.T.-K., 2019. A path-dependence perspective on the adoption of Internet of Things: Evidence from early adopters of smart and connected sensors in the United States. Government Information Quarterly 36, 321–332. https://doi.org/10.1016/j.giq.2018.09.010

Tang, T.L.-P., 1993. The Meaning of Money: Extension and Exploration of the Money Ethic Scale in a Sample of University Students in Taiwan. Journal of Organizational Behavior 14, 93–99.

Tao Zhou, 2011. Understanding mobile Internet continuance usage from the perspectives of UTAUT and flow. Information Development 27, 207–218. https://doi.org/10.1177/0266666911414596

Tauchert, C., Mesbah, N., 2019. Following the Robot? Investigating Users' Utilization of Advice from Robo-Advisors. CIS 2019 Proceedings. URL https://aisel.aisnet.org/cgi/viewcontent.cgi?article=1537&context=icis2019

Taylor, S., Todd, P., 1995a. Assessing IT Usage: The Role of Prior Experience. MIS Quarterly 19, 561. https://doi.org/10.2307/249633

Taylor, S., Todd, P.A., 1995b. Understanding Information Technology Usage: A Test of Competing Models. Information Systems Research 6, 144–176. https://doi.org/10.1287/isre.6.2.144

Teo, T.S.H., Lim, V.K.G., Lai, R.Y.C., 1999. Intrinsic and extrinsic motivation in Internet usage. Omega 27, 25–37. https://doi.org/10.1016/S0305-0483(98)00028-0

Tepper, T., 2022. Best Robo-Advisors Of February 2022 [WWW Document]. Forbes Advisor. URL https://www.forbes.com/advisor/investing/best-robo-advisors/ (accessed 2.17.22).

Thakur, R., Srivastava, M., 2014. Adoption readiness, personal innovativeness, perceived risk and usage intention across customer groups for mobile payment services in India. Internet Research 24, 369–392. https://doi.org/10.1108/IntR-12-2012-0244

Thompson, R.L., Higgins, C.A., Howell, J.M., 1994. Influence of Experience on Personal Computer Utilization: Testing a Conceptual Model. Journal of Management Information Systems 11, 167–187. https://doi.org/10.1080/07421222.1994.11518035

Thompson, R.L., Higgins, C.A., Howell, J.M., 1991. Personal Computing: Toward a Conceptual Model of Utilization. MIS Quarterly 15, 125. https://doi.org/10.2307/249443

Timothy Morey, Forbath, T., Schoop, A., 2015. Customer Data: Designing for Transparency and Trust. Customer Data: Designing for Transparency and Trust. URL https://hbr.org/2015/05/customer-data-designing-for-transparency-and-trust

Todd, T.M., Seay, M.C., 2020. Financial attributes, financial behaviors, financial-advisor-use beliefs, and investing characteristics associated with having used a robo-advisor. Financial Planning Review 3. https://doi.org/10.1002/cfp2.1104

Tversky, A., Kahneman, D., 1992. Advances in prospect theory: Cumulative representation of uncertainty. J Risk Uncertainty 5, 297–323. https://doi.org/10.1007/BF00122574

US Census Bureau, 2017. 2017 National Population Projections Tables: Main Series [WWW Document]. Census.gov. URL https://www.census.gov/data/tables/2017/demo/popproj/2017-summary-tables.html (accessed 12.27.22).

US Public Law, 1960. Section 10(a), no. 86–779, 74 Stat. 998.

Van de Wijngaert, L., Bouwman, H., 2009. Would you share? Predicting the potential use of a new technology. Telematics and Informatics 26, 85–102. https://doi.org/10.1016/j.tele.2008.01.002

Van Rooij, M., Lusardi, A., Alessie, R., 2011. Financial literacy and stock market participation. Journal of Financial Economics 101, 449–472. https://doi.org/10.1016/j.jfineco.2011.03.006

Vanguard, Spectrem Group, 2014. The affluent investor.

Venkatesh, Morris, Davis, Davis, 2003. User Acceptance of Information Technology: Toward a Unified View. MIS Quarterly 27, 425. https://doi.org/10.2307/30036540

Venkatesh, Thong, Xu, 2012. Consumer Acceptance and Use of Information Technology: Extending the Unified Theory of Acceptance and Use of Technology. MIS Quarterly 36, 157. https://doi.org/10.2307/41410412

Venkatesh, V., Chan, F.K.Y., Thong, J.Y.L., 2012. Designing e-government services: Key service attributes and citizens' preference structures. Journal of Operations Management 30, 116–133. https://doi.org/10.1016/j.jom.2011.10.001

Venkatesh, V., Davis, F.D., 2000. A Theoretical Extension of the Technology Acceptance Model: Four Longitudinal Field Studies. Management Science 46, 186–204. https://doi.org/10.1287/mnsc.46.2.186.11926

Venkatesh, V., Zhang, X., 2010. Unified Theory of Acceptance and Use of Technology: U.S. Vs. China. Journal of Global Information Technology Management 13, 5–27. https://doi.org/10.1080/1097198X.2010.10856507

Vergne, J.-P., Durand, R., 2010. The Missing Link Between the Theory and Empirics of Path Dependence: Conceptual Clarification, Testability Issue, and Methodological Implications. Journal of Management Studies 47, 736–759. https://doi.org/10.1111/j.1467-6486.2009.00913.x

Voorhees, C.M., Brady, M.K., Calantone, R., Ramirez, E., 2016. Discriminant validity testing in marketing: an analysis, causes for concern, and proposed remedies. J. of the Acad. Mark. Sci. 44, 119–134. https://doi.org/10.1007/s11747-015-0455-4

Voß, T., Hornuf, L., Dorfleitner, G., 2021. Recht der FinTechs. DE GRUYTER, Berlin.

Weber, E.U., Blais, A.-R., Betz, N.E., 2002. A domain-specific risk-attitude scale: measuring risk perceptions and risk behaviors. J. Behav. Decis. Making 15, 263–290. https://doi.org/10.1002/bdm.414

Weber, E.U., Hsee, C., 1998. Cross-Cultural Differences in Risk Perception, but Cross-Cultural Similarities in Attitudes Towards Perceived Risk. Management Science 44, 1205–1217. https://doi.org/10.1287/mnsc.44.9.1205

Weber, E.U., Milliman, R.A., 1997. Perceived Risk Attitudes: Relating Risk Perception to Risky Choice. Management Science 43, 123–144. https://doi.org/10.1287/mnsc.43.2.123

Weber, M., 1905. Die protestantische Ethik und der Geist des Kapitalismus. Archiv für Sozialwissenschaften und Sozialpolitik.

Webley, P., Lewis, A., Mackenzie, C., 2001. Commitment among ethical investors: An experimental approach. Journal of Economic Psychology 22, 27–42. https://doi.org/10.1016/S0167-4870(00)00035-0

Weijters, B., Rangarajan, D., Falk, T., Schillewaert, N., 2007. Determinants and Outcomes of Customers' Use of Self-Service Technology in a Retail Setting. Journal of Service Research 10, 3–21. https://doi.org/10.1177/1094670507302990

Weliver, D., 2021. The Best Robo-Advisors of 2021 [WWW Document]. Money Under 30. URL https://www.moneyunder30.com/robo-advisors (accessed 3.23.21).

Wood, R., Zaichkowsky, J.L., 2004. Attitudes and Trading Behavior of Stock Market Investors: A Segmentation Approach. Journal of Behavioral Finance 5, 170–179. https://doi.org/10.1207/s15427579jpfm0503_5

Wooldridge, J.M., 2019. Introductory econometrics: a modern approach, Seventh edition. ed. Cengage Learning, Boston, MA.

World Bank, n.d. Individuals using the Internet (% of population)—OECD members | Data [WWW Document]. URL https://data.worldbank.org/indicator/IT.NET.USER.ZS?locations=OE&name_desc=false (accessed 5.20.21).

Wu, M., Gao, Q., 2021. Human Aspects of IT for the Aged Population. Technology Design and Acceptance: 7th International Conference, ITAP 2021, Held as Part of the 23rd HCI International Conference, HCII 2021, Virtual Event, July 24–29, 2021, Proceedings, Part I, in: Gao, Q., Zhou, J. (Eds.), Lecture Notes in Computer Science. Springer International Publishing, Cham. https://doi.org/10.1007/978-3-030-78108-8

Xiao, B., Benbasat, I., 2007. E-Commerce Product Recommendation Agents: Use, Characteristics, and Impact. MIS Quarterly Vol. 31, 137–209.

Xue, J., Liu, Q., Li, M., Liu, X., Ye, Y., Wang, S., Yin, J., 2018. Incremental multiple kernel extreme learning machine and its application in Robo-advisors. Soft Comput 22, 3507–3517. https://doi.org/10.1007/s00500-018-3031-2

Yang, S., Lu, Y., Gupta, S., Cao, Y., Zhang, R., 2012. Mobile payment services adoption across time: An empirical study of the effects of behavioral beliefs, social influences, and personal traits. Computers in Human Behavior 28, 129–142. https://doi.org/10.1016/j.chb.2011.08.019

Ye, L.R., Johnson, P.E., 1995. The Impact of Explanation Facilities on User Acceptance of Expert Systems Advice. MIS Quarterly 19, 157. https://doi.org/10.2307/249686

Yi, M.Y., Fiedler, K.D., Park, J.S., 2006. Understanding the Role of Individual Innovativeness in the Acceptance of IT-Based Innovations: Comparative Analyses of Models and Measures. Decision Sciences 37, 393–426. https://doi.org/10.1111/j.1540-5414.2006.00132.x

Yoo, K.-H., Gretzel, U., 2011. Creating More Credible and Persuasive Recommender Systems: The Influence of Source Characteristics on Recommender System Evaluations, in: Ricci, F., Rokach, L., Shapira, B., Kantor, P.B. (Eds.), Recommender Systems Handbook. Springer US, Boston, MA, pp. 455–477. https://doi.org/10.1007/978-0-387-85820-3_14

Yoong, J., 2011. Financial illiteracy and stock market participation: Evidence from the RAND American Life Panel, in: Mitchell, O.S., Lusardi, A. (Eds.), Financial Literacy: Implications for Retirement Security and the Financial Marketplace. Oxford University Press, Oxford; New York.

Yu, C.-S., 2012. Factors affecting individuals to adopt mobile banking: Empirical evidence from the UTAUT model. Journal of Electronic Commerce Research 13, 18.

Yusuf Dauda, S., Lee, J., 2015. Technology adoption: A conjoint analysis of consumers' preference on future online banking services. Information Systems 53, 1–15. https://doi.org/10.1016/j.is.2015.04.006

Zhang, L., Pentina, I., Fan, Y., 2021. Who do you choose? Comparing perceptions of human vs robo-advisor in the context of financial services. JSM 35, 634–646. https://doi.org/10.1108/JSM-05-2020-0162

Zhang, M., Xin, G., Zhu, M., 2018. Content, Enjoyment or Payment? Factors Influencing Consumers' Purchase Intention in Mobile Reading: An Empirical Study from China. International Journal of New Developments in Engineering and Society 2. https://doi.org/10.25236/IJNDES.18229

Zhao, L., Lu, Y., 2012. Enhancing perceived interactivity through network externalities: An empirical study on micro-blogging service satisfaction and continuance intention. Decision Support Systems 53, 825–834. https://doi.org/10.1016/j.dss.2012.05.019

Zhou, T., 2012. Examining location-based services usage from the perspectives of unified theory of acceptance and use of technology and privacy risk. Journal of Electronic Commerce Research 13, 10.

Zhou, T., Lu, Y., Wang, B., 2010. Integrating TTF and UTAUT to explain mobile banking user adoption. Computers in Human Behavior 26, 760–767. https://doi.org/10.1016/j.chb.2010.01.013

Zubey, M.L., Wagner, W., Otto, J.R., 2002. A conjoint analysis of voice over IP attributes. Internet Research 12, 7–15. https://doi.org/10.1108/10662240210415781

GPSR Compliance

The European Union's (EU) General Product Safety Regulation (GPSR) is a set of rules that requires consumer products to be safe and our obligations to ensure this.

If you have any concerns about our products, you can contact us on ProductSafety@springernature.com

In case Publisher is established outside the EU, the EU authorized representative is:

Springer Nature Customer Service Center GmbH
Europaplatz 3
69115 Heidelberg, Germany

The manufacturer's authorised representative in the EU is Springer Nature Customer Service Centre GmbH, Europaplatz 3, 69115 Heidelberg, Germany. If you have any concerns regarding our products, please contact ProductSafety@springernature.com

Printed and bound by CPI Group (UK) Ltd, Croydon, CR0 4YY
02/10/2026
02227140-0003

Necessary Risks